BUSINESS WRITING

(Formerly published as *Business English*)

BUSINESS WRITING

Second Edition

J. Harold Janis

Howard R. Dressner

BARNES & NOBLE BOOKS

A DIVISION OF HARPER & ROW, PUBLISHERS

New York, Hagerstown, San Francisco, London

BUSINESS WRITING, second edition. Copyright © 1956, 1972 by J. Harold Janis. All rights reserved. Printed in the United States of America. No part of this book may be used or reproduced in any manner without written permission except in the case of brief quotations embodied in critical articles and reviews. For information address Harper & Row, Publishers, Inc., 10 East 53d Street, New York, N.Y. 10022. Published simultaneously in Canada by Fitzhenry & Whiteside Limited, Toronto.

First BARNES & NOBLE BOOKS edition published 1972

LIBRARY OF CONGRESS CATALOG CARD NUMBER: 72–83823

ISBN: 0-06-460151-X

79 80   12 11 10

Preface

Business Writing, which since its publication in 1956 has been successful as a learning tool, has now been revised and augmented. The new edition is designed not only to improve business writing skills but also to provide an up-to-date background for communication study. Four new chapters on report writing give due emphasis to this increasingly important medium; and additions to the section on the writing of résumés will help satisfy the needs of those who use this means to get new and better jobs.

The new plan of the book preserves the best features of the old. It offers a concise but complete treatment of the principles governing both business writing in general and specific types of business communications: order letters, inquiries and replies, credit and collection letters, adjustment letters, sales letters, sales promotion letters, and business reports.

Fully a hundred pages are still devoted to the fundamentals of grammar and sentence structure, word use, punctuation, spelling, and related matters. The book also provides a wealth of examples, including *do's* and *don't's* in parallel columns and *before* and *after* treatments of entire letters.

For purposes of both class review and independent study, *Business Writing* is divided into four parts. Part 1 offers an overview of communication in the modern business organization and sums up the relevant research findings in communication theory. Part 2 parallels many of the more popular texts: first, in its treatment of the qualities, mechanics, point of view, style, and construction of business letters; and, second, in its statement of the principles governing specialized types of correspondence. Part 3 treats the subject of reports, giving full attention to methods of research, organization of data, report language, and graphics and mechanical display. Part 4 is a complete handbook of English, with all the important rules explained, illustrated, and numbered for easy reference.

The reader will find that the principles are those proved effective over the years and that the examples follow the most widely accepted current practices. In matters of English usage, the distinction between the formal and the informal is often made in these pages, and the reader is encouraged by precept and example to employ the tone appropriate to the occasion. The long experience of the authors both in the classroom and in business insures that the book is sound and workable.

The completeness and self-teaching qualities of *Business Writing* make it suitable not only for those engaged in formal study of this area, but also for business men and women who wish to use it by themselves or in conjunction with company-sponsored training courses.

This book could not have been prepared without the help of a great number of people in a great number of places. The authors wish to express their indebtedness to the companies whose letters and experiences are here represented. They wish also to thank the many teachers and students both at New York University and elsewhere who were so generous in providing examples of effective writing.

J. Harold Janis
Howard R. Dressner

Table of Contents

About the Authors

J. Harold Janis is Professor of Business Communication and Vice Chairman of the Department of Business Administration at New York University. In addition to being author or coauthor of numerous other books in the field of business writing, including *Writing and Communication in Business* (Macmillan), he has written articles for *Reader's Digest, Nation's Business, Journal of Communication,* and other periodicals. For a time he served as consultant on letters and reports to the City of New York. More recently he has organized and conducted communication programs for some leading business institutions, including the Federal Reserve Bank of New York, Manufacturers Hanover Trust Company, American Telephone and Telegraph Company, the New York Life Insurance Company, and Merrill, Lynch, Pierce, Fenner & Smith.

HOWARD R. DRESSNER is Secretary of the Ford Foundation. He was formerly a member of the faculty of New York University where he specialized in the fields of business writing and speaking. He received his B.S. degree at New York University and his LL.B. from Columbia University. As a communications consultant, he served a number of leading corporations, including the First National City Bank of New York. He has written articles for such publications as *Nation's Business.*

PART 1
WRITTEN COMMUNICATION IN BUSINESS

PART 1
WRITTEN COMMUNICATION IN BUSINESS

The ability to write effectively is a valuable business asset. A great deal of business is transacted in writing, so that sooner or later almost every employee finds it necessary to put ideas on paper. The effective writer can use his skill to help increase his company's sales and profits by promoting good relations with customers, employees, and the general public. Proficiency in writing also gives the man or woman in business a personal advantage that contributes substantially to his or her self-confidence—a necessary quality for business success.

In recent years two developments have occurred which are especially important to business writers. The first is the rapidly expanding use of the computer. By taking over the routine clerical jobs, the computer has freed the office worker for the more creative tasks required by our growing business needs. Among these tasks are planning, investigation, and research; interpretation of data; decision-making and follow-up; and a wide variety of training, liaison, and promotional functions. All of these activities put a heavy emphasis on letters, memorandums, reports, and other written communications.

The second development of importance to business writers is the sharpened awareness of business writing as part of the larger phenomenon we call the communication process. The ever-increasing presence of television, motion pictures, and the other mass media, and of such instruments as the telephone, the tape recorder, and the Xerox copier, has stimulated a good deal of scholarly interest in the relationship of all factors that contribute to communication results. The writer can profit from this research.

In the next two chapters, we will give our attention to the expanding role of business writing and to the meaning of the communication process for the business writer.

1
The Scope and Functions
of Written Communication

The introduction of the electronic communication media should not be allowed to obscure the continuing and increasing need for writing in the business organization. For one thing, business could not operate without the convenient permanent record of its transactions that writing provides. Writing is easily encoded, transmitted, filed, and retrieved. More important, however, writing encourages thought and reason, and permits expression with the utmost clarity, precision, conciseness, grace, and tact. There are many places in the organization, including the higher echelons, where such qualities are especially valued and sought.

USES OF WRITTEN COMMUNICATION

Inevitably, a medium as useful as writing fills a variety of functions in the conduct of modern business. These functions may be broadly classified as follows: (1) to improve efficiency, (2) to promote understanding, and (3) to sell goods and services.

IMPROVING EFFICIENCY. Writing is indispensable for routine record-keeping and reporting, expressing company policies, issuing work assignments, and instructing employees. In some instances, efficiency is aided by the use of such printed forms as purchase orders, sales slips, inventory records, and receipts. In other instances, manuals are provided to insure efficient and uniform handling of routine problems. For example, instructions may be printed for every step in a complicated procedure or production process, or a carefully indexed series of form letters may be pro-

3

vided for use in certain repetitive situations. In still other instances, the work of the organization is performed by individually dictated letters and memorandums and carefully researched reports. Minutes of meetings, credit reports, and the reports of operations audits offer only a few examples of documents important to the continuing life of the organization and very demanding of the writer's skill.

PROMOTING UNDERSTANDING. An organization is not just a group of working people, but a group of people working together. Much that glues the organization together is accomplished on a person-to-person basis and in conferences and meetings. But a great deal of dependence is also placed on the written word. Part of the philosophy of employee relations is that the more information workers are permitted to have, the more interested they will be in their jobs and the more loyal they will be to the company. Happier workers tend to stay longer and produce more. In addition to the ordinary training manuals and printed job instructions, many companies also issue handbooks outlining the workers' rights, privileges, and duties. Other business publications include periodic news bulletins and company newspapers, magazines, and technical journals to which employees contribute. Most large organizations operate "suggestion systems" which make awards for employees' written suggestions for improving the work. Some heads of organizations also make it a practice to address letters to employees at their homes congratulating them on their job performance, on the celebration of an anniversary, or on the achievement of some community honor. Letters are similarly used to inform employees and their families of significant developments in the company.

Understandably, a company is dependent for its goodwill not only on its employees, but also on its customers, stockholders, suppliers, public officials, and the general public. Through its advertising, annual reports, announcements to the trade press, and general news releases, it seeks to keep all of its "publics" informed of its products, policies, and financial progress. Often special campaigns are mounted to combat bad publicity or promote corporate views on which greater public understanding is desired. The St. Regis Paper Company's emphasis on conservation of forest resources and the Mobil Oil Company's campaign to promote safe driving are but two examples of writing used to promote sympathy for corporate aims.

SELLING GOODS AND SERVICES. The writing that usually commands the largest space and the greatest public attention is that devoted to the sale of the company's goods and services. Anyone who opens the mailbox or reads newspapers and magazines knows how much of a company's time, creative talents, and financial resources are devoted to this function. Radio and television have, of course, made inroads on printed salesmanship, and many newspapers and magazines have suspended publication for lack of advertising revenue. Higher postal rates have also sent many advertisers to other media. Nevertheless, direct-mail and publication advertising remain in a remarkably healthy state. There is still no cheaper or more effective way to reach known customers than through mailed letters and circulars, and both mail and publication advertising have the longevity considered important in messages aimed at the most thoughtful, most literate, and most influential segments of the population.

COMMUNICATION FLOW

One of the best ways to study the uses of business writing is to observe the direction in which messages flow within a given organization.

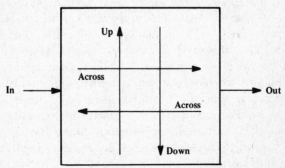

Fig. 1. Communication flow in the organization

EXTERNAL COMMUNICATION. A large body of messages travels between the organization and outside destinations. Included in this category is correspondence to customers, prospective customers, and others. Much of this communication is generated by inflowing correspondence, such as inquiries, orders, complaints, announcements, and requests of various sorts. Other external correspondence is initiated within the organization and consists in large part of sales letters, collection letters, requests for credit information, solicitation of bids on the purchase of goods and services, complaints and inquiries to vendors and contractors, inquiries to government agencies, and follow-ups on transactions in process.

In addition to letters, many other written forms also travel outside the organization. These include business proposals, reports to stockholders, technical reports for the guidance of users of the company's products, sales catalogues and circulars, newspaper and magazine advertising, and printed invitations, announcements, and brochures.

INTERNAL COMMUNICATION. Messages prepared for use inside the organization are designed to travel either up or down the organizational ladder or horizontally across departmental lines. The messages traveling upward usually consist of memorandums and reports for the information of those who must make evaluations and decisions. Thus a report on production difficulties may go from a supervisor to a department head who has the authority to remedy the trouble. Similarly a daily report on sales may travel from a retail selling department to a buyer who will use the information to make decisions about advertising, display, and reorders.

Written messages traveling downward through the ranks consist mainly of instructions, orders, and statements of policy. These provide guidance in technical matters and operating procedures, but they may also attempt to win co-operation and improve morale. Messages traveling horizontally are usually memorandums and reports designed to co-ordinate the activities of individuals and departments that operate on similar levels of authority but in different areas. For example, a manufacturing company's sales forecasts must be communicated promptly to the finance, manufacturing, advertising, and personnel departments because their plans are interdependent.

MESSAGE OBJECTIVES

No matter where it originates or what its specific use is, every business message is designed to achieve two main objectives:

(1) to communicate information, and (2) to influence the reader.

INFORMING THE READER. A business message is written in the first place because, presumably, the writer has something to say. To the degree that the content is important to the reader and communicated correctly, precisely, and clearly, it will be regarded as informative and thus, whatever else the consequences, have value for the reader.

Informative writing takes on special significance at the present time. Communication is so cheap, fast, and ever-present that there is a tendency to ignore it. Part of the writer's function is to make sure that his message gets the attention of the intended reader. At the same time, the writer must avoid the temptation to get attention at the expense of providing information. The absence of information is a common characteristic of consumer advertising which appeals largely to the emotions. Although emotional appeals are a legitimate function of communication, they should not be permitted to take the place of the "hard" information needed particularly in the decision-making processes. This principle is especially important in internal communications such as memorandums and reports which can have disastrous results if they do not carry full and accurate information.

INFLUENCING THE READER. In addition to providing information, the business message must influence the reader's response. This point is easy to comprehend in the instance of, say, an advertisement for soap or a collection letter where effectiveness can be determined by the number of bars of soap sold or the amount of money collected. But the matter of influence is less easy to understand in the instance of the reply to a casual inquiry that has no apparent business potential or of a report that is completely factual. Since neither message requires an answer, where is the influence exerted? The answer is in the attitude of the reader. If a letter satisfies the reader's needs, he will have positive feelings about the writer and the writer's organization—feelings that may ultimately be expressed in conversations with others, in a vote for management at a stockholders' meeting, or in some future choice of the company's products. A report that satisfies one's superior will have similar results. Even though no recommendation is made, the facts may influence a business decision and even lead to a promotion for the subordinate who wrote it.

What influences a reader, in addition to the information provided by the message, is sometimes hard to pinpoint. Certainly, it includes the consideration the writer shows for the reader's feelings and the manner in which the writer adapts to the reader's needs. Beyond that, influence depends on the writer's use of the psychology of persuasion, about which much has been learned in the past several decades. More will be said about this subject in the next chapter.

Review Problems

1. What are the advantages of writing in the organization? What are its uses? Can you think of any jobs that can be done better by speaking than by writing? Discuss.

2. What kinds of messages flow into the organization? What kinds flow out? Find an example of a common form of business writing that *cannot* be classified as a letter, a report, or an advertisement.

3. What kinds of messages travel upward in the organization? What kinds flow downward? Horizontally?

4. What are the two objectives of every business message? Examine three different business messages, preferably of different kinds, for the extent to which they fulfill these objectives.

5. By reference to library sources, write a short paper on the impact of the electronic media (including radio, television, and motion pictures) on written communication.

2
The Communication Process

So far the term *communication* has been used without any attempt to define it. It is time a distinction was made between writing —or speaking, for that matter—and communication. A very general but still valid point is that writing suggests putting thoughts into words. Thus it emphasizes a message-oriented concept. Communication, on the other hand, suggests the interdependence of sender and receiver—of writer and reader—and therefore emphasizes a human orientation as well. It is this concept of interdependence that identifies the communication process and controls modern communication thinking and practice.[1]

COMMUNICATION MODELS

A handy device for clarifying anything so complicated as the communication process is the use of "models." A model may be described as an abstract representation of the concept to be explained. The representation may be physical (as a terrestrial globe), mathematical ($\pi = 3.141592$), graphic (an organization chart), or verbal (a definition). Since all details cannot be represented and would in fact be confusing, the model includes only those details that are relevant to its purpose. In the treatment of

---

[1] Students who wish to learn more about aspects of the communication process dealt with in this chapter are referred to *The Process of Communication* by David K. Berlo (New York: Holt, Rinehart & Winston, 1960); *A Theory of Cognitive Dissonance* by Leon Festinger (New York: Harper & Row, 1957); *Communication and Persuasion* by Carl I. Hovland, Irving L. Janis, and Harold H. Kelley (New Haven: Yale University Press, 1953); and "The Mathematics of Communication" by Warren Weaver in Alfred G. Smith, ed., *Communication and Culture* (New York: Holt, Rinehart & Winston, 1966), pp. 15–24.

the communication process, a number of models—verbal and graphic—may be used. Each represents a distinctive view of the subject.

To initiate the study of the communication process, these definitions—or verbal models—may be offered:

1. Communication is the sending and receiving of messages.
2. Communication is social interaction through messages.
3. Communication is the use of messages to affect response.

THE SENDING AND RECEIVING OF MESSAGES. The first definition may be said to emphasize the mechanical or technical concept of communication. The aim of the communicator is to transmit a message from one point (A) to another point (B) with the greatest fidelity or the smallest loss of signal or meaning. This concept is explained in great technical detail in a landmark work of communication scholarship, *The Mathematical Theory of Communication*, by Claude Shannon and Warren Weaver.[2] To expound their theory, the authors use a graphic model of which a simplified version is shown in Fig. 2.

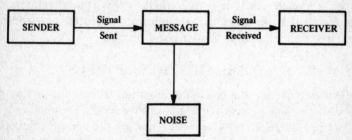

Fig. 2. The communication process (a technical model)

In the Shannon-Weaver model a distinction is made between the signal sent and the signal received. The difference is accounted for by "noise." Noise may be taken to mean any interference with the faithful transmission and receipt of the message. It is of two kinds: (1) mechanical noise, and (2) semantic noise. Mechanical noise is characteristic of all machine communication, which is subject to sound distortion, weak signals, interference (static), and

---

[2] University of Illinois Press, 1949. (A condensed and less technical version can be found in the Weaver article cited in footnote 1.)

the like. Mechanical noise is also present in human communication conducted without the intervention of machines. For example, a speaker may not be heard because of audible conversation in the same room or because of noise from traffic or building construction outside. Mechanical noise in a written message may be represented by a typographical error, a blot or strikeover, or any other damage that obscures the intended message.

Unlike mechanical noise, which is invariably represented by some physical manifestation, semantic noise is entirely in the mind.[3] It is the difference between the meaning intended by the sender and the meaning obtained by the receiver. Largely because of differences in life experience, the same words mean different things to different people. The point is that not only may vocabulary be deficient, not only are many words ambiguous in themselves, but the psychological overtones of words vary from person to person. There are many forms of verbal misunderstanding. A writer may, for example, say *credible* (believable) when he means *creditable* (praiseworthy), and the reader may take *creditable* to mean *credible*. Similarly, the writer may use *soon*, meaning "in the next few days," while the reader takes it to mean "in the next few weeks." But in addition, there are very abstract words like *free enterprise, honesty, democracy,* and *freedom,* which evoke the broadest range of difference because of the differences in the life experiences and values of the users.

For the writer, then, the concept of communication as "the sending and receiving of messages" is not as simple as it first seems. The most important fact about it is that it emphasizes (1) the need for fidelity or exactness both in the framing of the message and in its interpretation, and (2) the difficulties of achieving that fidelity both mechanically and verbally.

SOCIAL INTERACTION THROUGH MESSAGES. A second concept views communication as a social process in which the sender and receiver interact with each other. The product of their interaction is expressed in messages using language and signs of all sorts and any of the available channels of transmission, or media. A graphic model of this concept is shown in Fig. 3. The most distinctive

---

[3] The term *semantic noise* is derived from *semantics,* which is the study of the meaning of words and other symbols.

features of this model are **(1)** feedback, **(2)** empathy, and **(3)** the interdependence of sender and receiver.

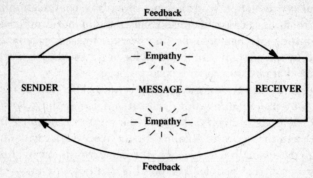

Fig. 3. The communication process (a social model). Sender and receiver transmit messages and use feedback and empathy.

Feedback. When the response to a message is used by the source as the input for future messages, the response is called feedback. This point is most readily illustrated by reference to oral communication. If a speaker's remarks are greeted by applause, he may continue in the same vein, confident that the audience is with him. If he sees the audience in the rear straining forward and cupping their ears, he senses he is not being heard and he raises his voice. As these examples show, the response or feedback performs two functions: (1) it tells the communicator to what degree his message has been effective, and (2) it helps to insure future effectiveness.

The difference between feedback in speech communication and feedback in written communication is that, in the first case, feedback is instantaneous, but in the second it is delayed. In fact, the lapse of time between the writing of a message and the receipt of a possible reply may be days, weeks, or longer. This is too late to make any needed corrections in the original message, but the reply may still permit correction to be made in a future message. Thus any response may still have value as feedback; the test is whether the writer uses what he learns from the response. In advertising, feedback is obtained by exposing trial copy to a small percentage of the audience. The lessons learned from the response are then incorporated in the final advertisement. Many costly mistakes in phrasing and in the use of sales appeals and illustrations are prevented in this way.

Empathy. Whether used by a speaker or a writer, feedback can come only in response to signals already sent. But would it not be helpful if one could judge *in advance* how a message will be received and thus be able to build effectiveness into the message in the first place? To a greater or lesser degree, every communicator is equipped to make such judgments. The means he uses is *empathy.* This is a psychological device by which the communicator develops expectations about the behavior of the receiver. He may exercise empathy by making inferences from his own experience, that is, by attributing to the receiver the feelings about the message that he himself might have. Thus, if he is writing a letter of condolence, he may recall how he reacted to condolence letters he received upon the death of a member of his family, and use that knowledge to anticipate the reaction to the letter he writes. He will be especially careful to avoid expressions that annoyed him and to include expressions that pleased him or those he wished the writers had used.

There are many other situations, however, for which the communicator's experience has not prepared him. In those circumstances, he must simply play-act or assume the role of the receiver. Thus, a writer may never have made a decision to institute a bonus plan that would cost his company two million dollars a year, but if he is advocating such a plan, he must be able to "get into the shoes" of the executive who is making the decision and marshal the kind of arguments that would make a favorable impression on him. In any situation, it stands to reason that the more one knows about the receiver, and the better he adapts to him, the more effective the message will be. Consequently, the successful writer is likely to be the one who studies the reader closely, inquires about others' experiences with him, and is generally sensitive to the motives and feelings of his fellow human beings. Such a writer may be said to have a large degree of empathy.

Interdependence of Sender and Receiver. Recognition of the place of feedback and empathy in the communication process makes it possible to describe three levels of communication:

1. The sender transmits messages as he pleases, without empathy for the reader and without using the response as feedback. This is

the lowest order of interdependence, using the receiver only as a receptacle for the sender's messages. It may arouse enmity and almost certainly is doomed to failure. It is called one-way communication.

2. The sender transmits messages with empathy and with the use of response for feedback. This is two-way communication, but not so effective as it can be, for this concept makes no provision for the reciprocal use of empathy and feedback by the receiver.

3. Both the sender and the receiver transmit messages, using empathy and feedback. Each puts himself in the place of the other, making predictions of how the other will respond, and communicating accordingly. This is two-way communication raised to the level of interaction, or reciprocal influence. On this level there is between both parties a bridge to which both parties have equal access. This is as close to the ideal of communication as the human condition permits.

THE USE OF MESSAGES TO AFFECT RESPONSE. This third definition, or model, of communication emphasizes the sender's purpose: to persuade the receiver (Fig. 4). The starting point is the re-

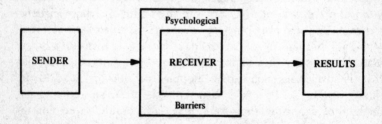

Fig. 4. The communication process (a pragmatic model)

ceiver's "image," which may be described as his beliefs, or his subjective view of the universe. These beliefs may be enlarged through the addition of new knowledge or they may be disturbed by the introduction of contradictory knowledge, which forces the receiver to reevaluate his previous position. In either case, persuasion is at work. However, it should be obvious that getting someone to accept new information is easier than getting him to accept contradictory information. It is to the latter problem that the business persuader must address himself most vigorously.

An example will help to demonstrate the problem and the nature of the solution. Mr. Jones uses gas to heat his home, but electricity to run the air conditioners in the two bedrooms. Advertisements for gas heat will not overtly change Mr. Jones's situation, but by providing new information about the quality or cost of gas heat or about the increased acceptance of gas heat in new communities, these advertisements will help to reinforce his previous conviction and make his loyalty to gas heat even stronger than it was. Should, however, the gas company try to get Mr. Jones to install a central gas air conditioning system, Mr. Jones will be faced with a conflict. He has already invested six hundred dollars in the electric air conditioners. It will cost him several times that amount to convert to central gas air conditioning. And then there are the imponderables: the cost of operating the system, its efficiency. It follows that the gas company will have a heavy job of persuasion in this instance.

The main problem of persuasion, then, is the resolution of conflict between what the receiver of the message already believes and what the sender would have him believe. As a matter of fact, psychologists make the point that there can be no persuasion until there is such conflict of beliefs, or—to use some of the other terms that are applied—*inconsistency* or *dissonance*. But if the persuader is expected to create such conflict, he is of course also expected to find ways of resolving it. Those ways include (1) source credibility, (2) motivation, (3) new information, and (4) force of the message.

Source Credibility. A message coming from a source whose credibility is accepted by the reader will tend to diminish inconsistency and move the receiver in the direction of message. Credibility is gained by (1) recognized expertness and (2) freedom from bias. An independent engineer employed to make a recommendation for the purchase of a computer may have both. The salesman-engineer for a computer manufacturer may have only the first. The "man-next-door" who touts his son's used car may have neither. A communicator who does not himself have strong credibility may be able to "borrow" it from another. In advertising, for instance, it is common to feature the endorsement of a respected individual as a substitute for the claims of the advertiser himself. In the office, a low-ranking employee with a good idea must often find a sponsor among the executive staff if he wishes it to be considered seriously by others.

Motivation. Even when the receiver feels he has no use for the belief put forward by the sender, he may yet want the benefits that acceptance will afford him. The Mr. Jones cited in the earlier example may be reluctant to switch to gas air conditioning, but he does want the comfort the change will provide. Emphasis on that comfort will help to resolve the conflict between his own belief and that of the gas company. In almost every instance of similar inconsistency, the receiver has some motive that can be tapped. It may be charity, vanity, curiosity, the instinct for survival, the prospect of personal gain, or any of a great number of other motives that control actions.

New Information. Very often a belief is based on old or inaccurate information. When better information is supplied, the old belief may easily give way. A company that avoids hiring handicapped workers in the belief that such workers are unreliable may relent when figures are shown that prove handicapped workers are more reliable in many ways than the unhandicapped. Of course, the motivation for hiring the handicapped will be stronger if the job market is tight.

Force of the Message. A belief expressed with unusual force or novelty may crumble the opposition to it. A report, for example, improves its chance of acceptance if it states its case with great clarity and logic. Similarly, a letter with gentle humor may overcome caustic criticism. Publication advertisements and radio and television commercials also demonstrate every day how repetition, suspense, humor, novelty, and sheer size or duration break down the consumer's resistance and make otherwise old or even repugnant ideas acceptable.

In summary, the view of communication as "the use of messages to affect response" presents the message as a bid for the mind of the receiver. It is not until the receiver relinquishes his contrary beliefs and accepts those of the sender that the message becomes wholly effective. This is a pragmatic view well suited to the needs of the business communicator. Its weakness, if any, is that it may encourage an aggressive attitude toward the receiver when, in fact, a less assertive approach might be more disarming and ultimately more persuasive.

TOOLS OF EFFECTIVENESS

While the foregoing communication models draw attention primarily to the relationship of the sender and the receiver, a large problem for the writer is how to weld all the elements of communication into an effective presentation. The tools he uses are (1) message content, (2) language or "code," (3) medium, (4) display, and (5) timing.

MESSAGE CONTENT. The factors that influence the message content include the purpose to be achieved, the reader's need for information, the policies of the sender's organization, the information available and suitable, the medium through which the message will be communicated, and the timing. Thus, to give some representative examples, the sale of a new technical product will call for a good deal of description and explanation; the reply to an inquiry will carefully include the data asked for; a refund on a bathing suit may be refused because of legal restrictions or store policy; unfavorable data regarding an employee may be kept out of a letter of reference to avoid the possibility of libel; and the timeliness of a newspaper may dictate a "sale" advertisement in that medium whereas a magazine would offer a more promising setting for goodwill or institutional copy.

Using the kind of information the circumstances dictate, the writer must organize it into a coherent whole. Much is written about the importance of choosing the right words, but a necessary —and often underestimated—prelude is to shape and form the message, to arrange and connect the parts. Once the reader detects the pattern of the composition, he has important clues to the writer's intentions and the effort to understand the message is considerably eased. The use of headings and subheadings, as well as topic sentences, connecting phrases, and the repetition of key words—all help to underline the structure of the message. These and other writing techniques are discussed in Chapter 6, "Plan and Construction of the Letter," and Chapter 16, "Organizing Report Data," and in Section VII, "Coherence and Emphasis."

LANGUAGE OR "CODE." Language is useful only when it is understood in the same sense by both the sender and the receiver. Thus it must utilize a code on which there is common agreement. It will not do, for instance, if the writer uses "operational difficulties" to

mean shortage of materials while the reader takes it to mean
worker dissatisfaction. Meaning depends partly on the context in
which words appear and partly on the individual experiences of
each party to the communication. Apart from their dictionary
meanings or "denotations," words also have subjective meanings
or "connotations." The latter are sometimes difficult to control,
although the writer is aided in the choice of words by his sensi-
tivity or empathy toward the reader. But in addition to his concern
for the reader, the writer must choose words to conform to the
character of the message and create a favorable impression of his
company and himself. The language suited to the announcement
of a mortuary will not be suited to the advertisement for a soft
drink; and a letter couched in the stilted language of an insurance
policy will not help to convey the warmth of either the writer or
the company.

MEDIUM. Every message must find its most effective medium,
whether it be print, sound, or picture. Within the general class of
medium, also, the most effective outlet, or channel, must be chosen.
Thus a written announcement will present the problem of whether
to send it out as a letter, a printed circular, a newspaper advertisement, or a magazine spread. At the same time, both medium and
channel will exert a strong influence on the composition of the
message and its display. A letter, for example, can be made to
sound much more personal than a printed circular or a publication
advertisement because each letter is addressed to a single individual. On the other hand, the letter is extremely limited in its
capacity for illustration and color, an important consideration if
one is selling a product like gourmet foods.

DISPLAY. As the preceding discussion suggests, display is an
attribute of the medium as well as the message. The medium, for
instance, determines the extent to which paper, color, and illustration can be used to heighten the effect of the message, but within
the limitations of any particular medium, a great deal of variety
is possible. One need not go further than the subject of letters and
reports to realize how much opportunity for display each medium
affords. Good paper, a well-designed letterhead, an attractive frame
of white space, and neat typing add immeasurably to the effect of
a letter. So, too, a handsomely packaged report—from trim cover to
easy-reading pages to compact tables and colorful graphs—pre-

dispose the reader to the message and make the task of persuasion that much easier.

TIMING. The time at which a message is received may also have much to do with its success. A letter of congratulation or condolence or a reply to a complaint or inquiry is best received promptly or the impact is diminished. A similar principle operates in placing advertisements. An umbrella advertisement attracts more interested attention when it is raining than when it is not, and advertisers whose equipment is used in sports events and technological breakthroughs most effectively boast of their contributions in the same issues of newspapers that report the events. As the examples indicate, some media permit more timeliness than others. A memorandum may be put in the hands of the intended reader within moments of completion. The reader of a letter or newspaper advertisement may have to wait for the next morning. On the other hand, a color advertisement in a national magazine will take a number of weeks between conception and publication.

Review Problems

1. What is a "model" and what forms does it take? Why is a model useful as a communication tool?

2. Give three verbal models (definitions) of communication, and explain their differences.

3. What are the obstacles to fidelity in the communication of written messages? Explain.

4. Define the following terms with relation to written communication: (a) noise, (b) feedback, (c) empathy.

5. Explain the concept of interdependence with relation to the communication process. What are the levels of interdependence? Which is the ideal level?

6. Discuss the relation of conflict to persuasion. By what means does the persuader attempt to resolve conflict?

7. Name the elements or tools that contribute to an effective written presentation. Find five different business messages, each of which is especially strong in one of these elements.

PART 2
BUSINESS LETTERS

PART 2
BUSINESS LETTERS

Among the forms of written communication in business, the letter is probably the most useful and the most common. A business letter is a private message designed to accomplish a specific purpose. As a rule, letters are individually dictated, typewritten, and signed. However, even *form letters*—those duplicated in large numbers—are private in the sense that each is enclosed in an envelope addressed to an individual.

An examination of successful business letters usually reveals certain common characteristics: (1) a definite purpose, (2) consideration for the reader, (3) natural style, (4) correct usage and form, and (5) attractive appearance. (See Fig. 5.)

DEFINITE PURPOSE. The businessman should write a letter only when he has a definite purpose and can clearly identify the response he seeks. In this way, he saves his and the reader's time and increases the likelihood of a favorable result.

CONSIDERATION FOR THE READER. Since it is the intention of every correspondent to produce results beneficial to his company, he must be aware of factors influencing the reader. One of these factors is courtesy. Another is the use of words and terminology that the reader can readily understand. Still another factor is the ability to see every transaction from the reader's viewpoint so that the benefits to the reader, not to the writer, are stressed.

NATURAL STYLE. In addition to presenting his ideas clearly,

South Connecticut Savings Bank

400 State Street
Hartford, Conn. 06006

January 19, 19--

Mr. Robert Anderson
238 Chapel Street
Hartford, Conn. 06012

Dear Mr. Anderson:

We shall be pleased to comply with your letter of
January 17 in which you inform us that you wish your
individual account changed to a joint account, with
Mrs. Anderson as co-depositor.

To make the change possible, you and Mrs. Anderson will
have to sign and complete the enclosed forms and return
them to us with your bankbook. A postage-paid envelope
is enclosed for your convenience.

As soon as we receive the signature cards and bankbook,
we shall change our records and return the corrected
book to you.

We appreciate the opportunity of adding Mrs. Anderson
to our family of depositors and we shall try to serve
her well.

Sincerely yours,

Albert Truslow

Albert Truslow, Cashier

AT:RB

Fig. 5. An effective business letter

the businessman's language should dispose the reader toward the
writer and his firm. Old-style "business English," with its stereo-

typed and impersonal phrases (e.g., "Yours of the 25th instant received and noted") has given way to a warmer and more natural style (e.g., "We are glad to reply to your letter of April 25").

CORRECT USAGE AND FORM. An effective letter is free of errors in sentence structure, word use, spelling, grammar, and punctuation. Facts, dates, names, figures, and titles should also be correct. Furthermore, the mechanical form of the letter (e.g., the details of the address, salutation, and complimentary close) should conform to modern standards. Deviations from the recognized rules or normal patterns of correctness in usage and form may distract the reader and leave a negative impression.

ATTRACTIVE APPEARANCE. A neat letter attracts favorable attention and, therefore, has a better chance of success than a slovenly one. The paper should be of good quality, and the printed heading should be attractive and distinctive in design. The margins should provide a pleasing frame for the letter, the typist's strokes should be of uniform weight, and there should not be either strikeovers or obvious erasures.

3
The Physical Form of the Letter

The reader of a business letter is influenced not only by its content but also by its physical form and appearance. A good first impression, particularly, depends on the care the typist has taken. Since this impression may have considerable bearing on the reader's final judgment of the message, it is worth while to check the various physical elements carefully before the letter is mailed.

To a great extent, current standards of acceptability determine the correct form of the letter. Thus, the policies of leading business firms provide guides to such factors as custom, appropriateness, and pleasing appearance. Although they differ in detail, the practices of these companies are sufficiently similar to permit the establishment of certain criteria for the physical make-up of letters. These criteria relate principally to (1) general appearance and (2) mechanical details.

GENERAL APPEARANCE

The most important physical characteristic of a letter is neatness. Whether or not a letter is pleasing to the eye depends mainly on the selection of stationery and on the quality of typing.

STATIONERY. To some extent the type of stationery varies with the purpose for which it is to be used. For example, the paper stock for interoffice messages need not be so good in quality as that for letters to customers. Similarly, the paper used in printed sales letters for mass circularization need not be so expensive as the paper used in the more personal types of letters.

Most business letters are typewritten on white bond paper, $8\frac{1}{2}$ by 11 inches in size. Many firms also stock a smaller size, usually $5\frac{1}{2}$ by $8\frac{1}{2}$ inches. This size is used for very brief messages of an informal nature. Generally, envelope sizes are standard and are referred to as "small" (No. $6\frac{3}{4}$) and "long" (No. 9 or 10). The long envelope is desirable when more than one sheet is enclosed. Occasionally, stationery of different size or color is used for special purposes, such as correspondence with branch offices and sales messages.

The letter sheet should be folded neatly to fit the envelope. When the small envelope is used, the letter is folded up from the bottom to about one-half inch of the top edge; then the sheet is folded twice across. When the long envelope is used, the sheet of stationery is folded twice horizontally.

TYPING. A letter that is well typed is clean and well spaced and has pleasing margins. Obvious erasures and strikeovers, a zig-zag right-hand margin, lack of space between paragraphs, and imperfect positioning on the page are evidences of carelessness and weigh against the content of a letter before a single sentence is read.

Fig. 7 is a neatly centered and typed letter. Note how the spaces between paragraphs and the regular right-hand margin make the letter inviting to look at and to read.

MECHANICAL DETAILS

Although tidiness is most important to the physical make-up of the letter, the correspondent must be concerned also with other factors, particularly those that are influenced by custom and tradition. These factors relate to (1) the indention, (2) the punctuation, and (3) the placement and the wording of the parts of the letter.

So that there may be a common ground for the discussion of these factors, see Fig. 6 in which the various parts of the letter are named. The parts of the letter are the *letterhead, date, inside address, salutation, body* or *message, complimentary close, signature,* and *initials.* Other devices, such as *postscripts,* notations of *enclosure, attention lines,* and *special references,* may also be used.

INDENTION. As Fig. 7 illustrates, the parts of the letter may be set in "block" style, that is, without indentions. In Fig. 8 the paragraphs composing the body of the letter are indented. This style

_____ (Letterhead) _____

_____

_____

_____ (Date) _____

(Inside Address) _____
_____
_____

(Salutation) _____

_____
_____
_____
_____
_____

(Body or Message)

_____
_____
_____
_____
_____

_____
_____
_____
_____
_____

_____ (Complimentary Close)

_____ (Signature) _____

(Initials)

Fig. 6. The mechanical parts of the letter

LOrraine 3-4760

Elite Department Store
100 Fifth Street
Cleveland, Ohio 44106

July 18, 19--

Miss Maude S. Oliver
Elite Department Store
100 Fifth Street
Cleveland, Ohio 44106

Dear Miss Oliver

First, let me congratulate you on having been selected,
from a number of applicants, to fill the position of
stenographer. I am sure that you will enter upon your
new duties with a keen desire to succeed.

Accompanying this letter is your copy of our Stenographers' Manual. It contains information about your business hours, holidays and vacations, absences, and
deductions for taxes, social security, etc. In addition,
it provides you with detailed instructions about the
physical form of your letters. You are at liberty to
take your copy of this manual home at night so that you
may read and study it at your leisure. But you should
always return it to your desk in order to be able to
refer to it quickly at any time.

So that you may carry on your work today, this letter
will serve as a model of the letter style that has been
fixed by the Elite Department Store. Although there
are several correct styles, we want you to follow the
form exemplified by this letter so that all of our letters
may be consistent in appearance.

If you encounter any difficulties in your work, do not
hesitate to consult me.

Sincerely yours

Edna Courtney

Chief Stenographer

Edna Courtney:DB
Encl.

Fig. 7. A letter in block style, open punctuation

Elite Department Store
100 Fifth Street
Cleveland, Ohio 44106

July 18, 19--

Miss Maude S. Oliver
Elite Department Store
100 Fifth Street
Cleveland, Ohio 44106

Dear Miss Oliver:

First, let me congratulate you on having been selected, from a number of applicants, to fill the position of stenographer. I am sure that you will enter upon your new duties with a keen desire to succeed.

Accompanying this letter is your copy of our Stenographers' Manual. It contains information about your business hours, holidays and vacations, absences, and deductions for taxes, social security, etc. In addition, it provides you with detailed instructions about the physical form of your letters. You are at liberty to take your copy of this manual home at night so that you may read and study it at your leisure. But you should always return it to your desk in order to be able to refer to it quickly at any time.

So that you may carry on your work today, this letter will serve as a model of the letter style that has been fixed by the Elite Department Store. Although there are several correct styles, we want you to follow the form exemplified by this letter so that all of our letters may be consistent in appearance.

If you encounter any difficulties in your work, do not hesitate to consult me.

Sincerely yours,

Edna Courtney

Chief Stenographer

Edna Courtney:DB
Encl.

Fig. 8. A letter in semi-block style, mixed punctuation

is called "semi-block." The block style is slightly more formal in appearance than the semi-block and is somewhat easier to type. Other styles of indention are used in business letters, but not with such frequency and consistency as the block and semi-block styles.

STYLES OF PUNCTUATION. So-called "open" punctuation is illustrated in Fig. 7. Except for abbreviations, no punctuation is placed after the lines forming the heading or date, inside address, salutation, or complimentary close. Somewhat more popular is standard or "mixed" punctuation, shown in Fig. 8. Punctuation is placed after the salutation and complimentary close. An older style, "closed" punctuation, which required punctuation after the date and each line of the inside address, as well as the other mechanical parts of the letter, is now seldom seen.

THE PARTS OF THE LETTER. Before typing the letter, the stenographer should estimate the amount of space the letter will occupy, then set her margins so that the letter will be properly centered. The side margins should be at least one inch wide and the bottom margin should be at least one inch deep. Although practices vary in setting up the specific parts of the letter, all of the following forms —provided they are followed consistently within the company— may be considered acceptable.

Letterhead. A company's letterhead is ordinarily printed or engraved at the top of the letter sheet. It should contain at least the name and address of the company and preferably the telephone number as well. Under appropriate circumstances, branch offices, cable address, and the particular department or office of the writer may be indicated. When a printed letterhead is not used, the address of the writer is typewritten directly above the date as follows:

```
                    1487 South Market Street
                    San Francisco, Calif. 94027
                    September 14, 19--
```

Date. The date should be placed several spaces below the letterhead. The line should begin halfway across the page, or farther to the right, but the end of the line should not project beyond the right-hand margin of the letter. No abbreviations should be used. *Correct*

```
                              February 16, 19--
```

Inside Address. The inside address consists of the name and address of the person or group to whom the letter is directed. It is placed at the left-hand margin several spaces below the date. The name of an individual is always preceded by a title of respect (*Mr., Dr., Professor,* etc.). A business title (*President, Secretary,* etc.) may follow on the same line or, if it consists of more than one word, on a second line. A company's name should be written in the same style as it appears in the company's letterhead, including abbreviations and punctuation. The words *Street, Avenue, North, South,* etc., and the name of the state may be abbreviated, but more often they are spelled out. Numbered streets and avenues up to and including *Tenth* are customarily spelled out. Street numbers are usually written with the endings *–st, –nd, –rd, –th.* The zip code number should be placed on the last line of the address following the city and state.

Correct

```
Mr. Walter Jones, President        Mr. Russell E. Compton
Jones Cement Company               252 West 34th Street
4400 Kensington Avenue             Toronto, Ontario
Chicago, Illinois 60013            Canada

Miss Phoebe Trasker                Dr. Jonas R. Kent
49 East Fifth St.                  Tivoli, New York 12583
Milwaukee, Wis. 53051

Busse Printing Co., Inc.           Dr. Jonas R. Kent
375 No. Buckeye Drive              Tivoli
Cincinnati, Ohio 45206             New York 12583
```

Salutation. The salutation is placed two spaces below the inside address and flush with the left margin. In general practice the salutation is followed by a colon (:). In the ordinary correspondence addressed to individuals, the salutation is *Dear Mr.* (*Miss* or *Mrs.*) —————————. Less formality may be shown by using the first name, as in *Dear Frank* or *Dear Lucy.* More formality may be shown by using such salutations as *My dear Mr.* (*Miss* or *Mrs.*) —————————, *Dear Sir* (or *Dear Madam*), and *My dear Sir* or *My dear Madam. Dear Madam* may be used in addressing either a single or a married woman.

In addressing a company or other organization consisting of both men and women, the writer should use *Gentlemen* (not *Dear Sirs*). If the organization consists entirely of women, the correct salutation is *Mesdames* or *Ladies*. When, however, the word *Corporation* or *Incorporated* is included in the name of the organization (as in "Helene Curtis, Inc."), the salutation should be *Gentlemen*.

Such salutations as *Dear Reader*, *Dear Customer*, and *Dear Subscriber* are pardonable in circular letters only.

Forms of address used in writing to special classes of individuals are illustrated below.[1]

Married woman or widow   *Divorced woman*

```
Mrs. William Smith                  Mrs. Mary Bates Smith
10 Grand Avenue                     10 Grand Avenue
Baltimore, Md. 21008                Baltimore, Md. 21008

Dear Mrs. Smith:                    Dear Mrs. Smith:
```

In the example above, *Bates* is the lady's maiden name and *Smith* the name of her former husband.

Minister of religion

```
Reverend David R. Kaye    Dear Sir:
9 Gerry Road              Reverend Sir:
Chestnut Hill, Maine      Dear Mr. Kaye:
                          Dear Dr. Kaye:
                          Dear Reverend Father: (Catholic)
                          Dear Rabbi Kaye: (Jewish)
```

President of the United States

```
The President             Sir:
The White House           Dear Mr. President:
Washington, D. C. 20500
```

---

[1] A more comprehensive list of forms of address will be found in *Webster's Third New International* (Unabridged) *Dictionary* (G. & C. Merriam Co., Springfield, 1967).

Cabinet Officer

```
Honorable Rufus S. Gordon        Sir:
Secretary of Defense             My dear Mr. Secretary:
Washington, D. C. 20301
```

Senator

```
Honorable Patrick D. Nigh        Dear Sir:
United States Senate             My dear Senator Nigh:
Washington, D.C. 20510
```

Member of Congress

```
Honorable Robert Gray            Dear Sir:
House of Representatives         My dear Mr. Gray:
Washington, D. C. 20510
```

Governor

```
Honorable John H. Temple         Sir:
Governor of New Jersey           Dear Governor:
Trenton, New Jersey 08608
```

Mayor

```
Honorable James M. Traynor       Dear Mr. Mayor
Mayor of the City of New York    Dear Mayor Traynor:
City Hall
New York, N. Y. 10007
```

Body.[2] The body of the letter contains the message. Except in very short letters, in which the body is occasionally double-spaced, the body of the letter is single-spaced with double spacing between paragraphs. Within the body, the names of the days and the months should be spelled out, and the endings *–st, –nd, –rd,* and *–th* should be omitted after the date.

Correct

```
last Wednesday; your letter of October 22
```

_____

[2] Other mechanical details of the body of the letter are treated in Part 4, Section X.

If the letter requires a second sheet, at least three lines of the body should be carried over. The second sheet does not usually have a letterhead. The name of the addressee, the page number, and the date should be typewritten across the top as follows:

```
Mr. Walter T. Brinkerhoff        -2-        May 25, 19--
```

Complimentary Close. The complimentary close usually begins two spaces below the last line of the body of the letter and about midway between the left- and right-hand margins. The most frequently used form of complimentary close is *Very truly yours*; *Yours very truly* is sometimes used. *Yours truly* and *Truly yours* are becoming rare. *Sincerely yours* or *Sincerely* is suitable when some friendly contact with the reader has already been established; *Cordially yours* or *Cordially* may be used in writing to a personal acquaintance. *Respectfully yours* is occasionally used in writing to an older person, an employer, a government official, or some other person toward whom it is desired to show special consideration. A comma follows the complimentary close except where open punctuation is used.

Signature. The signature consists usually of the name of the writer and his business title (if he has one). When a letterhead is not used or when the signature appears on a second or succeeding page, the name of the company is included. When a secretary signs a letter in the writer's absence, she writes his name in her own hand and puts her initials below the last few letters of the signature. Various styles of signature follow:

```
Very truly yours,                    Very truly yours,

John R. Smith                        Geneva Steel Works, Inc.

John R. Smith                        John R. Smith
Treasurer                            Treasurer


Very truly yours,                    Very truly yours,

Apollo Messenger Service             William S. Jones

by  William S. Jones                 William S. Jones
```

Very truly yours,   Very truly yours,

Mary C. Smith   *Mary C. Smith*

(Miss) Mary C. Smith   Mary C. Smith

Single woman

Very truly yours,   Very truly yours,

Mary C. Frye   *Mary C. Frye*

Mary C. Frye   (Mrs.) Mary Smith Frye
(Mrs. John D. Frye)

Married woman   *Divorced woman*

Initials. It is customary for the stenographer to place her initials
and those of the writer against the left-hand margin, two or three
spaces below the signature. If the name of the writer is not typed
below his signature, it is a good idea to type the full name in the
left-hand corner. Any of the following styles is acceptable.

TD:JRS	Thomas Dedham:JRS
td:jrs	
TD/JRS	TDedham
td/jrs	JRS

Special Devices. Some letters employ subject and file references,
attention lines, and notice of transmission by air mail, registered
mail, or special delivery. The exact position of these elements varies
from company to company. For example, the attention line, which
is centered two spaces below the salutation in the example immediately following, is sometimes centered above the salutation, is sometimes put on the same line with the salutation, and is sometimes
set against the left margin above or below the inside address or
below the salutation. The following examples show how the various
special devices may appear in the letter:

January 27, 19--

File No. 326 R

<u>AIR MAIL</u>

General Rope and Wire Co.
Hyannis, Massachusetts 02601

Gentlemen:

<u>Attention: Mr. George C. Brunswick</u>

January 27, 19--

<u>REGISTERED MAIL</u>

Mr. George C. Brunswick
General Rope and Wire Co.
Hyannis, Massachusetts 02601

Dear Mr. Brunswick:

<u>Subject: Contract No. 326 R</u>

Enclosures. When an enclosure is sent with a letter, a notation to that effect should be put directly below the initials, as in these examples:

TD:JRS Enc.	TD: JRS Enclosure	
		TD:JRS Enclosures: 2
TD:JRS Encl.	TD:JRS 2 encls.	

Postscript. A postscript may occasionally be used to emphasize an important point, not to call attention to something the writer inadvertently omitted from the body of the letter. The postscript (usually prefaced by the abbreviation "P.S.") is placed two spaces below the initials.

Correct

```
      TUCKER SUPPLY COMPANY
           24 Market Street
      Providence, R. I. 02706


                                          SPECIAL DELIVERY



                 Denton Manufacturing Company
                 1700 Springfield Avenue
                 Cincinnati, Ohio 45203



      Attention of Mr. Ralph Settle
```

Envelope Address. The envelope address, bearing the ZIP Code number on the same line as the city and state, should begin slightly below the middle of the envelope and should be well centered.[3] Postal instructions, such as Air Mail, Special Delivery, and Registered Mail, should be typewritten in capital letters just below the space for the postage. If there is an "attention" line in the inside address, the same line should be typewritten in the lower left-hand corner of the envelope. The return address, whether printed or typewritten, is usually placed in the upper left-hand corner.

Review Problems

1. Answer the following questions about the letter shown in Fig. 5:
   a. What is the purpose of the letter?
   b. In what ways does the writer show his consideration for the reader?
   c. How is the natural style of the letter evidenced?
   d. What factors contribute to the pleasing appearance of the letter?

2. Which of the characteristics of effective business letters are lacking in the following letter:

---

[3] The two-letter state abbreviations recommended for ZIP Code addressing are listed on page 379.

Dear Mrs. Miller:

We are in receipt of yours of the 18th advising that you wish to purchase two pairs of cafe curtains. If you will read our advt. carefully, you will see that these curtains do not come in orchid as you specified.

Awaiting further word from you, we are

> Very truly yours,

3. Rewrite the letter above in accordance with the rules for effective letters stated in the introduction to Part 2, "Business Letters."

4. Complete the following statements relating to the physical form of the letter:

    a. The size of standard letterhead paper is . . . .

    b. The side and bottom margins of a letter should measure at least . . . .

    c. A letter with indented paragraphs and with the lines of the inside address flush with the left-hand margin is said to be typewritten in the . . . style.

    d. The date line should be typewritten as follows (use today's date): . . . .

    e. . . . is a proper title in addressing senators, congressmen, governors, mayors; and other government officials.

    f. The correct way to address a letter to myself is as follows: . . . .

    g. Two correct salutations in addressing a man are . . . .

    h. Two correct salutations in addressing an unmarried woman are . . . .

    i. Two correct salutations in addressing a married woman are . . . .

    j. The most frequently used form of the complimentary close is . . . .

5. Correct the errors in the following parts of business letters:

    a. Warren Graves
       18 East 2nd Street
       New York, 10003

    b. Your letter of August 3rd

    c. Dear Miss:

    d. Dear Sirs:—

    e. Respectively yours,

    f. Very truly yours,
       Mr. Barry Smithers

    g. Dec. 14, 1971

    h. Mission Trucking Corp.
       Attention: James Katt
       100 Madison Street
       Duluth, Minn. Zip 55811
       Dear Mr. Katt,

    i. Honorable Governor Stephen Graham

    j. Mr. James S. Travers
      Secretary
      Delta Contracting Company
      Jackson 39206, Mississippi

4

Adaptation of the Letter to the Reader

For the most part business correspondents promote the interests of their firms. Paradoxically, however, business writers best accomplish this purpose when they demonstrate an interest in the reader. The writer should try to see the reader's point of view and to determine what and how to write in order to bring about the desired response.

OBJECTIVE AND READER

To help both himself and his reader, the writer begins by clarifying his objective. This he does by (1) formulating the purpose of the message, (2) obtaining all the facts essential to the transaction, (3) familiarizing himself with relevant company policies and procedures, and (4) discovering the interests of the reader.

FORMULATING THE PURPOSE. Before writing a letter, many correspondents find it helpful to formulate the purpose mentally in a single sentence: "This letter is intended to collect money the reader owes us," or "The purpose of this letter is to make a satisfactory adjustment of the reader's complaint," or "This letter is intended to obtain delivery of the goods by October 16 at the very latest." With a definite guide such as this, the writer is more likely to adhere to his aim and achieve the desired results.

The writer of the following letter apparently did not have a definite purpose in mind:

Vague

Gentlemen:

I saw your latest catalogue at the home of a neighbor
and thought it was very nice. As your records will
show, I have often ordered merchandise from you, but I
was not always sure of the right prices. Of course, I
could bother my neighbor, but I'd rather not.

Very truly yours,

The writer of the letter below leaves no doubt as to its purpose:

Definite

Gentlemen:

Will you be kind enough to send me your latest catalogue?

I saw a copy of it at the home of a neighbor and
realized how convenient it would be to have one for
myself. I do order from you frequently, as your records
will show.

Very truly yours,

OBTAINING THE FACTS. The correspondent who tries to put ideas
in writing before he has the essential facts is almost certain to confuse the reader. In many situations relevant information can be
found in other correspondence on the same subject or with the
same reader. The writer should study such information carefully
before he dictates his letter. In this way, he will have essential background facts, specific dates, and other references which he can use
to make his letter clear. The following is the type of letter that results when the writer has done a poor job of collecting information.

Vague

Dear Sir:

Thank you for your inquiry of September 29.

We can probably furnish you with the types of cigarette
lighters you described, but the question of delivery
schedule is a difficult one.

If shipment by air is feasible, we might be able to
meet the due date you mentioned.

As soon as we receive your instructions, we shall begin
processing your order.

Very truly yours,

This letter lacks clarity because the reader neglected to obtain more definite answers to these questions: (1) Can the types of cigarette lighters requested be furnished? (2) Is shipment by air feasible? Here is the same letter rewritten in clearer terms:

Definite

Dear Sir:

We shall be pleased to make up three dozen Flamex lighters according to the specifications in your letter of
September 29. If you will wire us confirmation of the
order by 12 noon on Wednesday, October 2, we will ship
the lighters by air express on October 21. They should
reach you the following day.

We look forward to the opportunity of serving you.

Very truly yours,

A writer who deals with technical subjects or with readers in technical fields should acquire some familiarity with the terms, processes, and machines or instruments used. He can acquire the additional knowledge he needs by studying reliable textbooks or other printed materials on the subject, by referring to a glossary or dictionary of terms used in the field, or by observing actual operations in the plant or the office.

FOLLOWING COMPANY POLICY. Sometimes correspondence is vague because the writer, not knowing his company's policies or procedures, refuses to commit himself. When the writer is uncertain as to his firm's policies, he should consult his supervisor or whatever references are available. In many companies, a printed manual provides answers to questions of policy and procedure. In other instances, records of past practices are to be found in the files.

Compare the next two letters.

Vague

Dear Mrs. Jones:

We are pleased when a customer writes to tell us her views on some aspect of our service.

Your suggestion regarding our merchandise tags should certainly have consideration. I am not certain whether the head of our dress department has the authority to make any change in the present system. Perhaps the suggestion can be passed upon by a member of our executive committee.

In any event, you can be sure the suggestion will be reviewed by someone in our organization authorized to do so. Please do not hesitate to write again if you do not hear from us within the next few weeks.

                              Very truly yours,

Here is the same letter rewritten to reflect a knowledge of company policy and procedures.

Definite

Dear Mrs. Jones:

We are pleased when a customer writes to tell us her views on some aspect of our service.

A meeting of the Suggestion Committee is scheduled for October 16, at which time your suggestion regarding the use of colored tags will be taken up. We have invited Mr. Edward Simmons, the head of our Ready-to-Wear Department, to be present and to express his views.

After the meeting, I shall write to you again to tell you the decision of the Committee. If your suggestion

is adopted, you will receive a cash award under the same
terms that apply to our Employees' Suggestion System.

Thank you again for your very evident interest in us.

Sincerely yours,

DISCOVERING THE READER'S INTERESTS. As we know, the effectiveness of a letter depends to a great extent on how well the writer
understands the reader's viewpoint. Thus, in addition to the other
information he must have, the correspondent should learn as much
as possible about the reader in order to determine the ideas that
will influence him. In illustrating this point, the executive of a
mail-order house once related that he had received a letter which
began, "The stores that sell your goods . . . ." He threw the letter
into the wastebasket. Inasmuch as his company sold its products
only by mail, he felt that the letter showed an abysmal ignorance
of the reader's point of view. Another letter to the same executive
began, "If you could cut your catalogue costs . . . ." It received
immediate attention and a favorable reaction.

It is the writer's job to discover the benefits to the reader and to
make sure that the reader understands them clearly. The writer of
the next message overlooked the reader's point of view and emphasized the benefit to the writer.

Poor

Dear Mrs. Royce:

The employees in our fur storage department will find
their jobs easier if you will request delivery of your
fur coat soon. As the days grow colder, the rush will
begin and it will become more and more difficult for our
clerks to keep up with the demands upon them.

Many women wait until the last minute. Don't be among
this group. We shall appreciate your co-operating with
us on this matter.

Very truly yours,

Here, on the other hand, is a letter that leaves no doubt that the
writer has considered the reader's point of view.

Good

Dear Mrs. Royce:

Right now is a good time to remember that winter is
hovering just a little to the north and that very soon
you're going to need the warmth and comfort of your fur
coat. Indian summer can be mighty pleasant weather-
but it's a wise woman who recollects that it always ends
in a frost.

Why not phone our fur storage department and request
delivery of your fur coat <u>before</u> the time you actually
need it? Then you're sure to be warm and cozy when the
first frost comes.

                                        Very truly yours,

    The particular kind of information which the writer obtains
about the reader will depend largely on the purpose of the letter.
Before dictating a collection letter, for example, the writer will
want information about the debtor's past record for paying his
bills. The writer will also want to know how long the debtor has
been a customer and what his financial standing is. Before composing a letter to sell tires, the writer must know whether the letter
is going to a private car owner, to the dealer in tires, or to the owner
of a fleet of cars or trucks used for commercial purposes. In each
of these instances, the reader's viewpoint will be different; consequently, the "selling points" should also be different. Similarly,
the writer must realize that the housewife will have one reason for
buying a refrigerator, the landlord another, and the pharmacist
still another. The following letter to a physician is effective because the writer has selected ideas of particular interest to his
reader:

Good

Dear Dr. Harvey:

Have you ever been confronted with the problem of temporarily preserving a pathological specimen in your
office?

The Frigidaire Water Cooler with refrigerated compartment provides, with no extra operating expense, a place
where vaccines, serums, glandular products, etc., may be
safely stored at an even, cool temperature. It also
provides healthfully cooled drinking water for you and
your patients.

The Frigidaire Water Cooler requires no attention. It
is clean and sanitary and takes up no more space than an
ordinary chair. Its operating cost is practically
negligible.

May we tell you more about the new Frigidaire Water
Cooler with refrigerated compartment? The Frigidaire
salesman will have more valuable data for you when he
calls.

Very truly yours,

THE "YOU" ATTITUDE

When a letter stresses ideas that suggest benefits to the reader
rather than to the writer, businessmen say that the letter has the
"you" attitude. This is another way of saying that the letter was
written with an *apparent* regard for the reader.

The writer whose letters consistently evidence an apparent regard for the reader usually has developed a *genuine* consideration
for people. His sincere desire to determine what concerns the
reader enables him to adapt his ideas effectively.

Generally, what concerns the reader most is himself. In his own
mind, he is the center to which events and people are related or unrelated. Thus, he is likely to be favorably impressed by a letter
which shows him how he can benefit himself or the people or the
things he cares about—his family, his home, his business, his community, his friends. Such a letter has the "you" attitude.

The "you" attitude has little relationship to the number of times
that the word *you* is used in the letter. For example, the following
letter can hardly be said to have the "you" attitude.

Poor

Dear Mr. Jones:

You did not pay sufficient attention to the letter sent
to you on July 12. Possibly you did not notice the due

date called to <u>your</u> attention in paragraph 2. <u>You</u>
should send us <u>your</u> check as soon as possible.

Very truly yours,

A letter in which the pronouns *we* and *I* are used may perhaps
contain a great deal of the "you" attitude.

Good

Dear Mr. Jones:

I believe that <u>our</u> letter of July 12 may not have
stressed sufficiently how important prompt payment is in
the protection of your investment with <u>our</u> company. I
hope <u>we</u> shall receive your check within the next few
days.

Very truly yours,

However, frequent use of *I*'s and *we*'s, especially at the beginnings of sentences and paragraphs, will seem to emphasize the
writer's point of view. Therefore, obvious repetition of these pronouns should be avoided. The two columns below point up the
ways in which sentences beginning with *I* or *we* can be restated
and improved by starting with *you*.

"I" or "we" attitude	*"You" attitude*
We are pleased to an- nounce....	You will be pleased to know....
I want you to contrib- ute....	You will no doubt want to contribute....
We follow this policy be- cause....	You will benefit from this policy because....
We sold 40,000 of these lamps last year.	You and other dealers like you bought 40,000 of these lamps last year.

ADAPTATION OF LANGUAGE

The preceding topics have dealt with the types of ideas that interest the reader and help produce a favorable response. A letter's effectiveness also depends on its language—intangible qualities of tone, appropriateness, courtesy, tact, and, as we shall see in Chapter 5, style. These qualities may be achieved instinctively, but results are more certain if the writer consciously studies the character and emotions of his reader and chooses his words accordingly.

USING SUITABLE VOCABULARY. Every word in a letter should be as meaningful to the reader as to the writer. This requirement does not rule out the use of many-syllabled words or technical terms. However, the writer who takes a genuine interest in the reader uses only those words and expressions with which the reader is likely to be familiar.

The banker who speaks to his commercial customers about "reconciling" their accounts would perhaps better use the word "comparing" in writing to the layman. "Open account" will make good sense to a businessman, but "charge account" would be more readily understood by the women customers of a department store. By the same token, "invoice" is a correct term for "bill," but the latter more nearly belongs in the vocabulary of the ordinary citizen.

Effective language, in other words, is relative, and what is suitable or clear to one reader may not be suitable or clear to another. The paragraph that follows is clear to the printer to whom it is written:

Technical

```
The copy would probably look best in 12 point Bodoni
Book with 2 point leading and lines not wider than 24
picas.  Please let us see some samples of 50 and 60 lb.
white wove stock before you proceed.
```

The paragraph below, although admittedly not so precise, is suitable to the layman.

Non-technical

We propose to use a type of good reading size and modern
feeling, with adequate margins and space between the
lines. We shall let you see samples of medium weight
soft white papers.

PRACTICING COURTESY. A well-mannered person says "please"
when he wants a favor, "thank you" when he receives a favor, and
"I am sorry" when he has unintentionally hurt someone or must
convey some unpleasant news. In the same way, the letter writer
should observe all the rules of ordinary courtesy.

Lack of consideration for the reader's feelings is a serious violation of courtesy. In the following letter, the writer commits this
breach.

Discourteous

Gentlemen:

If you don't want to give us this order that's all right
with us. We've been in business a long time without
your trade, and we expect we can get along some more
without it. Don't think, though, that you can send us
an order every time we cut our prices and then buy all
the profitable items from our competitors.

                              Very truly yours,

In general, any statements that indicate irritation, bad temper,
or suspicion should be avoided. The writer should, instead, strive
for expressions that show a willingness to help or to understand.

Discourteous	*Courteous*
It is foolish to think that we tried to deprive you of something that was rightly yours.	Let us assure you of our desire to be completely fair and honest with you.
You claim you didn't receive the refund we sent you.	We are sorry to learn from your letter that you did not receive the refund we sent.

Discourteous

If you know what's good for you, you'll see that we get that merchandise immedately.

Courteous

We are certain that consideration of your own interests will prompt you to ship these goods to us immediately.

In the following examples notice how changes in wording create differences in the degree of courtesy:

Unsatisfactory

We request that you send us

We have received your check

We are sorry if you were inconvenienced

You must have been ignorant of

You failed to send

More courteous

Please send us

Thank you for your check

We are sorry that you were inconvenienced

Evidently you did not know that

We have not received

To be courteous does not require fawning. The following letter is *too* courteous.

Dear Sir:

It was with profound pleasure that we received your order for a dozen amber goblets. Be assured that we shall work night and day to speed this order to you. Our greatest ambition is to please you.

Very truly yours,

ADAPTING LANGUAGE TO THE READER'S MOOD. In addition to being courteous, the writer should consider the reader's state of mind and adjust his language to fit the mood. He should be particularly tactful in approaching the sensitive reader, dramatic in appealing to the uninterested reader, and vigorous in stimulating action on the part of the reader who is dilatory or obstinate.

The reader's mood can often be anticipated from the letter the correspondent is answering. For example, a letter of complaint obviously indicates one mood while a letter of inquiry indicates another. Even if the writer has no other guide to the reader's state of mind, he will realize that the subject of his own letter will help to establish the mood. Thus, a credit refusal is apt to create bad feeling unless it is handled with a great deal of tact, but a letter that accedes to a customer's request needs only graciousness in order to succeed.

Differences in the reader's probable moods call for a variety of "tones," as illustrated in the following passages:

To an angry customer—sympathetic tone

We can well appreciate your feelings after your experience in our store last Wednesday.

To a "cold prospect"—stimulating tone

Don't wait. This offer positively will be withdrawn on May 15. So fill out the order card and mail it today-- right now!

To a poor credit risk—tactful tone

Although your personal references are excellent, we do not have enough business information of a positive nature to enable us to ship the goods on a credit basis. We hope conditions will permit us to open an account for you in the near future.

To a procrastinating supplier—insistent tone

We know that you have enough influence with the factory to secure immediate delivery for us. In view of your promise to deliver the goods by May 14, we are going to ask you to make good on that promise. Otherwise, you will have to share with us the responsibility of a lawsuit brought by our customer for breach of contract.

USING WORDS WITH PLEASANT CONNOTATION. Many words have both a denotation, or exact meaning, and a connotation, or suggested meaning. Thus the effectiveness of a letter is influenced not only by what words mean, but also by what they suggest to the reader. Words such as *pleasure, convenience, promptly,* and *service* are agreeable in what they connote; but *refuse, delay, recurrence,* and *impossible* give disagreeable impressions. The good writer naturally prefers words that arouse pleasant feelings. If he can not find pleasant words, he at least tries to avoid or modify unpleasant words. Contrast the following examples:

Bad suggestion   *Better suggestion*

We regret that we must re-   We regret that we are un-
fuse   able

In case of delay   Should the goods not arrive
                                    promptly

If you are dissatisfied   If you are not completely
                                    satisfied

We made a very careless   The error was ours.
error.

Good suggestion can also be achieved by the use of affirmative or positive rather than negative words and ideas. The store sign that reads "Closed until 9 a.m. tomorrow" is negative; the sign that says, "Open at 9 a.m." is affirmative. Both signs express essentially the same idea, but the latter is more inviting to favorable action. In a business letter, one writer will state, "We will not be responsible for loss after thirty days." Another writer will say, "Our responsibility for the safekeeping of these articles extends for thirty days." Here again the first statement is negative and almost antagonistic; the second is positive and reassuring. Contrast the next examples from the files of a municipal government agency.

Negative

Dear Sir:

We regret that we can not help you with your complaint
about the smoke nuisance in your neighborhood. This
kind of violation does not come within the jurisdiction
of this department.

                                   Very truly yours,

Positive

Dear Sir:

The smoke nuisance about which you have written to us
comes under the jurisdiction of the Smoke Control Bureau
of the Building Department.

We are taking the liberty of forwarding your letter to
Mr. George S. Laird of that office.

Thank you for writing.

                                    Very truly yours,

Contrast the negative and positive statements in the examples
below. Note the better impression made by the positive statements.

Negative   *Positive*

The Jot-It is not one of those third-rate ballpoint pens.	The Jot-It is the quality pen in the ballpoint field.
We assure you that there will be no further delay.	We assure you that these goods will be shipped at once.
We can not fill your order because you did not send payment.	We shall be glad to fill your order as soon as we receive your check.

Review Problems

1. Which of the following statements are correct?

a. In order to obtain the reader's point of view, the writer should learn
as much about the reader as possible.

b. The "you" attitude requires that you use the pronoun *you* more than
the pronoun *I*.

c. Adaptation to the reader requires that the writer ignore his own objective.

d. It is safe to assume that the reader is interested primarily in himself.

e. An argument that moves one customer will probably move all the others.

2. Look through the advertisements in a recent issue of a popular national magazine, and copy five sentences that show special consideration of the reader's point of view. Put in parentheses after each sentence the name of the product advertised.

3. Rewrite the following letter so that it will have the "you" attitude:

Dear Mr. Gordon:

On reviewing your account at our bank, we note that your balance has been less than $500.00 for some months. As we can not afford to service such a small account, we must ask you to increase your balance so that it meets our minimum requirement of $500.00. If you are unable to do so, we shall have to charge you $2.00 per month for service.

We are sure that you will see our point of view in this matter.

Very truly yours,

4. Select from the following sentences the words or phrases that you consider discourteous; then rephrase each sentence for better tone.

a. You claim that our delivery service was at fault.

b. We are surprised that you consider a cashmere sweater too fragile.

c. You must have known that we require complete specifications.

d. How much longer do you think we can wait for delivery of these containers?

e. I believe you are sadly mistaken about the facts.

5. Rewrite the following negative statements so that they will express the same ideas in a positive manner:

a. We can not accept orders after next Wednesday.

b. Our policy does not permit exchanges if clothing has been worn.

c. Permission to visit the factory after 6 p.m. can not be granted.

d. A business report with grammatical errors is bound to win disfavor.

e. We do not manufacture any of the items you ordered except the nylon nail brushes.

6. Which of the following words have a pleasant connotation? Which have an unpleasant connotation?

appreciate	must	profit
inconvenience	co-operation	approved
trouble	promptly	satisfactory
easy	delinquent	incompetent
reject	delay	safety

7. Assume that in response to a newspaper advertisement you made a reservation at The Hostelry, a hotel in Washington, D. C., for December 27–30. It is now December 20. In speaking to a friend about your plans, you learn that The

Hostelry is a third-rate hotel very inconveniently situated. As a result of your conversation you decide to make a reservation at another hotel and cancel the reservation at The Hostelry. Write a letter to The Hostelry, canceling your reservation.

8. Rewrite in better tone the following letter addressed to the District Director of the United States Internal Revenue Service in your city.

Dear Sir:

Last January—that's ten months ago—I filed a claim for a refund on my 19— taxes. When I received no answer, after six months, I wrote again. This time I was told that the office was being moved and that there would be a short delay before my claim could be attended to. Now it's four months later, and I still have no word from you.

Certainly you can't claim that you haven't had enough time to look into this matter. I'm a taxpayer, the same as anyone else, and I think it's high time you public officials moved yourself to do something for us without taking ten months and more.

If I don't hear from you within the next week, I'll take my complaint right to Washington. I know my rights and no small-time bureaucrat is going to deprive me of them.

Very truly yours,

5
Essentials of Style

The style of business writing is more or less formal depending on the personality of the writer, the purpose of the correspondence, and the character of the business firm for which the letter is written. A good style should embody (1) clear writing, (2) conciseness, (3) simplicity, and (4) individuality. Careful review and revision of each letter are also important.

CLEAR WRITING

When he is certain of what to say and how to approach the reader, the writer is faced with the problem of stating his thoughts clearly. The correspondent's writing should be exact in sentence structure, word selection, and punctuation [1] in order to be sure that he conveys his meaning accurately.

SENTENCE STRUCTURE. Faulty arrangement of words and reference of pronouns may be misleading or obscure the meaning. Notice the difference in clarity between the two versions of each of the following examples.

Misleading	*Clearer*
It is against our policy to sell left-over merchandise below cost.	It is our policy always to have full stocks of merchandise at fair prices.

---

[1] See Part 4, Sections VII, VIII, and IX.

53

We sell at retail <u>only</u> in Chicago.	We sell at retail in Chicago <u>only</u>.
He returned the stock certificates that he had received in error by <u>registered mail</u>.	He returned <u>by registered mail</u> the stock certificates that he had received in error.
Jones & Co. maintain excellent relations with their New York distributors, but <u>they</u> are still not doing as much advertising as <u>they</u> expect <u>them</u> to do.	Jones & Co. maintain excellent relations with their New York distributors, but <u>the distributors</u> are still not doing as much advertising as <u>Jones & Co.</u> expect <u>them</u> to do.

PUNCTUATION. Incorrect marks of punctuation or lack of necessary punctuation may cause the reader at least temporary misunderstanding.

Confusing	*Clearer*
Before you order your stock records should be consulted.	Before you order, your stock records should be consulted.

EXACT WORDS. Words and expressions may be unclear not because they are technical or polysyllabic, but because they can mean more than one thing to the reader.

Inexact

We have your <u>recent</u> letter.

(How recent? April 30? May 6? May 10?)

Please send us a <u>supply</u> of leaflets for distribution to our customers.

(Exactly how many are wanted? 50? 100? 5000?)

Our <u>local</u> warehouse will handle your needs.

(Is that the warehouse near you or the one near the customer?)

You can count on <u>quick</u> delivery.

(An hour? Five days? Two weeks?)

The applicant is <u>well-educated.</u>

(At which schools? What degrees?)

Ours is a <u>new</u> business.

(Established yesterday? Five years ago?)

CONCISENESS

The effort the writer expends in making his message concise ultimately saves the reader's time—always an important consideration in business.

Concise writing in business consists of using as few words as possible without sacrificing courtesy and clarity. For the most part, conciseness is achieved by (1) omitting unnecessary details, (2) condensing unimportant ideas to their essentials, and (3) eliminating unnecessary words.

OMITTING UNNECESSARY DETAILS. Too many details in a letter are as undesirable as too few. Notice, in the following section of a letter addressed to a dealer, how unnecessary are the last two sentences in the first paragraph. Actually, the letter could be improved by omitting them.

We are sorry that we are out of this particular style and will not have another supply until the first of the year. If we were going to fill your order, we would of course send you the advertising matter you requested, but since you will not have the goods for another six months, we think we ought to hold up the advertising, too. As a matter of fact, we may have some fresh advertising material by that time and will send it to you then.

Perhaps, in the meantime, you could select from our catalogue a substitute for the style you wanted. We can supply you immediately with advertising on any style you choose. Please let us know if we can be of help.

CONDENSING UNIMPORTANT IDEAS. At times too much space is taken up in a letter with an explanation of necessary but comparatively unimportant ideas. The writer should treat such details as briefly as possible.

Lengthy

```
In this envelope you will find enclosed an order blank
and a self-addressed, stamped envelope.  Please fill in
your name and address on the order blank, making sure
you give us your postal zone number; then enclose the
blank in the envelope.  Do it today if you want it to
reach us in time to ship your order so you will get it
by Friday.
```

Concise

```
Just fill in the order blank and mail it in the enclosed
postpaid envelope.  Act today in order to receive
delivery of your order by Friday.
```

ELIMINATING UNNECESSARY WORDS. Often the writer will use two or three words when one will do. This practice is most clearly seen in so-called "business-like" phrases such as those in the left-hand column below.

Wordy	*Concise*
attached hereto	attached
enclosed herewith	enclosed
letter under date of	letter of
letter with regard to	letter about
check in the amount of	check for
during the course of	during
in the event that	if
in the process of tabulating	in tabulating

SIMPLICITY

In modern business practice, correspondents strive for reading ease in their writing. Writers may achieve relatively simple styles by using (1) short sentences and short paragraphs, and (2) the active voice.

USING SHORT SENTENCES AND PARAGRAPHS. Because they are easier to read and understand, short sentences and paragraphs are generally preferable to long ones in business letters. Satisfactory averages are about twenty words per sentence and five or six lines per paragraph.

The disadvantage of an exceedingly long sentence or paragraph is readily apparent in the following one-sentence letter. It contains 101 words.

Bad

```
Dear Madam:

We are sorry to learn that the curtains you recently
purchased from us were imperfect when you received
them and while apologizing for any inconvenience you
may have had on this occasion, we have already made
arrangements to pick up the merchandise at your home
and, as soon as we receive it, we will have it credited
to your account and if you will give us the description
of the curtains you originally ordered as to style,
price, size, and color, we will prepare a perfect set
of curtains to your specification and send them to you
as soon as possible.

                                Very truly yours,
```

Here is the same letter with only slight changes in wording, but broken into several sentences and paragraphs.

Better

```
Dear Madam:

We are sorry to learn that the curtains you recently
purchased from us were imperfect when you received
them.  Please accept our apologies for any inconvenience
caused you.

We have already made arrangements to pick up the mer-
chandise at your home.  As soon as we receive it, we
shall have it credited to your account.
```

If you will describe the curtains you originally ordered
by specifying style, price, size, and color, we shall
prepare a perfect set of curtains to your specification
and send them to you as soon as possible.

Very truly yours,

EMPLOYING THE ACTIVE VOICE. Another means of achieving
simplicity is to use the active voice in preference to the passive
voice (see Part 4, Section V). This is done by making the actor
the subject of the sentence.

Passive (*indirect*)	*Active* (*direct*)
The order was not received by us until October 7.	We did not receive the order until October 7.
Payment was approved by Mr. King.	Mr. King approved the payment.

In situations requiring special tact, the experienced business
writer may use the passive voice.

Active (*too blunt*)	*Passive* (*better*)
You did not enclose check with your order.	The check was not enclosed with your order.
Mr. Green apparently failed to mark the appointment on his calendar.	The appointment was apparently not marked on Mr. Green's calendar.

INDIVIDUALITY

The writer achieves individuality in business correspondence by
expressing himself in somewhat the same language he would use
if he were conversing with the reader. In essence, individuality
requires the use of fresh (not stale) expressions, everyday words
and phrases, and personal pronouns.

USING FRESH EXPRESSIONS. The main reason for lack of individuality in business English is the mistaken adherence of a number of writers to the idea that correspondence is written according
to a rigid, unchanging formula. Instead of writing as he might talk,

the correspondent relies on a set of shopworn phrases, as illustrated in the following letter:

Lacks individuality

Dear Sir:

We wish to acknowledge receipt of your credit application dated February 16 giving trade and bank references,
and we thank you for same. Please be advised that
credit accommodations are herewith extended as per your
request and order has been shipped.

Hoping you will give us the opportunity of serving you
again in the near future, we remain

                                        Very truly yours,

   This letter, conveying essentially the same message, is more nearly conversational.

Improved

Dear Mr. Smith:

Thank you for sending so promptly the trade and bank
references we had asked for. I am glad to say that
your order has already been shipped on the terms you
requested.

We hope you will give us the chance to serve you again.

                                        Very truly yours,

   Good writers take care to avoid stale expressions. Examples of stereotyped phrases and suggested antidotes follow:

Stereotyped	*Improved*
We wish to acknowledge re- ceipt of	We have received
We have your order and wish to thank you for same	Thank you for your order

Stereotyped	*Improved*
Kindly advise	Please let us know
Your letter of recent date	Your recent letter, (or preferably, Your letter of April 5)
We have not been favored with an answer.	We have not received your answer.
We beg to inform you that	You will be interested to learn that (or omit entirely)
Thanking you for your kind attention to this order, we remain	We shall appreciate your careful attention to this order.

Other stereotyped expressions like the following should also be avoided:

Stereotyped

would advise	contents noted
would say	under separate cover
said letter	hand you herewith
and oblige	favor (for "letter")
pending receipt of	wish to state

SELECTING EVERYDAY WORDS AND PHRASES. Business correspondence is more effective when it is natural and friendly than when it is pompous. Some writers use multisyllabic words and legal-sounding phrases in the mistaken belief that such expressions sound important and "businesslike." Terms such as these should be avoided.

Latinistic and legal-sounding

ultimo	therefor
proximo	aforesaid
as per	aforementioned
in re	above captioned
pursuant to	hereinbelow set forth
duly	deem it advisable

Latinistic and legal-sounding

hereby	held in abeyance
thereto	said person
thereof	herinafter discussed

The use of a long word when a short word would do may make the letter appear pretentious. The individuality of a letter, therefore, may be increased by employing short, easily understood words wherever possible. This does not mean "writing down" to the reader, but rather making it easier for the reader to grasp the message.

The following example is obviously cumbersome and hard to follow:

The comptroller proposed a suggestion regarding a departure from our standard procedure with respect to remuneration for overtime employment. Subsequently, as a preliminary measure, we forthwith instituted an investigation to ascertain the number of the company's employees that would be affected.

Here is the same passage rewritten in simpler (and fewer) words. Observe how much easier it is to read and understand.

The comptroller suggested a new way to issue salary for overtime. The first thing we did was to find out how many of our people would be affected.

Compare the difficulty of the words and phrases in the first column below with the relative simplicity of those in the second column.

Your communication	Your letter
After a comprehensive appraisal of the circumstances	After studying the facts
Please endeavor to terminate the investigation as expeditiously as possible	Please try to end the investigation as soon as you can

| Take it under advisement | Think it over |
| Commenced operations | Began work |

USING PERSONAL PRONOUNS. Although tact may occasionally require an indirect approach, the individuality of the letter is usually increased by liberal use of the personal pronouns *you, we,* and *I.* At times a writer, either through false modesty or the mistaken belief that he is avoiding personal responsibility, may write in such an impersonalized style as "*It* is believed" instead of "*I* believe," or "*It* would be appreciated" instead of "*We* should appreciate," or "*There* has recently arrived" instead of "*You* recently sent us."

Understandably, a writer wishes to avoid a succession of *I's* or *we's* (see p. 44), but unless he has a sound reason for doing otherwise, he should use personal pronouns when appropriate. In this way, he helps to make the letter interesting, direct, and personal, as these additional examples illustrate.

Impersonal	*Personal*
This is in reply to	We are replying to
Receipt is acknowledged of	We have received
It is the understanding of the writer that	I understand that
It would be considered a great favor if you	You would do us a great favor if
There is available to you	You have available

CAREFUL REVIEW AND REVISION

Many errors in style are not evident to the writer until he has had an opportunity to review his work. Reviewing a letter may reveal to him that the message is not clearly and concisely transmitted or that it is not expressed in the most simple and most natural way. Sometimes the correspondent may remedy the faults of a letter by changing the arrangement of words, by correcting the punctuation, or by substituting nouns for pronouns; in other cases, he may improve the letter considerably by condensing or combining related ideas, or by eliminating unnecessary or incorporating essential details.

Perhaps reviewing a letter may also enable the writer to discover additional faults in sentence structure and word usage. He may find it necessary to make substitutions which will increase the directness and individuality of the message: a shorter word or sentence for a long one, a fresh word for a hackneyed one, a personal pronoun for an impersonal one, or the active voice for the passive voice.

When circumstances permit, the correspondent may find it helpful to read the letter aloud. If the letter does not "sound" right, it probably will not "read" right.

The mechanical requirements of the letter and the typing should not be overlooked. Careful proofreading will help the writer to correct potentially embarrassing transcriptional and typographical errors and to avoid confusing the reader.

Review Problems

1. Assume that you have just read in today's *Daily Gazette* the following advertisement placed by Gaines Brothers, a large department store in your city:

PERSONAL STATIONERY

Beautifully imprinted with your name and address. Single sheets, size 6″ × 7½″ or folders of the same size in white, gray, buff. Imprinting in black, blue, or red. 75 single sheets and 50 envelopes or 50 folders and 50 envelopes, $4.95. Mail orders accepted, accompanied by check or money order.

Write a letter to Gaines Brothers, 100 Main Street, ordering the stationery according to your own taste.

2. Assume that in writing a report about a business problem you have come across a book that you would like to obtain for your own library. Inquiries among a number of bookstores and the publisher reveal that the book is out-of-print. Write a letter to a local dealer who specializes in out-of-print books, asking whether he can secure a copy for you. Use an actual book as the subject of your inquiry. Be specific as to the title, author, publisher, edition number, and date of publication.

3. Express the following ideas in more specific terms. Invent any necessary details.

    a. Please let us hear from you soon.
    b. Several copies of this letter will be sufficient.
    c. We expect to establish a new branch somewhere before long.

   d. These gloves come in a full assortment of fabrics.

   e. I am a college man (or woman).

   4. Rewrite the following sentences for greater clarity. Assume any facts which seem necessary.

   a. Once inside the customer gained the impression of spaciousness.

   b. We shall be very glad to send you the goods which you ordered on Friday.

   c. Tom and Harry sent their reservations a week ahead, but they failed to arrive in time for the convention.

   d. In reconsidering our proposition, I knew Mr. Grimes would give considerable weight to our extensive experience with pension members.

   e. The commission should be divided equally between Mr. Ramsey of the main office and Mr. Grace and Mr. Hart of the Syracuse branch.

   5. Rewrite the letter below to give it more individuality.

Gentlemen:

As per your favor of June 4, inquiring about shipment of two dozen children's hats, style 084–12, wish to advise that same was shipped yesterday by Railway Express.

Hoping this is satisfactory, we are

                                                  Very truly yours,

   6. Rewrite the following sentences so that the verbs will be in the active voice:

   a. Your letter was not received by our main office until November 15.

   b. It has been noted that you desire your mail addressed to your home in Berkeley.

   c. The cancelled check was returned by us to you on Tuesday by air mail.

   d. His application will not be seen by the personnel manager until Wednesday.

   e. The bid submitted by you must be reviewed by the Executive Committee.

   7. Rewrite the following sentences in better style:

   a. There has recently come to our attention the fact that the Dahl Company is opening a new branch factory in Roanoke, Va., and is seeking to establish a connection with a reputable banking institution in that area.

   b. Upon receipt of your signed authorization, we shall make the stock purchases outlined in this letter and notify you when we have done so, and if there are any questions that you may have in your mind about this matter, it would please us to have you get in touch with us.

   c. This will acknowledge receipt of your letter sent under date of March 16, which we are glad to answer, relative to information about our new vertical files which have just been introduced on the market.

   d. Subsequent to receipt of your communication of April 11, we commenced proceedings to effect collection of the accounts hereinbelow set forth.

   e. Kindly advise if said premises have been vacated by you as per our agreement and oblige.

6
Plan and Construction of the Letter

Like a building or a book or any other creative work, a letter requires careful planning and construction. First, the writer selects only relevant facts and adheres to a single objective. Second, he arranges these ideas in such a way that the reader is led in an orderly manner through the opening, body, and close. Third, the writer employs conjunctions, connecting sentences and paragraphs, repetition, and other devices to make the transition between ideas logical and smooth. Fourth, he emphasizes the important ideas by putting them, forcefully expressed, in the opening and close, and by apportioning space among them according to their importance.

COMPLETENESS

A letter may be considered complete when (1) it presents all the essential ideas and (2) it has one objective only.

ESSENTIAL IDEAS. The necessary ideas in a letter are (1) those intended to inform the reader and (2) those designed to influence or to motivate the reader to act in the writer's favor.

Information. The facts the writer chooses to include are dependent upon the specific aim of the letter. Thus, a collection letter should include information such as the amount owed and the length of time the account has been overdue. Similarly, a direct mail sales letter should contain complete descriptions, prices, and instructions for ordering. Also, an answer to an inquiry must cover all the points raised by the inquirer, as well as any others that seem to be relevant.

Motivation. A genuinely effective letter surpasses the function of informing the reader; it influences the reader's emotions in order to resolve his doubts, win his goodwill, and persuade him to act. Hence, it motivates the desired response on the part of the reader. In a collection letter, it may not be enough to tell the debtor how much he owes; in many instances, he should also be told why it is important to pay or what he will lose if he does not. In sales letters, as in other types of advertising, information about a product is often supplemented with proof of the claims made and with strong emotional stimuli. (An encyclopedia, for example, may be bought not on the strength of a description of its contents, but because of an appeal to the reader's pride or to his desire for self-improvement.) Similarly, replies to inquiries may answer all the questions asked and yet be ineffective because the writer fails to recognize the reasons for the requests and, therefore, does not helpfully interpret the information he provides.

The letter below contains the necessary facts about the delinquent account and an appeal for payment based on the reader's desire to maintain a good credit standing. Much of the effectiveness would be lost if the motivation in the second paragraph were omitted.

Dear Mr. Dodge:

We regret that we must once more call to your attention the unpaid balance of $9.00 on the Krono Watch which you purchased last June.

We are sure that your failure to pay this balance is an oversight on your part, for we are confident that you would not knowingly do anything to injure the high credit rating you have established.

Now, while the matter is before you, won't you please make out your check and mail it to us.

                              Very truly yours,

SINGLE OBJECTIVE. In order to be completely effective, a letter should concentrate on a single objective. Ideas that do not help to accomplish this objective divide the reader's attention and, therefore, should be omitted. In the following letter, it would have been wise to omit the sales message in the last paragraph.

Dear Mr. Jones:

We are sorry to learn that the Wilmot Electric Shaver you purchased several weeks ago has not been giving you complete satisfaction.

May we suggest that you return the shaver to our store at your earliest convenience. If a defective part is causing the difficulty, we shall of course send it to the manufacturer for adjustment.

When you stop in, we think it will be to your advantage to look at the new Franklin men's traveling kits now available at a special low introductory price. These compact easy-to-handle kits hold an electric shaver as well as the other accessories a man needs on business or pleasure trips.

                                        Very truly yours,

From a practical point of view, a letter with more than one message often fails to receive prompt attention because it must be relayed from one department to the other. The following letter was delayed in the bookkeeping department for several days before it was sent to the sales department. The writer would have received a prompter reply to his request for a catalogue if he had asked for it in a separate letter.

Gentlemen:

Please refer to your invoice covering our purchase order #2193, dated December 9. You will find that we were charged at the new rate you had indicated would not go into effect until December 15.

If your invoice is in error, please let us know how we should handle payment.

Incidentally, can you mail us another copy of your current catalogue? We sent the copy we had to our Chicago office.

                                        Very truly yours,

EFFECTIVE ARRANGEMENT

After the writer has decided what ideas he will put into his letter, he should arrange those ideas in the way that will be most effective. In this respect, his first concern is with the organization of the letter as a whole, but he must also be conscious of the need for good arrangement within the smaller units of the letter.

ARRANGEMENT OF THE WHOLE. The majority of business messages have three parts: the opening, the body, and the close. The subject of the letter is introduced in the opening; it is elaborated upon by means of additional information presented in the body; and the reader's response is stimulated by the message in the close. The opening and the close are usually, but not always, separately paragraphed. The body may consist of any number of paragraphs.

In the letter that follows, the opening, body, and close are labeled to emphasize the separation of the various functions.

Dear Dr. Martin:

Opening

May we suggest the facilities of the Central Towers Hotel for the meetings, conferences, luncheons, or dinners which your Association plans from time to time.

Body

Many organizations consider the Central Towers as headquarters for all their business and social events. Our private lounges and ballroom are highly suitable for such occasions.

We can accommodate meetings, luncheons, and dinners of from 10 to 250 people. Our rooms are, we believe, among the most beautiful in the city, and we are sure that our excellent service and delicious food would appeal to your members.

Close

If we can help in any way, just call our Banquet Department, ELdorado 8-4000 or stop in at the hotel whenever you are in the neighborhood.

                                        Very truly yours,

ARRANGEMENT WITHIN THE LETTER. Paragraphs [1] and other parts of the letter present their own problems of arrangement within the organization. Generally, their order is patterned after the four forms of discourse: narration, exposition, description, and argumentation.

Narration. Narration may be briefly characterized as story-telling. Although "stories" of fact or fiction are occasionally used in business letters, particularly as a means of getting attention in sales letters, narration more regularly takes the form of a chronological account of events relating to a particular transaction. In narration, we usually employ the past tense and depend for effectiveness on the use of specific details. Here is an example taken from a letter having to do with terms of payment. Note that the last two sentences are in chronological order.

Good

```
Our terms are 2 per cent ten days, net thirty.  Inasmuch
as the invoice was dated September 10, the discount
period expired on September 20.  Your payment was not
made, however, until October 3, fully two weeks after
the expiration of the discount period.
```

It is obvious that the statement of facts according to the time of their occurrence provides an orderly movement from one idea to another. If the facts in the preceding example were not told chronologically, this is what would happen.

Poor

```
Our terms are 2 per cent ten days, net thirty.  The dis-
count period in this case began on September 10, but you
did not make payment until October 3, fully two weeks
after September 20, the date on which the discount
period expired.
```

Exposition and Description. In business, as elsewhere, the correspondent uses *exposition* to inform and explain. Through *description* [2] he characterizes a situation, product, etc. Description

---

[1] See Part 4, Section VII.
[2] See Chapter 12, "Sales Letters."

is often necessary in expository writing and may appeal both to the physical senses—sight, taste, etc.—and to the emotions.

When explanations and descriptions require more than a single sentence, the writer usually starts with a broad statement and then supplies the details. He may develop expository paragraphs by means of facts, reasons, illustrations, comparisons, and statements of cause and effect. Specific and vivid words are essential when the business correspondent writes in one or both of these forms of discourse.

In each of these examples, the first sentence presents the generalization, and the sentences which follow contain the details.

Exposition

The majority of our customers prefer the special checking account. The reason is that no minimum balance is required. All that is needed is enough to cover the amounts on the checks drawn. Checks may be bought in books of 20 for $2.00 per book. There is no charge for deposits.

As you requested, we are putting you on our mailing list to receive our bulletin. It is published on the 15th of each month except June, July, and August. There is no charge for single copies.

Exposition and description

We set out to give you more for your money in fine auto seat covers than you can find anywhere else in America. They are handsomely tailored of a sturdy fabric in colors that blend beautifully with any car interior. The firm, closely woven fabric is actually 60 per cent heavier than the fabric in most other seat-covers and, because they are tailored from actual measurements of the make and model of your car, these covers hug your seats with smoothly fitting perfection! Cushions and backrests are woven fiber--cool and comfortable-- specially finished to repel water and dust. Armrest covers are included for cars having center armrests in rear seats.

Argumentation. Reasoning or *argumentation* is employed whenever a conclusion requires the support of evidence. Here, two opposite forms of argument—*deduction* and *induction*—are possible.

In deduction, the writer makes a broad statement (conclusion) and then supplies the facts, reasons, or details on which the statement is based. In induction, the writer immediately states the facts and afterward sets forth the conclusion. The deductive order is often used when the conclusion is favorable to the reader, as when a request is granted. The inductive order is frequently employed when the conclusion is unfavorable to the reader, as in the case of a request denied.

Favorable conclusion—deductive order

We are glad to inform you that your request for the franchise of Wellington Television in the Philadelphia area has been granted. Our representative will stop in to see you on April 23, if the date is convenient for you, to make confirming arrangements.

Your franchise will be an exclusive one in the greater Philadelphia area. All our advertising in the area will feature the name and location of your store.

Unfavorable conclusion—inductive order

According to state law, articles for personal use, such as combs and hair brushes, may not be accepted for exchange or credit. Signs prominently displayed in our drug department give notice to that effect. The ruling applies whether or not the goods have been used and is intended for the protection of all customers. Under the circumstances, we are sure you will understand why we can not accept the return of the hair brush you bought from us last week.

SMOOTH CONNECTION

With the arrangement of ideas fixed in his mind or put on paper in the form of a brief outline, the writer is ready to dictate or type his letter. At this point, one of the principal problems he will encounter, in addition to presenting the message clearly, is that of bridging his ideas logically and smoothly. There are many ways in which such connection can be achieved.

CONNECTING WORDS AND PHRASES. The easiest and most obvious way to connect ideas is by the use of conjunctions such as *and, but, for, or, nor, if, as, since, because, when, while,* and *although;* conjunctive adverbs such as *moreover, furthermore, however, accordingly,* and *so;* and connecting phrases such as *in addition to, at the same time, on the other hand,* and *in conclusion.*

CONNECTING SENTENCES AND PARAGRAPHS. A whole sentence and even a paragraph may be used to show the connection or transition between two parts of the letter. Notice the transition provided by the underscored sentences here.

Connecting sentence

It is too bad we were not able to buy the machine when it was offered. <u>Even if we had, however, I doubt that it would have been instrumental in solving all of our production problems.</u> We would still need an extra press to handle two- and three-color work because, efficient as the Mentor is, it is still uneconomical for anything but four-color operations.

Connecting paragraph

Cost is the most important consideration in deciding whether or not the department should be reorganized. A thorough study of this factor must be made by the controller. He should be prepared to start his survey no later than Wednesday of next week.

<u>Quite apart from how much the reorganization will cost are several problems involving personnel. These should be considered at the same time.</u>

One personnel problem concerns the necessity of transferring several 25-year employees to departments in which they have never worked before.

USING PRONOUNS AND REPETITION. Pronouns show connection because they serve as substitutes for names or ideas already mentioned. Repetition of a word also helps to establish connection. Occasionally a demonstrative pronoun—*this, that, these,* or *those* —will be used with the word that is repeated. Notice how the pronouns and the repetition of words in the following passage help to bridge the ideas.

<u>Mr. Brown</u> would like the opportunity to present to you at your office the laboratory <u>record</u> of last Monday's test. <u>He</u> believes <u>this record</u> will convince you of the

desirability of using the S42 formula in th
of your paint products.

NUMBERING IDEAS. Numbering a series of rel
matically provides connection. However, the numbered ideas
should be expressed in parallel fashion.

Not parallel

```
This plan has three advantages:
     1.  Promoting goodwill at low cost.
     2.  The increase of consumer participation.
     3.  It will arouse interest on the part of em-
ployees.
```

Parallel

```
This plan has three advantages:
     1.  Promotes goodwill at low cost.
     2.  Increases consumer participation.
     3.  Arouses interest on the part of employees.
```

CORRECT EMPHASIS

Correct emphasis aids the reader in evaluating the relative importance of the ideas in the letter. The writer achieves correct emphasis mainly by (1) making effective use of the beginning and end of the letter and (2) apportioning space in accordance with the importance of the ideas treated.[3]

EMPHASIS AT THE BEGINNING AND THE END. The beginning of a letter is important because it makes the initial impression on the reader; the end is important because the impression it leaves frequently remains with the reader for the longest period of time.

The Opening. The opening should be as specific, as personal, as positive, and as cordial as the subject allows. The writer should avoid the temptation, which is especially strong at the start, to use trite and stereotyped expressions.

In the following examples of letter openings, note the faults and how they have been corrected:

---

[3] See also Part 4, Section VII.

eotyped

We wish to acknowledge receipt of your letter of
May 18th with check for
$19.60 enclosed and wish to
thank you for same.

More natural

We appreciate your letter
of May 18 and the check for
$19.60 you sent with it.

Unsympathetic

We have your letter of
March 9 in which you say
that the goods you ordered
on February 25 have not yet
arrived.

More cordial

We regret to learn from
your letter of March 9 that
the goods you ordered on
February 25 have not yet
arrived.

Too impersonal

We are always sorry when-
ever a customer decides to
close his account with us.

More personal

We are sorry to learn that
you have decided to close
your account with us.

Too general

Thank you for your order.

More specific

Thank you for your order
for two silver candle-
sticks, Style B, at $100.00
the pair, as advertised in
the New York Times, November 16.

Negative

We regret that we can not
comply with your request
for a charge account at our
store.

More positive

We have given careful consideration to your request
for a charge account.

In some instances it is possible to begin the letter with a direct
request, a reminder, or a notice of action taken or planned.

Good

Please send us three copies of Hemingway's The Old Man
and the Sea.

Good

Last week we sent you a letter we had received from
Mr. H. R. Crowley of Boston, Mass., in respect to his
application for a position in our New York office.

The chair that you referred to in your letter of January
7 was shipped by express from our Grand Rapids factory
on January 6.

The Close. An effective letter ending will (1) tell the reader
what action is expected of him or (2) if no direct response is required, leave the reader with some expression of regard, assurance,
appreciation, willingness to help, or the like. Many times the two
purposes are combined. In other instances, particularly in very
short letters or letters of a strictly informative nature, the writer
often states his last fact and then stops, without any special formality.

Good closes

Please sign and mail the enclosed form. Your order will
be shipped at once.

We shall appreciate your check for $35.00 by return
mail.

We insist that you telegraph your supplier at once and
then notify us of the action he is going to take.

Thank you for your interest in writing.

Please let us know if we can be of further assistance.

I hope this information will be helpful to you.

We assure you that your report will be treated in strict
confidence.

We look forward to the opportunity of serving you.

It was nice of you to write. Please give my regards to
Mr. White and the others.

If the close is to be emphatic, it must consist of a complete sentence, not a participial fragment.

Poor closes   *Better closes*

Hoping to hear from you   We look forward to hearing
soon, we are . . .   from you soon.

Assuring you of our desire   We assure you of our desire
to help, we remain . . .   to help.

EMPHASIS BY PROPORTION. The importance of an idea is associated with the amount of space given to it. Thus, the writer should
apportion the space in the body of his letter so that the important
ideas occupy relatively more space than unimportant or negative
ideas. Elaboration upon a pertinent idea should not involve monot-
onous repetition or other forms of wordiness, but should be accomplished through the addition of reasons, facts, or examples.

In the letter that follows the writer was wise to elaborate on the
advantages of the hotel and the desire to be convention host. Thus,
the disappointing news in the beginning is effectively counteracted.

Good proportion

Gentlemen:

We should certainly like to be host to the New York
Statistical Association during its annual convention.
We are, however, completely booked for the first week
in July. Under the circumstances, perhaps your group
will find it possible to schedule its convention one
or two weeks later than originally contemplated.

In addition to the many conveniences with which you are
already familiar, the Hotel Franklin has recently added
several programs and facilities that will add to the
comfort and enjoyment of your members. Our new indoor
swimming pool will be open at no charge to all convention guests. Air conditioning is now standard equipment in all rooms of the hotel. And the opening of the
new and palatial Festival Dining Room has made it possible
to accommodate large groups on the American Plan.

In order that you may have time to consider a possible
change in dates, we are reserving the weeks of July 11
and 18 and will hold those periods open for the next
ten days.

If either of these two weeks meets with your approval,
you can be sure of a most successful convention at the
Hotel Franklin. Please let us hear from you soon.

                              Sincerely yours,

Taking too much space for unimportant or negative ideas is just
as undesirable as devoting too little space to important ideas. The
excessive use of negative ideas in the first letter that follows puts
the emphasis on the wrong values. The improved version benefits
considerably from drastic rewriting.

Disproportion of negative ideas

Gentlemen:

We are sorry to learn from your letter of January 11
that our credit memorandum of December 28 was not dispatched to you by air mail in accordance with the standing instructions in our file.

We are embarrassed to discover that these instructions
were overlooked in this instance, and we can but offer
our apologies for the mistake on the part of our clerk
in handling this transaction.

Needless to say, we have brought this matter to the
attention of the parties concerned, and we hope that
this will not happen again. We appreciate your letting
us know about this mistake, however, for we want to
see that in the future the credit memorandums are sent
to you in accordance with your wishes.

                              Sincerely yours,

Improved

Gentlemen:

We are sorry to learn from your letter of January 11
that our credit memorandum of December 28 was not dispatched to you by air mail, in accordance with the
standing instructions in our file.

You may be sure that in the future we shall make a
special effort to see that the credit memorandums are
sent to you in the manner which you have specified.

Sincerely yours,

Review Problems

1. Which of the following statements are correct?

   a. A good letter concentrates on one main idea.

   b. The common literary forms, such as narration and description, have little place in a business letter.

   c. When you must say "no" to the reader, it is a good idea to say it in the beginning of the letter.

   d. Conjunctions are not the only way to provide connection between words.

   e. The amount of space you give to an idea is closely related to the emphasis it receives.

2. Rewrite the following letter openings for greater effectiveness:

   a. After looking into the matter, we are sorry that we must decline to accept the return of the brown suede shoes which you say do not fit properly.

   b. Your order for two dozen linen handkerchiefs, initialed "R," was received today.

   c. In reply to your advertisement in this morning's *Courier,* I am very much interested in obtaining a job as stenographer.

3. The following letter is neither well-planned nor well-constructed. Rewrite the letter for greater effectiveness.

   Gentlemen:

   We regret to advise that we are not complying with your request of April 18 that we appoint a chairman for the purpose of soliciting individual contributions from our employees in support of the Community Chest, as the matter of solicitations among employees is decided upon by our Employees' Association, which has agreed to make such solicitations only for specific national charities.

   However, we are pleased to report that our company has been supporting the Community Chest campaign for many years and we plan to do so again this year.

Sincerely yours,

4. Rewrite the following letter for better selection, arrangement, connection, and emphasis of ideas. It is addressed to a dealer in household appliances.

   Dear Mr. Judge:

   Your letter of March 10 received. You asked about our line of electric refrigerators for next year.

We have discontinued manufacture of refrigerators. They used to come in sizes from 4 cubic feet to 11.5 cubic feet. Many of the larger models had across-the-top freezers. The prices ranged from $200.00 to $600.00 at retail.

We discontinued our line of refrigerators so that we could devote more attention to our line of farm implements. We have been making farm machinery since 1885. Only recently we opened a new plant in Hamilton, Ohio. It is the largest factory of its kind in the world.

With appreciation for your interest, and hoping this answers your inquiry, we are

Very truly yours,

7
Inquiries and Replies

Inquiries and replies are among the most common types of business letters. They are also among the most important. If an inquiry is properly written, it may bring valuable business information and the opportunity to save money or to make a profit. If a reply is effectively composed, it may build goodwill and increase sales.

INQUIRIES

The clearer and more complete the inquiry is, the more satisfactory the answer will be. Letters seeking information fall into two broad categories: (1) general inquiries and (2) sales-related inquiries.

GENERAL INQUIRIES. Almost all firms receive inquiries that promise little or no direct return to them. Often, the information requested is necessary for private or business research. For example, a college student may write to a company for information he wishes to include in a term report; a teacher may ask a national magazine for a copy of an article that appeared in a back issue; a personnel executive may request information about an employee-suggestion plan from the personnel director of another company.

In a general inquiry, the writer should state why he needs the information and why he has selected the reader as his source; moreover, the writer should indicate his awareness of the imposition on the reader and tender his appreciation or offer to reciprocate, or both. The wise writer will make a great effort to be clear and concise so he will not waste the reader's time.

Good

Gentlemen:

I am a student working toward a Bachelor of Science degree in Business Administration at New York University.

To fulfill the requirement of a term report in my marketing course, I have chosen the topic, "Special Distribution Problems in the Soft Drinks Industry." Because your company has such a long record of successful accomplishment in this field, I thought you might be able to furnish me with pamphlets, booklets, or other information on this subject.

I shall greatly appreciate your co-operation.

Very truly yours,

SALES-RELATED INQUIRIES. Sales-related inquiries are written in regard to a product or a service purchased or being considered for purchase. To obtain a satisfactory response, the writer of the inquiry should state his request specifically and courteously.

The letter that follows may not bring exactly the information desired because the writer states his request too generally:

Gentlemen:

Will you please tell me what happens to a policyholder if he does not pay his premium on time. I have heard a lot of conflicting statements and thought you might help me.

Very truly yours,

This letter is more specific:

Gentlemen:

The premium on my policy, No. 0643R, is due on July 16, including the grace period.

I am not sure at this time whether I shall be able to forward you a check on that exact date, although I may be able to send it to you shortly after.

```
Will you please tell me what, if anything, the penalty
will be if payment is a few days late and what steps
should be taken so that the policy will not lapse.

                              Very truly yours,
```

Because of its obvious discourtesy, the following letter would probably bring a grudging response or none at all:

```
Gentlemen:

Your ads brag about how great your company is and here
is your chance to prove it.

If those nylon cord tires are as good as you say, how
many miles could I get out of them?  I don't see any-
thing in your ads about their being punctureproof,
although you do mention that they are blowoutproof.
What do you say to that?

                              Very truly yours,
```

The courtesy in the next letter is obvious.

```
Gentlemen:

I have been very much impressed by your ads for Dura
nylon cord tires, although I can not recall having seen
any reference to the mileage that can be expected from
them.  Also, your ads mentioned that the tires are
blowoutproof, but said nothing about their being punc-
tureproof.

Will you please tell me what the guaranteed mileage is
and whether or not they are punctureproof as well as
blowoutproof.

                              Very truly yours,
```

REPLIES TO INQUIRIES

The imaginative correspondent knows that every inquiry he answers (whether obviously sales-related or not) may carry the seed of future business. Inquirers who are not themselves customers or potential customers may be in a position to influence others to buy. The correspondent's first objective, therefore, is to build goodwill. His second objective is to influence the sale, if the inquiry opens up the opportunity for new or additional business. The success of both objectives depends largely on his adherence to these principles: (1) answer promptly, (2) reply courteously, (3) respond completely, (4) provide additional information if it is relevant, and (5) follow up the answer.

ANSWER PROMPTLY. A prompt reply reaches the reader while his interest is still high. Furthermore, he may have addressed the same request to several persons or companies and, if it is satisfactory in other respects, the first response the reader receives is most likely to win his favor. A prompt answer is psychologically effective, too, because it gives the impression that the company acts promptly in other matters.

If the information requested is not immediately available, it is good policy to write an interim letter saying that the desired information will follow soon. The letter below gives only part of the data wanted by the inquirer, but indicates that the rest will be sent shortly.

Dear Mr. Felix:

Thank you very much for your letter of April 9 in which you ask when the new frost-free Arctic refrigerator will be available for retail distribution in your area.

We are sure now that we will have limited quantities ready for our franchised dealers before October 31. However, we shall be able to answer your question more specifically--with exact dates and quantities--next week when our own production schedule will be firm.

Until then, when we shall write to you further, please accept our assurance that the new Arctic will be all that you want in a goodwill-building, profit-making re-frigerator.

Sincerely yours,

REPLY COURTEOUSLY. No matter how much or how little information can be given, a courteous reply to an inquiry creates a favorable impression. Particularly is this so in answers to inquiries that are not sales-related. Here, the reader does not expect extraordinary consideration, and he is especially grateful for whatever help he receives.

Good

Dear Mr. North:

We are glad to reply to your letter of February 28 requesting data on marketing problems in the soft drinks industry.

The enclosed copy of our latest annual report should prove helpful, particularly the information on pages 7-11. We also suggest that you write Magna Soda Foundation, Inc., 155 East Maitland Street, New York, N.Y. 10017. This organization, which represents a number of branches of the industry, may be able to furnish you with further information along the lines that you are seeking.

We should enjoy looking over a copy of your report when it is completed.

                                            Very truly yours,

On occasion, the firm's correspondent can not give the answer the inquirer desires. Even then, a courteous explanation should be given, as in the next letter.

Dear Mr. Reed:

We appreciate your letter of April 20 inquiring about the availability of a television set, console type, in a black wood cabinet.

With regret we must tell you that we do not have such a model in our line and are not contemplating one this year. If you are not able to find a suitable cabinet, you may want to purchase one of our modern consoles and have it refinished by a cabinetmaker near your home.

In any case, thank you for your interest.

                                            Very truly yours,

RESPOND COMPLETELY. As in other types of business correspondence, in order for a reply to be really helpful, it must be

complete. Omissions such as overlooking rates in response to an
inquiry about hotel accommodations, failing to include available
colors in a reply regarding fabrics, and neglecting secondary-
school requirements in responding to an inquiry about college ad-
mission, limit the value of the answer and handicap the reader in
his decision. The following reply supplies the reader with all the
information he needs:

Dear Mr. Burns:

On the basis of the information in your letter, we have
prepared the attached itinerary for your consideration.
We believe that it covers the areas in which you are
most interested.

From New York the cost of air transportation to and
from Mexico City will be $235.00 to $270.00 per person
depending on the choice of return route. The cost of
ground arrangements, including round-trip air fare between Mexico City and Oaxaca, will be $285.00 additional
for each of two persons. Included are all hotel accommodations and meals, sightseeing, guides, and transfers.

Please examine the itinerary. If you have any further
questions, please let us know and we shall try to answer
them to your satisfaction.

We appreciate this opportunity to be of service, and we
assure you that we will do everything possible to make
your trip a success.

Sincerely yours,

When the inquiry calls for an exceedingly long answer, it is
sometimes desirable to substitute printed literature. The most
important test of the usefulness of printed materials is whether or
not they answer the reader's questions. When a brochure, booklet,
or pamphlet is available, the writer may still send a "covering
letter" to call attention to the printed reply and to give the response a personal tone. The writer shows additional concern for
the reader's problem if he indicates where in the printed statement
the desired information can be found. A letter like the following
is faulty because, although it is courteous, it leaves to the reader
the task of finding the answers:

Dear Mr. Trimble:

Perhaps the best way to answer your inquiry of September
17 about our Employee Pension Plan is to send you our
Employees' Handbook, which gives all the details. A
copy is being mailed to you today.

We appreciate this opportunity to be of help.

                                        Very truly yours,

In the letter below, the writer has made it easy for the reader
to find the answers he wants.

Dear Mr. Trimble:

Perhaps the best way to answer your inquiry of September
17 about our Employee Pension Plan is to send you our
Employees' Handbook, which gives all the details.

A copy is being mailed to you today. In it you will
find our Pension Plan discussed on pages 71-86. Your
question about the employee's alternatives under the
plan is answered on page 73. We think you will also be
especially interested in the degree of employee partici-
pation since the start of the plan in 1949. This information you will find in the chart on page 82.

We appreciate this opportunity to be of help.

                                        Very truly yours,

To insure telling a complete story, many companies use form
letters as replies. Form letters are acceptable if they answer the
inquiries logically. Actually, they have two advantages: (1) saving
time and (2) assuring a carefully prepared letter. But form letters,
by their very nature, can not anticipate the exact substance of each
request; thus, it is very important that they be used discriminately.
Sending a form letter when it does not fit the situation, as in the
following illustration, is a sure way of earning the reader's ill
will. This letter of inquiry was addressed to the Chamber of Commerce of a large state. Let us suppose that the state was Montana.

Gentlemen:

During my vacation this summer I plan to visit Montana

and would appreciate it if you would furnish me with
pertinent travel information. I would also appreciate
advice regarding the availability of motels as I am
planning to travel by automobile and will have my wife
and two daughters with me.

I would be grateful for any information you can give me.

                                        Very truly yours,

Here is the incomplete reply.

Dear Mr. Frank:

We are pleased to receive your inquiry indicating your
interest in vacationing in Montana. We feel that our
state possesses ideal facilities to fit any desire for
relaxation and recreational activities.

We welcome you, in advance, to beautiful Montana and
hope that your stay here will be a pleasant and memora-
ble one.

                                        Sincerely yours,

GIVE ADDITIONAL INFORMATION. Many inquiries are satisfac-
torily answered only when the letter of reply gives information over
and above that which is actually requested. It is possible that the
inquirer has misdirected his letter, or has asked about a discontinued product or service, or has inadvertently not been complete
in stating his needs. It is also possible that the writer of the reply
can direct the reader to other and more fruitful sources of information, or suggest the need for other products or services of
which the reader is unaware, or provide many other kinds of unsought but welcome assistance.

The following inquiry, very general in nature, offers the writer
of the reply an opportunity to give additional information:

Gentlemen:

I am thinking about having a Wintaire Heater-Humidifier
installed in my home.

Will you please send me whatever literature you have

available in order that I may consider further whether
it will suit my needs.

                                        Very truly yours,

   The response reprinted below risks losing a sale, but it also
prevents a ruined appliance and a dissatisfied customer. Notice
that, as in other answers to consumers' inquiries, the name and the
address of the local dealer are included.

Good

Dear Mr. Davis:

We were gratified to learn of your interest in the Wintaire Heater-Humidifier. It should do much to increase
your comfort indoors during the winter months.

The enclosed folder provides you with detailed specifications, including operating instructions. Please note
that the Wintaire operates on alternating current (AC).

If you will consult your local Wintaire dealer, Mr.
Stanley Cross, 947 West Eighth Street (VIllage 6-9430),
he will be glad to check the kind of current (AC or DC)
supplied to your home and, if necessary, provide an
adapter to enable you to use the Wintaire.

Mr. Cross will also be glad to demonstrate the Wintaire
and point out its many desirable features, including
safety, portability, and economical operation.

Visit Mr. Cross soon, or call him on the telephone. It
is the best first step you can take to controlled
humidity and temperature in the winter months ahead.

                                        Very truly yours,

   FOLLOW UP ON SALES-RELATED INQUIRIES. When a response to
a sales inquiry does not result, within a reasonable time, in some
affirmative action on the part of the reader, the writer may send
a follow-up letter.[1] In so doing, he may simply ask the reader if

---

[1] For a further treatment of follow-up sales letters, see Chapter 12, "Sales
Letters."

any further help or information can be given. Better still, without asking, he may use the follow-up letter to provide additional information. Here the writer offers a personal interview as a means of elaborating on the initial response and giving the reader an opportunity to raise further questions.

Good

Dear Mrs. Smith:

Several weeks ago, we mailed you our booklet, "The Happy Years," after you had indicated an interest in sending your eight-year-old daughter to Camp Wingate this summer.

Although we have tried to anticipate your questions in our booklet, there may be many more which you and your daughter would like to ask. For that reason, we believe it would be worth while for you to meet with our director, Mrs. Julia Sells, in your own home.

Like you, we want to be sure that the Wingate program will mean a summer of pleasant activity for your child. Would you call Mrs. Sells at GIbralter 1-4396 for an appointment at your convenience?

Sincerely yours,

P. L. Greene

Camp Wingate

Many times, as a follow-up to a sales-related inquiry, a company salesman is asked to call on the inquirer. At other times, a copy of the company's reply is sent to the local distributor, who is expected to supplement it with another letter, a telephone call, or a local salesman's visit.

As a result of the latter practice, this letter from a local sales representative followed by ten days a letter and printed literature from the company's home office.

Good

Dear Sir:

I am the Wonderwood sales representative serving this area. By this time you have undoubtedly received lit-

erature and other data in reply to your recent inquiry.
Enclosed you will find the names and addresses of build-
ing-materials dealers in our area who sell the 33 types
and thicknesses of Wonderwood. You will find any one
of them eager to be of service.

All-wood Wonderwood is truly "the building material of a
thousand uses." There is a particular Wonderwood product suitable for every building or remodeling job from
the attic to the basement: walls, wainscots, ceilings,
exterior siding, cabinets, built-ins of all kinds, indoor and outdoor furniture, work surfaces, handyman
projects, repair jobs--there is just no end to the list.
And Wonderwood is so durable! These amazing hardboards
withstand all kinds of use and abuse, including extremes
in weather and humidity.

Select a dealer now. Ask him to show you samples of
genuine Wonderwood, particularly the proper type and
thickness for the job you have in mind.

                                        Sincerely yours,

Review Problems

1. Name the following:
   a. Two possible results of a well-written inquiry.
   b. Two possible results of a well-written reply to an inquiry.
   c. Two kinds of inquiries.
   d. Two qualities required of all inquiries.
   e. Five principles affecting replies to inquiries.
2. Think of some question you would like to have answered by a company
whose product you own (for example, the maker of your washing machine,
refrigerator, television set, hot water heater) or whose service you buy (for
example, your insurance company, your electric or gas supplier, your laundry)
and write a letter incorporating your inquiry.
3. Assume that you are working in the registrar's office of a school or college
and that you have received the following letter from George Bly of 565 Temple
Avenue, Your City:

Gentlemen:

Will you please let me know if you have evening courses in business correspondence? If so, I should like to know the hours and tuition.

I am 21 years old and am a high school graduate. I am at present working
for White & Tuttle Tool Co.

Write the reply.

4. Assume that you are a college student and have written to a well-known company for a copy of its stenographers' manual for study by your class. You have received the following reply:

Dear _____:

You will find enclosed our stenographers' manual as requested in your letter of October 17. As this represents a considerable expense to us, we are reluctant to pass out copies indiscriminately. We hope that all your classmates will share your copy and that we will not have to answer further requests from your school.

Very truly yours,

Rewrite the letter to show how much better the company might have handled the situation.

5. Criticize the next inquiry sent to a summer resort.

Gentlemen:

Please send rates and information about accommodations.

Very truly yours,

6. Assume that you are a correspondent for the Goodwin Department Store in your city. You have received the following letter from a mail-order customer who lives in a town about 100 miles away:

January 8, 19—

Goodwin Department Store
Your City, Your State

Gentlemen:

I have been looking everywhere for a pair of 14-inch drum-shaped lampshades in the color of the wallpaper sample I am enclosing. Could you tell me if you have such shades? Please also tell me the kind of material they are covered in and the price.

Very truly yours,

Assume further that you have no lampshades in the color requested. You do, however, have a silk material in a plum color (very close to the shade of the wallpaper) which the customer might buy if she would care to make the lampshades herself or have them made locally (your store does not make lampshades to order). The plum-colored silk material is $8.80 per yard. One yard is required for each lampshade. The 14-inch drum-shaped lampshade frames are $5.75 each. Write the reply to the customer's letter, returning her wallpaper sample and enclosing a swatch of the plum-colored silk.

8
Orders and Remittances

Much business activity revolves around the preparation of letters dealing with orders for and payments for merchandise. Unfortunately, the great volume of such letters may cause the business correspondent to compose them with less than customary forethought and care. As a matter of fact, letters about orders and remittances affect so many of the company's customers and suppliers that any improvement in writing these letters is certain to result in increased goodwill towards the company.

Order letters should be exact, and replies to them should be cordial and tactful. Letters about remittances must also be accurate and diplomatic, particularly where differences respecting terms and amounts of payment are involved.

ORDER LETTERS AND REPLIES

Because order letters and replies to them involve such matters as the description of merchandise, catalogue numbers, amounts of money, terms, and delivery dates, they must be written with great attention to detail. Simultaneously, the writer must strive for the same qualities of courtesy and individuality which characterize his other correspondence.

WRITING ORDERS. An order letter needs to be correct, complete, and definite so that the reader may fill it exactly as the writer wishes. Incompleteness or errors may mean further correspondence, shipping delays, complicated billing, repacking and reshipping, and loss of business.

Only by thorough checking of every order letter can inaccuracies be avoided. Even a careless typographical error—"60 dozen" shirts instead of an intended "6 dozen"—adds needless extra steps to the completion of a transaction. Many order letters are worthless because they omit important details. Although the writer may have a definite item of merchandise in mind, the reader of an order letter often must select it from a stock of dozens, even hundreds, of items. If one or more necessary specifications are omitted, the order may be filled incorrectly, or it may be delayed until the customer provides the needed information. In other instances, the failure to state the manner of packing or shipping may also cause delay and extra expense.

In the following letter, the writer has not specified the quantity, and, therefore, the supplier can not fill the order without further inquiry:

Gentlemen:

Please furnish us with your Hercules picture hooks, style 1500, on or before January 19. Either brass or silver finish is acceptable.

Very truly yours,

In the next example, the writer is so indefinite in his instructions that the reader is at a loss to know how to proceed in filling the order.

Gentlemen:

Please send me several boxes of your yarn in one of the brighter colors. I will pay for the order when the yarn is received.

Very truly yours,

The questions raised by this letter are: How many boxes? What quality or type of yarn? What specific color? Is the order to be sent collect or is it to be billed and paid for later? Following is the same letter rewritten in clearer terms:

Gentlemen:

Please send me by parcel post collect three dozen balls

```
of your Millicent No. 6-B yarn in peppermint red or
bright orange.
```
Very truly yours,

Whenever an order letter includes cash or a check or money order, or samples of color or material, reference to the enclosure should be made in the letter. In that way it can not be overlooked or inadvertently thrown away.

If there is the possibility that an order can not be filled exactly as prescribed, the writer should state an alternative. For example,

```
If you do not have fifty 2-lb. tins, one hundred 1-lb.
tins will be satisfactory.
```

Many companies doing a large mail-order business provide order forms for their customers. These are designed to bring forth all the details the company needs to fill orders correctly, such as item, quantity, catalogue number, size, color, style, and amount and mode of payment. Customers should use the forms in preference to letters whenever possible. Large buyers usually have purchase order forms printed for their own use. Using these forms helps to systematize purchase records, assists in writing orders accurately, and insures that purchases are made in accordance with the policies printed on the forms.

REPLYING TO ORDER LETTERS. Under ordinary conditions, an order letter does not require a reply, and none is expected. There are circumstances, however, when a reply to an order is needed or would be helpful. Such instances occur when a customer places an initial order or requests confirmation of an order, when an order is lacking in clarity, and when an order can not be filled.

Acknowledgments. A letter of acknowledgment offers the opportunity to say "thank you" to a new customer and to make him feel that his business is valued.[1] Naturally, a perfunctory letter of this sort is hardly better than none at all.

Perfunctory acknowledgment

```
Gentlemen:

This is to acknowledge your order of September 17 for
twenty gallons of our #888 light green paint.  Shipment
will be made by October 1, as requested.
```

[1] See Chapter 13, "Sales Promotion Letters."

Assuring you of our desire to serve you, we are

                              Very truly yours,

Improved acknowledgment

Gentlemen:

It is a pleasure to receive your order for twenty gallons of our #888 light green paint. The order is now being packed for shipment. You should receive it well before October 1, the date you specified.

Since you are a new customer, we should like to take this opportunity to assure you that we will do everything possible to provide you with top quality paint products and efficient service.

In another envelope we are sending you a complete catalogue of our paints and varnishes. You will find it convenient for reference.

We look forward to the opportunity of serving you again soon.

                              Sincerely yours,

Occasionally, a customer will request confirmation of an order to insure delivery of goods as specified. Under such a condition, the supplier may find it to his advantage to write a personal letter, even though he has printed forms for acknowledgment.

Good

Dear Mr. Rickey:

We want to assure you that your supplementary order of March 6 for 12 dozen men's straw hats will be shipped on April 20 along with your order of January 18. We are also increasing to 10,000 your order for our summer envelope stuffer imprinted with your name.

It is good to know you anticipate a successful season and we wish you success. Mr. James Olson, our new representative in your area, will call on you soon with

the fall line. We are sure he will be very attentive
to your needs.

                                        Very truly yours,

    Requesting Additional Information. When an order is incomplete, a reply must usually be written to secure clarification or essential information. A positive approach, courtesy, and a good measure of tact are assets in this type of letter. The writer should especially avoid emphasizing the fault in the original letter and, instead, should concentrate on ways to speed the order to the customer in compliance with his wishes.

Tactless reply

Gentlemen:

We have received your order of November 28 for two
dozen Model B super-speed broilers. Unfortunately, you
neglected to indicate which size or sizes you want--
small, medium, or large.

Until we receive this information, we can not fill your
order. Also, if your reply is going to be delayed,
please give us another delivery date, because it will be
impossible for us to deliver your order on the date requested.

                                        Very truly yours,

Improved reply

Gentlemen:

We are pleased to have your order of November 28 for
two dozen Model B super-speed broilers. So that we
may deliver this order on the date you requested, will
you indicate by return mail which size or sizes you
want--small, medium, or large.

We were going to ship eight broilers of each size, but
hesitated because in some localities one size in particular is in heavy demand.

Thank you for your co-operation in this matter.

                                        Very truly yours,

Refusing Orders. When, through no fault of the customer, an order can not be filled, the writer should explain why. If an item is out of stock, he should tell when it will be back in stock. If an item has been discontinued, he should say so and, if possible, offer a substitute. Patience in explaining the exact circumstances helps the customer and paves the way for future sales.

Insufficient explanation

Gentlemen:

In reply to your request of April 12 for three American Group coffee tables, we regret to inform you that this number has been discontinued.

Very truly yours,

Improved explanation

Gentlemen:

Although we appreciate your order of April 12 for three blond mahogany coffee tables in the American Group, we regret to tell you that the line has been discontinued.

It has been replaced by the Home Life series, which is also available in blond mahogany, as well as walnut and limed oak. The discontinuance of the American Group is in keeping with our practice of changing our contemporary line of furniture every four years. Except for several small bookcases, we no longer have any American Group pieces in stock.

You will find enclosed a catalogue of our new Home Life series. The coffee table is shown on page 4. Should you wish us to substitute this table for the model you ordered, please let us know.

Very truly yours,

REMITTANCE LETTERS

Inasmuch as almost all types of remittance letters involve money matters—transmitting and receiving payment and handling errors and irregularities in payment—accuracy is a prime requirement.

ACCURACY NECESSARY. The need for accuracy in letters of remittance is apparent not only in the writing of amounts, but also in the statement of dates, terms, invoice numbers, and the like. People are extremely sensitive about the payment of bills; therefore, it is wise to take care to insure correctness and to avoid controversy or ill will. A competent writer follows the practice of re-examining all the details of a transaction before writing a remittance letter; he also reviews it carefully after it is written.

TYPES OF REMITTANCE LETTERS. Remittance letters are used to (1) transmit checks and money orders, (2) acknowledge receipt of payment, (3) note errors in billing, and (4) call attention to errors in payment.

Transmitting Payment. On the checks themselves or on enclosed "advices" provision is generally made for noting the particular bill or bills which the remittance covers. Even so, an accompanying letter is often sent, especially if the writer desires to make a particular comment about the transaction. The first illustration below shows a simple letter of transmittal; the second adds a gracious comment. Both letters are examples of acceptable business practice.

```
Gentlemen:

We are enclosing our check for $395.00 in payment of
your invoice of March 16 covering our purchase of a
Zenith Electric Typewriter.

                                Very truly yours,


Dear Mr. James:

You will find enclosed our check for $1750.00 covering
your legal services for the first six months of this
year.

This is a good opportunity to tell you that we have en-
joyed working with you and are looking forward to the
benefit of your advice for a long time to come.

                                Sincerely yours,
```

Acknowledging Payments. Acknowledgments of payment, like letters transmitting payment, are not usually necessary. If sent, they should be more than perfunctory messages. Acknowledgments of payments are particularly appropriate when one wishes to express special appreciation or when additional assurance about the merchandise or service seems to be in order. In either case, the letters should be friendly and natural.

Perfunctory

Gentlemen:

Your check for $3,430.00, dated April 10, is acknowledged. This constitutes payment of our invoice No. 1050B, dated April 3.

                                        Very truly yours,

Improved

Gentlemen:

Thank you for your check of April 10 for $3,430.00, in payment of our invoice No. 1050B, dated April 3.

We look forward to the opportunity of serving you again.

                                        Sincerely yours,

Another effective letter

Gentlemen:

We appreciate your promptness in sending us your check for $1,470.30 in payment of the heavy-duty compressor that we recently installed for you.

The service agreement, which formed part of the transaction, extends for a full year from the date of installation. Please do not heaitate to call on us if you have any questions regarding the operation of the machine.

We are confident that you will be completely satisfied with long years of service from this compressor.

                                        Very truly yours,

Noting Errors in Billing. When the recipient of a bill believes an error has been made, he should write in a calm, matter-of-fact style so that the reader's attention will be focused on the error

rather than on the writer's emotions. The acknowledgment of
such an error should be equally serene. It should include a simple
apology and a statement regarding the correction. A new invoice
or bill is usually enclosed.

Notification of error in billing—good
Gentlemen:

We have just received your invoice No. 473B, dated
April 16 and amounting to $45.60, representing the pur-
chase of a C-2 blower for our Colvex Dryer.

Your sales department records should show that this
attachment was a replacement for a defective part and
that we were allowed a $25.00 credit on the new blower.

Under the circumstances we are returning the invoice to
you and are asking you to issue a corrected bill for
$20.60.

                                          Very truly yours,

Acknowledgment of error in billing—good

Gentlemen:

We regret that through our error, you were not credited
with the $25.00 allowance for the defective C-2 blower.

A corrected bill for $20.60 is enclosed. For discount
purposes you may regard the date of this letter as the
invoice date.

                                          Sincerely yours,

   Calling Attention to Payment Errors. When an error in payment
has been detected, as with an error in billing, the letter which calls
attention to the mistake requires calmness and courtesy.

Error in payment—a good reply
Gentlemen:

Thank you for your check for $35.00 in payment of your

January account. We were about to credit your account
with this payment when we noticed that the check was not
signed.

We are sending the check back to you for your signature.
Will you please return it to us in the stamped envelope
which we are enclosing for your convenience.

                                    Very truly yours,

When terms are misunderstood, a clear and tactful explanation
is necessary, especially so that similar erors will be avoided in the
future.

Misunderstanding in payment—a good reply

Gentlemen:

We have received your check for $760.10 in payment of
our invoice of November 12 for $940.50, covering your
half-page advertisement in the Metropolitan Times on
November 10.

In the letter accompanying the check, you say that you
should have been charged the retail, rather than the
national, rate because your products are sold in the
city's stores. We should, on the other hand, like to
call your attention to our rate card which defines local
advertising as that which is "placed and paid for by
retail merchants." Inasmuch as your company is a manufacturing and not a retail organization, we are sure you
will agree that the national rate should be charged.
If, in the future, you decide to let your retail outlets
place the advertising for your products in their own
names, we shall of course bill these stores at the
retail rate.

In view of this explanation, we are returning your check
and ask that you send us another for $940.50, the full
amount of the invoice.

                                    Very truly yours,

In the following letter, which also involves a misunderstanding
of terms, the customer's check is accepted in full payment, but the

writer takes the trouble to explain the policy involved, so that the error will not be repeated.

Good

Gentlemen:

Thank you for your check for $299.76 in settlement of our invoice dated September 8.

Although your remittance was not mailed until several days after the expiration of the discount period, we have credited your account with full payment. At the same time we should like to point out that under our terms of 2 per cent 10 days, net 30, the discount period begins with the invoice date and your check should therefore have been sent in not later than September 18.

Our practice of asking all customers to observe our terms closely has been favorably received because it in-dicates our earnest desire to deal equally with every-one. Under the circumstances, we are sure you will co-operate with us by making future payments in accordance with our terms.

                                          Very truly yours,

Review Problems

1. Which of the following statements are correct?

a. Letters about orders and remittances are routine in nature and there-fore do not require as much care as other types of correspondence.

b. Under ordinary circumstances, a letter need not be written to acknowl-edge an order.

c. If an order is not clear, it should be filled as well as possible.

d. When an error in billing is made, the best way to secure prompt cor-rection is to write a forceful complaint.

2. Write a letter to a local department store, ordering an article advertised in the evening newspaper.

3. Assume that you are working in the order department of the Ideal Pub-lishing Company. You have today (November 26) received the following letter:

475 Duquesne Avenue
Pittsburgh, Pa. 15024
November 24, 19—

Ideal Publishing Company
485 Fourth Avenue
Boston, Mass. 02116

Gentlemen:

Please send me a copy of the paper-bound edition of *The Home Workshop* by Charles Harris. Enclosed is my check for $2.00 to cover the cost.

Very truly yours,
Seymour Graves

Write a letter to Mr. Graves telling him that the paper-bound edition is out of stock and that you do not expect to have another printing before next March. Ask if Mr. Graves would like the cloth-bound edition at $7.00. Return the check for $2.00.

4. Assume that you are the Circulation Manager of your favorite magazine. You have just received an initial subscription order (with check enclosed) for a year's subscription. The order has come from Mr. Darrel R. Hynes of 985 Bascom Road, Tulsa, Oklahoma 74103. Write a letter of acknowledgment.

5. Assume that you are employed in the Bookkeeping Department of the Bryant Heater Company of Brookline, Mass. You have today (March 30) received from the Ratchet Plumbing Company of 8700 Commonwealth Avenue, Boston, Mass. 02110, a check for $687.63 in payment of six water heaters you shipped to them on March 3 and for which you billed them $721.50. On a slip of paper attached to the check the customer has written, "Have deducted $33.87 for trucking charges." Assume that your catalogue, from which the Ratchet Plumbing Company had ordered, has a notice on page 3, under the heading "Terms," which reads "Customers must pay shipping charges." The same notice is printed on all your invoices. Write a letter to the customer asking for a check for $33.87, the amount deducted.

9
Credit Letters

Credit has been defined as "A promise of future payment in kind or in money given in exchange for present money, goods, or services." [1]

The importance of credit in modern business can not be overstated. Literally billions of dollars worth of goods and services are exchanged annually on this basis. Credit is the instrument which enables producer, manufacturer, retailer, and consumer to obtain goods at a time when they can be profitably or enjoyably used, even if ready cash is not available. With only a relatively few exceptions, all business concerns buy or sell (or buy and sell) on credit. At one time or another, most consumers, also, purchase goods and services on credit.

Although the promise to pay is essential to any credit transaction, the ability and the intention of the debtor to live up to his promise are even more important. The evaluation of such ability and intention is the job of the credit man.

CRITERIA FOR JUDGING CREDIT RISKS

The credit man judges a "promise to pay" on the basis of three criteria commonly known as the "3 C's of credit": (1) capital, (2) capacity, and (3) character.

CAPITAL. *Capital* is the net financial worth of a person or company. It consists of the total value of all assets—including cash, goods, and property—minus the total of all outstanding debts.

---

[1] Sloan, Harold S., and Zurcher, Arnold J., *Dictionary of Economics,* an Everyday Handbook (5th ed.; New York: Barnes & Noble, Inc., 1970).

CAPACITY. *Capacity* is the ability to manage one's personal affairs or the affairs of one's company so as to be able to pay debts when due. Capacity may depend on the individual's education, competence, or experience, or a combination of these factors. The capacity of a worker depends on his ability to hold a job; the capacity of a company may depend on such factors as its location, its sources of materials, the markets for its products, and the technical skill or business acumen of its personnel.

CHARACTER. *Character* is reputation, especially with respect to the manner in which debts are discharged. The debtor who pays his bills promptly and conducts his business honestly is sure to be well-regarded by credit managers. Conversely, the debtor who is slow in paying, or given to personal excesses or to unethical business practices, is considered to be weak in character and, therefore, a bad credit risk.

SOURCES OF CREDIT INFORMATION

Information concerning the capital, capacity, and character of a company may be obtained in many ways. Although the sources of credit information may be more numerous, it is often more difficult to obtain information about individuals.

INFORMATION FOR A COMPANY. In obtaining credit information for a business firm, the company itself may be asked to supply a financial statement or bank or trade references. Inquiries can be directed to the sources named by the prospective debtor or to banks and credit agencies with which the creditor regularly does business. The credit agencies may be private organizations (such as the well-known Dun & Bradstreet, Inc.), or they may be trade associations of which the firm is a member.

INFORMATION FOR AN INDIVIDUAL. Obtaining credit information for individuals is usually more difficult than for companies. Commercial banks will provide information for individuals maintaining regular checking accounts, or for those transacting other business with banks, or for those in business circles. Facts regarding capital, capacity, and character may also be obtained from employers, landlords, and real-estate records. In large cities, data may be obtained from the local retail credit bureaus, many of which are co-operative agencies run by the merchants; in smaller cities and towns, data must be sought from the merchants directly.

AIMS OF THE CREDIT MAN

Using capital, capacity, and character as his guideposts, the credit man has two main objectives: (1) to limit financial losses to his firm resulting from the extension of credit and (2) to increase the volume of credit sales.

MINIMIZING FINANCIAL LOSS. The indiscriminate granting of credit invites poor credit risks and ultimate loss. The credit man never grants credit until he has thoroughly acquainted himself with all the facts. When the information he receives indicates that the credit risk is greater than he is willing to accept, the credit man has two courses open to him: (1) He may refuse credit entirely. Or (2) he may limit the line of credit. When credit is refused, the prospective customer must find another source of credit or buy for cash, if he is to obtain the goods at all. When the line of credit is limited, the amount of goods the customer may buy for credit is restricted to only part of what he wants or requires. Any purchases exceeding the credit limit must be paid for in cash. In this way, a merchant who orders $2000.00 worth of goods may be limited to a credit line of $1000.00. If the merchant wants the whole order, he is required to pay $1000.00 cash. By the same token, when the merchant pays $700.00 toward the reduction of his credit or "open" account, he is permitted to buy on credit an equivalent amount of goods against the account.

INCREASING SALES VOLUME. The credit man increases sales volume for his firm in several ways, among which are (1) granting credit liberally, (2) providing credit information for company salesmen, and (3) writing letters that promote goodwill.

Granting Credit Liberally. The credit man grants credit as liberally as possible without taking undue risks. The more credit he grants, the more business he creates for his firm. Even when he must refuse credit, however, the opportunity to make a sale is not entirely lost. If he is tactful and persuasive enough, he may yet induce the customer to buy for cash.

Notifying Company Salesmen. Periodically, the credit man informs his company's salesmen of the conditions of their accounts, thus enabling them to concentrate their efforts on good credit risks. In some instances, he may originate lists of desirable credit risks and pass them along to the sales department. Since the credit position of the customer or prospective customer may change overnight, the credit man must be constantly aware of significant changes and must notify the sales department accordingly.

Promoting Goodwill. The credit man writes letters that promote goodwill and increase sales. By his alertness to the opportunities to write such letters and by his skill in writing them, he advances harmonious and profitable relations.

TYPES OF CREDIT LETTERS

Generally speaking, the credit man's letters fall into six categories: (1) letters requesting information, (2) letters giving information, (3) letters granting credit, (4) letters refusing credit, (5) letters inviting new credit accounts, and (6) letters reactivating old accounts.

LETTERS REQUESTING INFORMATION. In his effort to secure credit information, the credit man will write either to the customer or to a third party, or both. The need for a credit inquiry usually originates with a request for credit. Thus a merchant may write as follows:

```
Gentlemen:

Please ship by express on open account four Dexter Air
Conditioners, Model 3HT, at $227.60 each, as listed in
your latest trade catalogue.

                                    Very truly yours,
```

If the merchant is already an established credit customer, this letter presents no special problem. If, on the other hand, the merchant is ordering for the first time and is unknown to the credit man, a credit inquiry is necessary. First, the credit man may consult one of the credit rating books published by Dun & Bradstreet, Inc. or by his trade association; or he may seek to obtain a special report from the bank or credit agency with which he customarily deals. Should he be unable to obtain from these sources sufficient up-to-date information about the merchant's financial worth, reputation, and ability to pay, the credit man will then direct an inquiry to the merchant himself. If he is not careful, he may dictate a letter such as the following:

Gentlemen:

We have your order for four Dexter Air Conditioners,
Model 3HT, which you asked us to ship on open account.

Since we have never done business with you, we made
several inquiries about your credit standing, but no
one seems to have any information about you. We shall,
therefore, have to hold up your order until you can
supply us with your most recent financial statement and
several trade references.

If, after further investigation based on this information, we find your credit position satisfactory, we
shall be glad to ship your order on open account.
Otherwise, we regret to say that we shall have to insist
on cash in advance.

                                        Very truly yours,

A better letter, such as the one below, would avoid such tact-
lessness and assume, at least for the time being, that the reader will
qualify for the open account.

Gentlemen:

We are pleased to have your order for four Dexter Air
Conditioners, Model 3HT.

To help us fill your order on open account as promptly
as possible, will you please send us a recent financial
statement and the names of three firms which now sell to
you on a credit basis. You may find the enclosed form
convenient for submitting this information.

The four air conditioners you ordered have been held
aside for you so that you can be certain of obtaining
the models you desire. We look forward to the opportunity of serving you.

                                        Very truly yours,

Should the merchant supply the trade references requested, the
credit man will then direct an inquiry to each of them. The kind
of response he receives depends largely on how courteous and spe-

cific he is in his letter of inquiry. The credit man who asks a favor as if he is giving a command is sure to meet resistance. On the other hand, the credit man who is courteous but vague about his requirements may get a willing answer, but one that is so general as to be almost useless.

The letter below is neither courteous nor specific.

Gentlemen:

We have received an order from the Bower Electrical Co. Since your name was given as a reference, we are writing to obtain all the information you can give us about your dealings with this company. Please answer immediately in the envelope provided.

                              Very truly yours,

The next inquiry is both courteous and definite and is, therefore, much more likely to elicit the kind of response desired.

Gentlemen:

We have received an initial order from a firm with which we understand you are at present doing business, the Bower Electrical Company of Fort Worth, Texas.

In seeking to establish a line of credit, the Bower Company submitted the name of your concern as a reference.

So that we may fill the pending order as promptly as possible, we respectfully request your co-operation in furnishing pertinent information on the Bower Company. We would like to know particularly how long you have done business with the company, what credit limit you have placed on this account, how promptly terms are met, and what amount is currently outstanding.

Thank you for your co-operation in this matter. We hope you will some day give us the opportunity to reciprocate.

                              Very truly yours,

In retail practice, the credit or "open" account is usually referred to as a "charge account." A customer applying for such an account may write:

Gentlemen:

Will you please be good enough to open a charge account
for me at your store. I have been a cash customer of
yours for many years but would now like to enjoy the
convenience of charging my purchases.

If there is any information about me you would like to
have, please let me know.

                                    Very truly yours,

                                    Dora C. Grant

                                    (Mrs. John R. Grant)

If the credit manager of a department store in a large city received such a letter, he would probably telephone the Retail Credit
Bureau in his city to find out whether Mrs. Grant has any other
accounts in the city and, if so, what her credit record has been.
Very often the information supplied by the Retail Credit Bureau is
all the credit man needs. If the Bureau has no information about
Mrs. Grant, the credit man will write to her somewhat as follows:

Good

Dear Mrs. Grant:

We are glad to know that you wish to open a charge account with us. As you are already aware, you are certain to find such an account a great convenience to you.

So that we may be in a position to open your account as
soon as possible, will you please give us the information requested on the enclosed card and return the card
to us in the accompanying stamped envelope.

You may be sure that we are most eager to add your name
to our growing list of charge customers.

                                    Sincerely yours,

The card enclosed will be very much like the following:

I should like to have a charge account entitling me to charge
my purchases at Blank Brothers.

Signature _____

Employer's Name _____

Business address _____ Telephone _____

Home address _____ Telephone _____

Name and address of my bank _____

_____

After the filled-in card is received from the customer, the
credit man may make one or two inquiries by mail or telephone
to the references given on the card. A letter to the bank reference
may read as this one:

Gentlemen:

Mrs. John R. Grant, who has applied for a charge account
at our store, has told us that her husband has a checking account with you.

We should appreciate your telling us how long Mr. Grant
has had the account and how much his balances customarily average.

You may be sure that we shall be glad to return the
favor at any time.

                                        Very truly yours,

LETTERS GIVING INFORMATION. The credit man is frequently
called upon to furnish information about his own firm. Or he may
be asked to furnish information about a company with which his
firm does business. In either case, he is aware that his own best
interests are served if he responds as courteously and completely
as possible.

In a letter concerning his own firm, the credit man should state
the information requested and insofar as possible let the facts
speak for themselves. No matter how deserving of credit the

writer's company is, the letter should be cordial in order to start
business relations on a pleasant basis. Expressions of impatience,
arrogance, or indignation are unnecessary.

Poor

Gentlemen:

I find it hard to believe that a question is raised
about our company's credit standing. I would suggest
your credit department engage in at least a cursory examination of available information before sending a request of this kind.

However, in order to speed delivery of material which
we have already indicated we need in a hurry, you will
find attached the financial statement requested in your
letter of October 10.

I trust we can now get on with the business of having
the merchandise packaged and delivered.

                              Very truly yours,

   By demonstrating his understanding of the need for credit information and his willingness to co-operate, the writer is more
likely to establish a relationship that will influence the reader favorably in future transactions between the two companies.

Good

Gentlemen:

We are of course glad to submit the information you requested with regard to the establishing of an open account
with your company.

You will find attached our most recent profit and loss
statement and balance sheet. Named below are companies
with which we have done business on credit for at least
five years:

                    Smith, Jones, and Black, Inc.
                    Lyndon, Texas

```
                    Bell & Co., Inc.
                    17 State Street
                    New York City

                    Album Company
                    Fredo, Ohio
```

We shall be glad to provide additional information, if
you should have further questions on this matter.

                                        Very truly yours,

A letter answering a request for credit information about a third
party should be objective, prompt, and specific.

Objectivity. The answer to a request for credit information
should be *objective*. The inquirer is interested primarily in an
honest report and evaluation of his prospective customer's financial
ability. To color or to distort the facts in favor of or against the
third party not only does a disservice to the reader, but may subject the writer and his company to a lawsuit for fraud or libel.
Notice the emphasis on facts and the absence of editorial comment
in the letter from a bank to a customer who requested credit information about a third party.

Gentlemen:

We are glad to answer your letter of April 22 regarding
The Brady Corporation, 145 Auburn Street, New York City.

This corporation was organized approximately three and
one half years ago to engage in the export business.
Although the company specializes in automotive parts and
equipment, it also handles a general line of merchandise.

A good account has been carried with us since January
19--, with balances in satisfactory proportions. The
company does not borrow from us.

The financial statement of the corporation as of February 29, 19--, submitted to us in confidence, discloses
a satisfactory condition and a net worth in low five
figures. Mr. Frank Paul is the president and principal
at interest, and our general impressions of him are entirely favorable. On the basis of our experience, we

believe The Brady Corporation is a reputable organization.

We hope this information will prove helpful.

                                    Very truly yours,

Observe the treatment of unfavorable information in the following letter, written by a department store in response to a request for information about one of its customers. General practice favors disguising or omitting the customer's name when an unfavorable report is written. Many companies prefer to give negative reports over the telephone.

Good

Gentlemen:

We are sorry to say that our experience with Mr. R.W., about whom you inquired in your letter of July 17, has been unsatisfactory.

The account has been open for three years and on several occasions we have had trouble in effecting settlements. Mr. R.W. still owes $132.50 for purchases made over seven months ago. The account is now in the hands of our attorneys for collection.

May we ask that you treat this information as strictly confidential.

                                    Very truly yours,

Promptness. The answer to a credit inquiry about a third party should be *prompt*. Sometimes a delay in sending credit information destroys the inquirer's chance for a profitable business transaction. Furthermore, the writer is more likely to obtain prompt replies to his own requests if he shows similar consideration.

Specificity. The answer should be *specific*. Note the comparative value to the credit man of the expressions in the two columns below.

General	*Specific*
He is an unsatisfactory payer.	He is a "slow" payer, but dependable.

General	*Specific*
Mr. Blank is a regular customer.	Mr. Blank has been a steady customer for the past five years.
The XYZ Company is one of our big buyers.	The XYZ Company placed $120,000.00 worth of business with us last year.
We have had some trouble with this account.	Three months ago we were compelled to make collection through our attorneys.

LETTERS GRANTING CREDIT. Since they are ordinarily addressed to *new* customers, messages granting credit offer unusually good opportunities to create favorable impressions. At this time, the writer can express his pleasure in opening the account and his anticipation of a pleasant relationship. The following letter is routine and lacking in cordiality:

Gentlemen:

Your order per your letter of November 16 is being shipped today. Terms are 2/10.

Please remit check payable to The Carver Company, Inc.

                                        Very truly yours,

The letter below is even worse because it is negative.

Gentlemen:

Although we have rather serious reservations about certain aspects of the credit information you submitted, we have decided to extend a limited line of credit for the time being.

You will have to prove to us over the next several months that this privilege is warranted.

Our invoice will accompany the shipment which you can expect on November 14.

                                        Very truly yours,

In the next letter, the writer not only begins affirmatively, but also mentions an added benefit of the credit privilege.

Good

Gentlemen:

We are able to make immediate delivery of your order for
24 Prince George desks. On the basis of the information which you so promptly provided us, we are glad to
send this merchandise on our regular credit terms of 2
per cent 10 days, net 30.

As a regular customer, you will receive advance notices
of our national promotion efforts so that you may take
steps to relate your own merchandising to them.

It is our hope that this order represents the first step
in the establishment of a long and pleasant business
relationship.

                              Very truly yours,

Letters to customers of retail stores often indicate the manner in which purchases may be charged and the way in which they will be billed.[2]

Good

Dear Mrs. Marr:

We are pleased to tell you that your charge account is
now open and ready for your use. We are sure you will
find it a great convenience.

The Charga-Plate enclosed, bearing your name, address,
and account number, should be presented to the clerk
whenever you charge a purchase. A statement will be
sent to you regularly each month.

---

[2] The Truth-in-Lending Act of 1968 tells exactly what must be disclosed to
the consumer when credit is extended, arranged, or just offered. Full information will be found in the pamphlet "What You Ought to Know About Federal
Reserve Regulation Z—Truth-in-Lending." For a free copy, write to the Board
of Governors, Federal Reserve System, Washington, D.C. 20551.

Thank you for this opportunity to be of service.

                              Sincerely yours,

In some instances, although credit is granted, limitations are imposed. Under these circumstances, the writer should state the limitations in a straightforward manner.

Good

Gentlemen:

Thank you very much for submitting the financial statements and trade references we requested in regard to your establishing a line of credit. We are pleased to inform you that merchandise up to the amount of $1500.00 can be furnished you on open account.

Inasmuch as your present order amounts to $2165.50, a cash payment of $665.50 should be made upon delivery of the goods. Or, if you prefer, you may instruct us to reduce your order by that amount. The balance can of course be paid according to our regular terms of 2 per cent 10 days, net 60.

Please let us know your wishes as soon as possible so that we may ship your order promptly.

We look forward to serving you as a steady and valued customer.

                              Very truly yours,

LETTERS REFUSING CREDIT. Writing a letter that declines credit is always a challenge to the correspondent. This is so because the writer must be able to retain the reader's goodwill despite the refusal. Moreover, if he still values the reader's order, he must attempt to obtain it on a cash basis.

Since the credit man is sending bad news, he is less likely to offend if he organizes his ideas inductively (see p. 71); that is, stating the pertinent facts first and the conclusion later. To begin the letter, "I am sorry to inform you that we can not ship the merchandise you requested on open account," may so jar the reader's feelings that he will not respond favorably to the rest of the letter, no matter how friendly and constructive it is. Even when the in-

118CREDIT LETTERS

ductive order is used, diplomatic phrasing is required. Lame excuses like, "We have decided temporarily not to open any more new accounts"; over-directness in stating unpleasant facts; and harsh finality in the refusal should be avoided.

The tone of the following letter is sympathetic. Notice especially, in the third paragraph, how the writer has subordinated the refusal of credit to the desirability of the merchandise.

Gentlemen:

We appreciate the promptness with which you provided the credit information which we requested in our letter of March 18.

In accordance with our general policy, we have carefully studied the information and have been in touch with the companies which you listed. In most respects, your past record is entirely satisfactory. However, we are reluctant to extend credit because of the difficulties you have experienced at times in disappointing seasonal dips.

Even though we can not extend credit privileges at the present time, we should like very much to ship the goods to you on C.O.D. terms. As you mentioned in your order, you can use the merchandise most profitably during the current month. Along with the added advantage of the 2 per cent discount for cash, you can turn over the goods quickly at this season and make a handsome profit.

The merchandise has been held aside for you and is ready for immediate shipment. If you will indicate by return mail or telegram (collect) your approval of C.O.D. terms, we can make delivery in time for you to put the goods on sale before the end of next week.

We hope you will give us the opportunity to serve you.

Very truly yours,

Although such a vigorous approach is not ordinarily warranted in the case of the consumer, it is still possible for the credit man to turn the reader's attention in the close to the thought of doing business on a cash basis—as in the letter below.

Dear Mrs. Bond:

Your recent application for a charge account has been
given careful consideration.

As is our custom before a new account is opened, we have
endeavored to acquire information that would serve us as
a basis for credit. Such information as we have thus
far obtained does not permit us to form a positive conclusion. Perhaps, in the future, conditions may change
as to allow us to open an account for you.

Meanwhile, we hope you will continue to avail yourself,
as you have in the past, of the excellent merchandise,
the attractive prices, and the friendly service of the
Brody Department Store.

Very truly yours,

INVITING NEW CREDIT ACCOUNTS. Individuals with credit accounts tend to buy more frequently and to buy more at a time than
cash customers. Accordingly, the alert credit man does not merely
respond to requests for credit; he also searches for opportunities to
build new credit accounts. For this purpose, letters are very useful.

The credit man may use letters to invite new accounts either
among present cash customers or among persons who, to his
knowledge, are not regular customers. Letters inviting credit accounts are especially common in retail-store practice.

Good

Dear Mr. Staley:

Perhaps you have already visited our new Fifth Avenue
store at 51st Street. It seems as if all New York has
looked us over since our opening.

If you did see the store, it will require no urging on
my part, I am sure, to convince you that this should be
your store for wearing apparel--and that you will find
a charge account a real convenience in shopping.

The charge account application card enclosed will take
only a moment to fill out and return. Won't you do it
now?

Very truly yours,

REACTIVATING OLD CREDIT ACCOUNTS. When a reliable credit customer stops using his account, the credit man has another opportunity to take constructive action. He may ask in a letter if the company or store has in any way been at fault. Or he may attempt to reactivate the account by stressing a positive reason why the customer should resume activity.

Good

Dear Mrs. Lacy:

In checking our records we note that your account with our store has not recently been used. We take this opportunity to remind you that Dior's new spring collection offers a fashion-compelling reason for you to renew old acquaintances.

For your own shopping convenience, please being along your Account Card. If you have mislaid it by any chance, a telephone call to our accommodation desk will speed a new one on its way.

As always, we welcome the opportunity to serve you.

                                              Cordially,

Review Problems

1. Which of the following statements are correct?
   a. The three C's of credit are capital, character, and courtesy.
   b. The two main jobs of the credit man are to keep down losses and help increase sales.
   c. A credit man called on for information about one of his customers should always give a frank opinion.
   d. It is good practice for the credit man to try to convert cash customers into credit customers.
   e. When the credit man refuses credit, he should give up also any idea of selling to the customer on a cash basis.

2. Assume that you are the credit manager of an exclusive department store in your city. Write a form letter to be sent to selected club women, telling them that you have taken the liberty of opening a charge account for them. Ask them to stop at the manager's desk on the first floor for their charge account identification plate.

3. Assume that you are employed by James Stahl & Co., manufacturers of rubber boots. You have today received an initial order for 6 dozen boots amounting to $388.00 from the Atlas Shoe Stores, 475 Grand Avenue, Minneapolis 7, Minn. 55415. Upon consulting Dun & Bradstreet, you find that this

firm is highly rated. Write a letter to the Atlas Shoe Stores thanking them for their order and telling them that shipment will be made within one week.

4. Assume that you are the proprietor of the Palm-Breeze Hotel in Miami, Florida. You have just received an eight-weeks' reservation from Mrs. Carrie Meyers of 4975 Knickerbocker Road, Teaneck, N.J. 07666. She has given the Teaneck National Bank as a reference. Write to the Teaneck National Bank, asking for information about Mrs. Meyers' financial responsibility.

5. Assume that you are the vice-president of the Teaneck National Bank and have received the letter mentioned in Problem 4. Mrs. Meyers has dealt with your bank for a great number of years. She keeps an account with balances averaging in medium four figures and, in your opinion, she is entitled to the usual credit courtesies. You have a high regard for her personally. Write a reply to the Palm-Breeze Hotel.

10
Collection Letters

Collection letters become necessary when credit customers fail to pay their accounts promptly. Collecting "past-due" accounts is usually a function of the credit department, although a special person or staff may be assigned to the work.

The individual in charge of collecting past-due accounts should be familiar with the factors that make collections successful; he should choose carefully his means of follow-up and should adapt his message to his readers; and he should be willing make exceptions to the normal collection pattern in order to meet special circumstances.

FACTORS IN SUCCESSFUL COLLECTIONS

Success in collecting past-due accounts by letter or other means depends principally on three factors: (1) knowledge of one's customers, (2) systematic follow-up, and (3) good tone.

KNOWLEDGE OF CUSTOMERS. Successful collections require not only a broad knowledge of human nature, but also a knowledge of the specific business backgrounds and the paying habits of one's credit customers. The writer of collection letters should realize that people are sensitive about their credit standings and must therefore be handled with great tact. He should realize, too, that these same customers are inclined to be dilatory. Generally, business houses more readily than individuals recognize the importance of paying promptly, but even well-rated accounts, business houses and individuals alike, sometimes fail to pay their bills on time.

It takes knowledge and insight on the credit man's part to distinguish between the classes of risk and consider their differences. Many companies classify customers as (1) very good or "gilt-edge" risks, (2) good risks, and (3) poor risks. The *very good risks* have ample capital and capacity, and usually pay very promptly—discounting all their bills if they are business firms. The *good risk* has adequate capital and capacity and a fair reputation for prompt payment. The *poor risk* just barely meets the creditor's requirements with respect to capital and capacity and is inclined to be slow in meeting obligations.

Regardless of the class of credit risk dealt with however, allowances should be made for special circumstances. Even one who pays promptly will need an extension of time if his business has suffered from fire or tornado or other natural hazard, or if business conditions in his area are temporarily depressed, or if illness or other personal misfortune has struck him. The correspondent must know or discover such circumstances if he is to adapt his collection messages to his readers and collect the most accounts and, in addition, retain the goodwill of his company's debtors.

SYSTEMATIC FOLLOW-UP. Having a good record of collections depends a great deal on the training customers receive. This training is imparted by a planned series of letters and other follow-up forms that constitute the collection system. Through the collection system, customers come to know that the creditor *expects* prompt payment. They are reminded when payments become past due and receive letters regularly if they do not respond. Meanwhile, the pressure on them increases steadily until finally they are threatened with action against them—action which is ultimately taken. Because it is consistent and unremitting, customers acquire a respect for the collection system and for the creditor who employs it. From the creditor's point of view, systematic follow-up results in fewer overdue accounts and fewer letters to write. For it is only natural for customers of limited resources to pay their most insistent creditors first. By being politely and judiciously insistent, the collection man insures that he will not be ignored.

The timing of follow-up messages is an important factor in the success of the collection system. Generally, the length of the system and the time between letters should be determined by the established habits of the customer, by competitive practices, and by the nature of the credit business. (For example, an installment collection business requiring weekly payments will move considerably faster in collecting money than a department store that requires the full payment of charged purchases every month.) In addition, the following rules should prove helpful: (1) The better the risk, the longer the time before legal action is threatened; conversely, the poorer the risk, the shorter the time before legal action is threatened. The theory here is that a good risk has financial resources and that collection will eventually be made. A poor risk, on the other hand, has only limited resources, and if they are not tapped promptly, they may be dissipated. (2) The better the risk, the longer the time between letters. Thus a good risk may be sent a letter once a month early in the system while a poor risk may be sent a letter every two or three weeks. (3) The further advanced the system, the shorter the interval between letters. If early in the system letters are sent once a month, they may be speeded up to two, three, or even four a month after several months have elapsed.

GOOD TONE. Collection letters even more than other types of correspondence require good tone. This quality depends on a genuine respect and consideration for the reader as an individual and the use of temperate language—especially in trying situations. Common errors in tone include scolding, bullying, sarcasm, and other language abuses.

Bad

Don't you realize the injury you are doing to yourself by withholding payment?

We'll show you that you can't abuse credit and break promises.

I am tired of wasting money on stationery and stamps to remind you of your overdue account.

Please don't hurry on our account. We're only the creditors.

Tactful language and good tone are illustrated in letters marked *good* throughout this chapter.

The fact that no one likes to receive a collection letter puts the writer in a difficult position. If he tries too hard to be agreeable, he may weaken the letter to the point where it does not bring the payment desired. If he is only as firm as circumstances warrant, he may cause embarrassment or worry. Ordinarily, he attempts to use a tone that will not cause irritation, resentment, or indifference. Rarely will a reader respond to a collection letter with enthusiasm, but the correspondent is successful if he receives a favorable response without offending the credit customer.

TYPES OF COLLECTION FOLLOW-UPS

The collection system may gain interest and effectiveness through the use of a variety of follow-up forms and methods. These include (1) printed notices, (2) form letters, (3) personal letters, and (4) telegrams, telephone calls, and personal visits. The more personal the approach, the stronger the effect. Hence the practice of using printed reminders and form letters early in the system and more personal letters later. In collection messages, as contrasted with other types of letters, the personal touch is not usually welcomed by the customer and, indeed, may prove embarrassing to him.

PRINTED NOTICES. Usually, *printed notices* are the mildest of reminders and are effective early in the system when it may be presumed that most past-due accounts are the results of oversight. A common form of printed notice is the rubber-stamped legend on the monthly statement.

PAST DUE

or

PAST DUE
Please remit

More elaborate reminders are sometimes printed on gummed labels which are affixed to the statement. One reminder reads:

Just a Friendly Reminder

—that this account is past due—
and that payment would be
greatly appreciated.
—Thank you

A number of companies, including many departments stores, use a series of collection messages on cards.[1] These may have blank spaces to be filled in with pertinent data. The tone becomes increasingly severe in successive cards, although threats are usually left to the more personal types of follow-up. The following is a typical card series:

```
            Robert Greer & Co.

             500 State Street

          Boston,  Mass. 02105




   The balance indicated below is now past
   due.  Payment will be appreciated.

   Balance to_____

   $_____
```

```
            Robert Greer & Co.

             500 State Street

          Boston,   Mass. 02105

   We are calling your attention again to
   the balance of your account,which is
   now considerably overdue.  Please send
   us your check at once.


   Balance_____

   $_____
```

---

[1] Collection cards should be enclosed in envelopes. In many states the libel laws prohibit the sending of collection notices on post cards. It is also unlawful in some states to print on an envelope such a notice as, "We collect bad debts." In general, the debtor should not be exposed to public embarrassment except as it may come to him through court action.

```
          Robert Greer & Co.

          500 State Street

          Boston, Mass. 02105


Your balance of $_____which dates
back to_____is still unpaid in spite
of our several reminders.  We must in-
sist that this matter receive your im-
mediate attention.
```

FORM LETTERS. *Form letters* save considerable expense in dealing with large numbers of past-due accounts. They also provide an effective follow-up system. These letters are printed, or otherwise duplicated, with blank spaces for the date, inside address, salutation, and specific information the creditor may want to give in respect to the condition of the account. If form letters are carefully processed and filled in, they will look like individually typed letters, although the personal effect is neither necessary nor especially desirable in the early part of the system.

Below is an example of a form letter used by a furniture house which allows customers to purchase on the installment plan. Space is allowed for filling in the date, inside address, salutation, and amount overdue.

DALY BROTHERS
90 Geyer Street
Jackson, Mississippi (39200)

```
In looking over your account, we note there still re-
mains a small balance of $_____  now overdue for some
time.
```

```
We will appreciate, therefore, your remitting this sum
within the next few days.

Thank you for your co-operation.

                                        Very truly yours,



                                Daly Brothers
```

PERSONAL LETTERS. When printed reminders and form letters fail to bring response, or when the circumstances of collection are highly individualized, *personal letters* are necessary. Personal letters are often prepared as the occasion requires. But more often they are copied or are adapted from "guide" (pattern) letters that the company has developed over a period of years and that reflect the firm's policy. Guide letters are classified forms or paragraphs from which the collection man selects the one or ones best suited to a particular siuation. He indicates to his stenographer what dates and amounts are to be inserted in the appropriate places and, in some instances, chooses from a selection of alternative phrases. If necessary, he recasts sentences and paragraphs. The letter the reader receives is individually typed and can not be distinguished from a personally dictated letter. Even a large company may find that 50 to 100 guide letters will expedite 90 per cent or more of its collection correspondence.

TELEGRAMS, TELEPHONE CALLS, AND PERSONAL VISITS. *Telegrams* [2] are sometimes used as a follow-up to letters, especially when collection is urgent. Thus, the message of a telegram might read:

HAVE YOU COMPLIED OUR REQUEST JANUARY 18 ANSWER IMPORTANT

Telephone calls and *personal visits* to a customer should be made only after careful consideration, for they are intrusions on privacy and may cause resentment. However, both methods are useful, because they get answers where letters often fail. Personal calls, in addition, may be instrumental in obtaining immediate payment. It is a fact that some small merchants and salaried employees actu-

---

[2] See *Letters For All Occasions,* an Everyday Handbook (New York: Barnes & Noble, Inc., 1952), pp. 175–186.

ally prefer to pay a collector and they wait for his visits. Company salesmen are often charged with collecting past-due accounts when they solicit new business from a credit customer.

COLLECTION APPEALS

In trying to obtain payment of a past-due account, the writer of collection letters uses a variety of appeals. A number of these appeals are mild; a number are strong. Several work well with certain customers; others do not. Choosing the right appeal at the right time is part of the strategy of successful collections. The main appeals in order of severity are (1) reminders, (2) inquiries, (3) appeals to sympathy, (4) appeals to fairness, (5) appeals to self-interest, and (6) appeals to fear.

REMINDERS. In the reminder, the writer briefly calls attention to the fact that the account is overdue and asks for payment. He also refers to any previous notifications.

Good

```
Dear Mrs. Gold:

Recently your attention was called to the overdue bal-
ance of your charge account.  Settlement should have
been made several months ago.

We hope to receive your check for $87.55 within the
next few days.

A prepaid envelope is enclosed for your convenience in
remitting.

                              Sincerely yours,
```

Often reminders suggest customers' oversights. Such reminders are sometimes called *appeals to goodwill*, because they take for granted the customers' good intentions. By attributing to the reader a common (and, presumably, excusable) human failing, the writer hopes to avoid a more serious implication.

Good

```
Dear Mr. Day:

This is intended merely as a friendly reminder of your
```

past-due account of $45.00 which we believe you have
overlooked.

Now that it has been brought to your attention, we are
sure you will want to bring your account up-to-date.

If by chance your check is already in the mail, please
disregard this reminder and accept our thanks.

Sincerely yours,

INQUIRIES. When the creditor believes there may be a valid
reason for nonpayment, he will write a letter to elicit an explanation from the debtor. Such a *letter of inquiry* (*courtesy letter*) is
often written early in the collection system when the customer's
former record of payment has been good. As a case in point, it is
possible that the customer did not receive the goods or the bill or
that an adjustment is pending. The letter of inquiry is also used
toward the end of the system. At this time, the letter may inquire
into the ability of the reader to pay, and it may suggest that special
consideration will be shown if the customer will only write and
explain his situation.

Good (*an early inquiry*)

Dear Mr. Ray:

On September 12 we wrote to you in regard to your past-
due account of $149.50. Until now we have not received
a response.

If there is some reason why payment has not been made,
we should appreciate your writing to us.

Otherwise we shall assume that nonpayment is due merely
to an oversight and that we will have your check within
the next few days.

Very truly yours,

Good (*inquiry preceding the threat*)

Dear Mr. Kurt:

We are considerably disturbed by your failure to answer
any of our letters regarding payment of your account,
which is now past due in the amount of $96.25.

The matter is so serious that we want to give you another opportunity to communicate with us before we take
further action. If there is any reason why you can not
send us your check, you should notify us now. Simply
jot down a few words at the bottom of this page and return it to us in the envelope enclosed.

On your answer depend our future relations with you.
We ask you to mail your reply at once.

                                        Very truly yours,

I can not send you payment now because:

I expect to send $_____on _____

I am enclosing $_____

APPEALS TO SYMPATHY. Though infrequently used, *appeals* to
sympathy can be helpful in soliciting payment of small debts. In
such an appeal, the writer points out that although the reader's
debt is small, the company has a large number of such outstanding
accounts and, thus, the aggregate is important to the company's
operations. In this type of letter, the correspondent does not emphasize the reader's point of view, but he makes his appeal to
sympathy effective by putting the reader in the position of a
helper rather than of a debtor.

Good

Dear Mr. David:

Won't you please take care of the enclosed bill--before
you forget it?

The amount is insignificant, we know, and we dislike to
bother you about it. But your little debt, plus your
neighbor's perhaps, plus all the rest, runs into many
thousands of dollars. The total is extremely important
to us in running our business efficiently.

By sending us your check today, you would really be
helping us a lot. Thank you for your co-operation.

Sincerely yours,

APPEALS TO FAIRNESS. An appeal to fairness says in effect, "We
gave you goods, service, and credit. It is only fair that in return
you pay us what you owe." Because people genuinely desire to be
fair and resent any implication to the contrary, this appeal must
be handled diplomatically. Sometimes the point is made that it
is unfair for one customer to take several months to pay his bills
while other customers are required to pay promptly.

Good

Dear Mrs. Robin:

We are sorry that we must again call your attention to
your unpaid balance of $66.00 which has been past due
since last January.

Your account was opened with the understanding that we
would serve you to the best of our ability and that you
in turn would make payment in accordance with our regular terms. We believe that we have lived up to our part
of the agreement. In fairness, we believe that you
should live up to yours.

Please send us your check for $66.00 at once.

Very truly yours,

APPEALS TO SELF-INTEREST. Used mainly in collections from
business firms, *appeals to self-interest* must be employed with great
care, not only because of the effect on the reader, but also because
of the legal risk on the part of the creditor. Businessmen are so
dependent on credit that they are very sensitive to collection appeals that suggest injury to their credit standing. Occasionally, the

reader is told that a credit agency will be notified if payment is not made promptly. Here the implication is that an unfavorable report to a credit agency will make it difficult for the debtor to obtain credit from other sources. It is important to note that a creditor may report delinquencies if inquiries are made; he may also notify a co-operative credit association, of which he is a member, about overdue accounts. However, the collection man may not, under laws governing extortion, threaten to volunteer unfavorable information to unauthorized sources as a consequence of non-payment.

Good (*appeal to businessman*)

Dear Mr. Wright:

Your credit standing is such a valuable asset that we should dislike to see it injured by your failure to pay your long past-due balance of $243.65.

Not only is your ability to secure more goods from us at stake, but also your ability to secure credit from other sources which may come to us for a report about you.

We know you will understand the seriousness of this matter and send us your check for full payment by return mail

                                        Very truly yours,

Self-interest is less effective as an appeal to consumers, but it is used when circumstances warrant.

Good (*appeal to consumers*)

Dear Mr. Jay:

As members of the Retail Credit Association of this city, we are bound to report to the central office of this organization all delinquent accounts.

We have afforded you every opportunity to pay arrears and keep your credit record clear, but you have neglected to avail yourself of this chance.

The files of the credit bureau are maintained for use of
members and all credit applications are cleared through
this bureau.

Immediate attention on your part will enable us to with-
hold reporting your account to the association.

Very truly yours,

APPEALS TO FEAR. The strongest of the collection appeals is the
appeal to fear, or the *threat*. This is usually a declaration of in-
tent to place the account in other hands for collection, if payment
is not made immediately or within a specified time. The company's
attorney or collection agency takes over when the creditor's own
methods fail. Since the appeal to fear is the creditor's last resort,
before entailing collection fees that may run as high as 50 per cent
of the amount owed, it is used only after a great deal of thought.
Before deciding to use the threat, the creditor may elect to send
several appeals to self-interest and several inquiries about the
reason for nonpayment. Of course, a number of threats may be
used, too, but they quickly lose their effect once the debtor realizes
that they are not as "final" as they appear to be.

Good

Dear Mr. Gray:

Your account in the amount of $98.50 is now so delin-
quent that we must insist on immediate payment.

We have repeatedly and unsuccessfully brought this matter to your attention. We are disappointed that we
have had no co-operation whatever from you.

It is not our desire or custom to be other than considerate of our customers. Legal action, unfortunately,
is now our only recourse.

Unless we receive payment in full by October 24, we
shall be forced to turn this matter over to our attor-
neys.

Very truly yours,

After the account is put in the hands of an attorney or collection agency, a considerable length of time may elapse before legal proceedings, if any, are instituted. In the meantime, the attorney or agency usually sends out another series of letters attempting to persuade the customer to pay voluntarily. Following is one of several letters sent by the attorney for a department store to one of its debtors.

Good

Dear Mr. George:

My client, Goode & Co., has informed me that letters regarding your indebtedness to them have not received your attention.

Therefore, I must inform you that unless full payment of your arrears is made immediately, I shall find it necessary to follow the instructions of my client and institute collection proceedings without further delay.

                                        Very truly yours,

HUMOR AND NOVELTY

Occasionally, writers try to make capital of humor and novelty in their collection follow-ups. All that can be said in this respect is that people differ widely in their response to such letters. When the amount owed is small and of no serious concern to either the creditor or the debtor, a jogging in a light vein may have its appeal. On the other hand, one can never tell when the debtor will take offense.

The two letters following are offered as dangerous examples of the humorous approach:

Dear Sir:

How do you do?
Some pay bills when due.
Some pay when overdue.
Some never do.
How do you do?

                                Very truly yours,

Gentlemen:

Can you give us the name of a good lawyer in your community? We may have to sue you.

                              Very truly yours,

Generally speaking, novel treatments are less likely than humorous ones to be offensive. There is, for example, the wordless letter
consisting of the salutation "Dear Sir," followed by a large por-
trait of a young lady with a hand cupped to her ear, a complimentary close and signature, and the amount due noted in the lower
left-hand corner. Another example is the so-called "half-and-half"
letter. The letter is divided in two columns, one headed, "This is
our story," and the other, "Now you tell us yours." The creditor's
letter appears under the first heading. There is blank space under
the second heading for the debtor's reply.

Less novel, but probably more effective, are collection letters
that dramatize the message, but remain within the bounds of
good taste.·

Acceptable

Dear Mr. Green:

Have you ever passed an old friend on the street, called
out, "Hello, Bill, how are things?"--and have him walk
straight ahead, without saying a word in return?

We've brought this up because we find ourselves in a
similar situation. You see, we wrote you a few weeks
ago about your unpaid balance of $34.75. So far we
haven't heard a word.

Maybe you had something else to think about the day you
got the letter, or somehow you have misplaced it.
Anyway, this amount is now considerably overdue--and
we're "speaking to you" again, by way of this letter,
and hoping to get a check soon.

Won't you say "Howdy" in a clear, friendly voice by
placing your check in the enclosed envelope and dropping
it into the nearest mailbox today? We will sincerely
appreciate it.

                              Very truly yours,

SPECIAL COLLECTION CIRCUMSTANCES

Collection work entails much more correspondence than the letters already described appear to indicate. One reason is that replies to collection letters are continually being received and many of them must be followed up by further correspondence. Another reason is that there are alternative ways of collecting a debt, and these may be employed when circumstances warrant. Situations calling for special handling are described below.

ACKNOWLEDGMENT OF PARTIAL PAYMENT. Frequently, a customer pays only part of his past-due account, making it necessary to acknowledge this payment and to ask for the balance.

Good

Dear Mr. Sand:

Thank you for your check for $24.00 which was received on May 10. There now remains to be paid $16.00 in your past due account.

Considering the length of time since your account became due, we hope that you will make a strong effort to send us the small balance.

May we expect your check for $16.00 by May 24 at the latest?

                                        Very truly yours,

EXTENSIONS OF TIME. When a debtor writes that he is unable to pay, he may ask for an extension of time. The collection man may grant or deny this request, but, in either case, he should give a reason.

Dear Mr. Rowe:

After careful consideration of your letter of August 1, we are glad to inform you that we are granting your request for more time in which to pay your past-due account of $95.40.

In times of sickness, exceptions can be made to even

our strictest credit rules without working an injustice
to our other customers who rely upon us to give all
the same credit treatment.

In return for this exception made in your favor, we feel
sure you will take care of this obligation by November
1, the date you suggest.

We extend our sympathy and our sincere wishes for a
quick recovery.

                                        Sincerely yours,

DEFERMENT OF ORDERS. Often a customer with a past-due account will order more goods on credit. In this circumstance, the
correspondent may combine an acceptance or refusal of the order
with a request for payment of the past-due balance.

Good (refusal of order)

Gentlemen:

Thank you for your order of July 28.

In looking over your account, we find that our invoice
of June 2 amounting to $54.15 is as yet unpaid. As this
account is thirty days past due, it would not be in accordance with our rules (which benefit all our trade)
to give you an additional extension of credit.

The condition of your account may have escaped your
attention; hence we feel sure, now that we have reminded you of it, that you will send us your check for
$54.15. By so doing, you will be conforming to our
credit rules and will enable us to pass your order to
our shipping department for immediate forwarding.

                                        Very truly yours,

NOTES AND DRAFTS. Customers who can not meet their obligations may proffer a note or series of notes or be forced by the
creditor to react to a draft. Notes are written promises to pay
either on demand or on the dates specified in them. They generally bear interest and must either be paid when due or be renewed for another term. The creditor may ask for a note as a
condition of purchase or after an account has become overdue. A

draft [3] is a document placed with the creditor's bank and directed to a bank in the debtor's community; it calls on the debtor to pay a stated sum, usually upon presentation. The draft can not force a debtor to pay, but his refusal to honor it gives notice to his local bank that he is a poor credit risk. Because of the possible consequences, the debtor should be notified in advance that the bank draft is to be issued. The use of drafts is confined largely to wholesale and manufacturing businesses.

Good (a threat to draw)

Gentlemen:

Although we have many times urgently requested payment of your long-overdue account in the amount of $286.65, we have not yet had the satisfaction of a reply.

We must now inform you therefore that we shall draw on you on April 15 through the Security Bank of Great Falls.

Please arrange to honor the draft upon presentation.

Very truly yours,

Review Problems

1. Which of the following statements are correct?

a. The most important thing a collection man should know is the paying habits of his customers.

b. When collection letters are written too systematically, the customer begins to anticipate them, and hence they lose their effectiveness.

c. Customers are more likely to resent form collection letters than personal collection letters.

d. The appeal to self-interest is considered a strong collection appeal.

e. Humorous collection letters have an almost universal appeal.

2. Write a letter to a friend in a distant city who borrowed $20.00 from you, when he visited you a few months ago, but has not repaid you. Use the appeal to sympathy.

3. Assume that you are working for the Hall Department Store in your city. Write a series of two printed reminders to be sent to charge customers one month and two months respectively after their accounts have become past due. Assume that the reminders are to be sent to well-rated risks only.

[3] Sloan, Harold S., and Zurcher, Arnold J., *Dictionary of Economics,* an Everyday Handbook (5th ed.; New York: Barnes & Noble, Inc., 1970).

4. Assume that the Continental Tire Company of Champaign, Illinois 61820 bought $1,000.00 worth of office furniture from your company—the Woods Desk Company of Grand Rapids, Michigan—on March 6. It is now July 15 and you have not received payment. Your terms were thirty days. You have already sent a statement stamped "past due," a form letter, and a personal letter appealing to the customer's self-interest. Write a second personal letter, again using the appeal to self-interest.

11
Adjustment Letters

Although responsible business firms, both large and small, make every effort to conduct their activities in such a way as to keep complaints to a minimum, it is inevitable that complaints will be received. Handling complaints is another important business function which requires considerable correspondence. In large companies, a special administrative unit known as the Adjustment Department (or Complaint and Adjustment Department) carries out this function. If complaints are treated sympathetically and reasonably, they can ordinarily be turned to the advantage of the recipients. At worst, they will not cause irreparable injury.

ATTITUDE TOWARDS COMPLAINTS AND ADJUSTMENTS

In former days, businessmen received complaints with a great sense of self-righteousness and with deep suspicion of the customers who sent them. Today, a more characteristic attitude is that complaints perform two valuable services for the company: (1) they provide a means of discovering and correcting poor service and defective merchandise. And (2) they provide an opportunity to win back the goodwill and business of the complainants.

Many companies are so convinced of the value of complaints that they actually go out of their way to invite them. These companies believe that the majority of dissatisfied customers do not voice their complaints, but simply withdraw their patronage. Let-

141

ters to inactive accounts are one way to discover what is wrong and to win back lost business.

Good

Dear Mrs. Kane:

We observe with considerable regret that your charge account has been inactive for some months.

You may think that one account makes very little difference in a large business such as ours. We want to assure you, however, that our regret over the loss of a long-time customer is infinitely greater than our pleasure in gaining a new one, a fact which prompts us to ask if there is anything we can correct or explain.

You see, it is our policy to "build for tomorrow in the service of today," and if we have erred in that service your constructive criticism would be helpful.

On the other hand, if nothing has occurred to disturb our pleasant relations--and we hope this is the case-- may we look forward to further opportunities of demonstrating that our customers do enjoy many distinct advantages in the matter of quality, value, and service?

Very truly yours,

P.S. Your comments on the reverse side of this letter will be warmly appreciated.

ANALYSIS OF COMPLAINTS

In dealing with a complaint, the first step is to investigate all the pertinent facts. A determination can then be made as to (1) whether or not the complaint is justified and (2) whether or not an adjustment can be granted.

IS THE COMPLAINT JUSTIFIED? Experience proves that most complaints are justified. They are usually the result of a fault in the merchandise or a fault in the service supplied by the seller or a third party (for example, the transportation company). Merchandise faults include defective, damaged, or incorrect goods.

Service faults include delay in delivery, failure to deliver at all, and discourtesy on the part of employees.

Complaints that are the result of misunderstandings or other faults in which both buyer and seller have participated may be regarded as just or unjust depending on the circumstances. For example, the complaint of a customer who wishes to return merchandise bought under terms of "all sales final" may be just if the customer was not informed of the terms, unjust if the sales slip is so marked.

If the buyer is completely at fault or has in some way misrepresented the case, the complaint is ordinarily considered unfair. Unjust complaints are occasionally fraudulent, but more often they result from the fact that customers take undue advantage of company policies, especially those relating to the return of merchandise. In this way, a customer may give a rug hard use for five years and then, when it begins to show signs of wear, may insist it is defective. Another customer may buy a suit and have it altered to fit and decide later to return it because he does not like the color.

CAN AN ADJUSTMENT BE GRANTED? Granting an adjustment may involve refunding money, giving new merchandise, performing an additional service, or simply acknowledging the error and assuring the reader that care will be taken to avoid repetition.

A just complaint results, of course, in an immediate adjustment. When the complaint is the fault of the transportation company, however, the customer may under the terms of purchase be required to file a claim against the carriers and to await an adjustment from them. Under these circumstances, the seller may still offer to send a duplicate of the item ordered to tide the customer over until the claim is adjusted.

When both parties to the transaction share the fault, the seller must weigh the degree of error on each side in order to determine what adjustment to make. Only when the customer is largely (or wholly) at fault can adjustment be refused in good conscience. In circumstances when the customer is not entitled to an adjustment, however, the management may still weigh the cost of making an adjustment, the length of time during which the complainant has been a customer, and similar factors before making a final decision.

ADJUSTMENT PRINCIPLES

To do a creditable job, the writer of adjustment letters should follow certain basic principles. These are (1) answer complaints promptly, (2) give the customer the benefit of the doubt, (3) accept blame gracefully, and (4) be diplomatic.

ANSWER COMPLAINTS PROMPTLY. Since the complainant is already displeased, making him wait a long time for an answer only intensifies his displeasure and makes him less amenable to a reasonable settlement. A prompt reply, on the other hand, makes the customer feel that the company is considerate of his interests and anxious to settle the complaint. When an adjustment must be delayed for any reason an acknowledgment should be dispatched immediately to assure the customer that his complaint is being considered.

Good

Dear Mrs. Walters:

Thank you very much for writing to us about the carpet of our manufacture that you purchased from the Wynn store in St. Louis.

We regret the difficulty you have had and want to be of assistance. We are now trying to obtain from the Wynn Store further information relating to the transaction.

We are anxious to settle this matter to your satisfaction. You will hear from us again very shortly.

                                        Very truly yours,

GIVE THE CUSTOMER THE BENEFIT OF THE DOUBT. One of the faults in handling complaints is the assumption that the customer is wrong until the facts prove otherwise. A more enlightened view is that the customer is right unless the facts prove him wrong.

Poor

Dear Mr. McCoy:

We are at a loss to understand your criticism of our

Theater Spice Drops which you say you recently purchased.

We take great care in the preparation of our product and
constantly endeavor to place only fresh merchandise in
the hands of customers.

Is it possible that you purchased the candy some time
ago and have confused it with a more recent purchase of
another kind?

In any event, we are sending you two boxes of our Spice
Drops with the hope that these will satisfy you.

Very truly yours,

Better

Dear Mr. McCoy:

Although we regret the experience you have had in your
recent purchase of Theater Spice Drops, we are pleased
that you took time out to bring the matter to our attention.

We can assure you that we take every possible step to
see that only fresh merchandise reaches our customers.
On the rare occasions when this objective is not
achieved, we are glad to have our customers tell us so.

Under separate cover, we are sending you two boxes of
fresh Theater Spice Drops. We know you will enjoy
them. May we take this opportunity to tell you how
much we appreciate your patronage and to express the
hope that you will allow us to serve you for many years
to come.

Sincerely yours,

ACCEPT BLAME GRACEFULLY. The majority of customers will
forgive the seller if he accepts the blame for a mistake readily and
with dignity. However, a customer will resent the seller's attempt
to make light of a complaint, to pass off the blame to subordinates,
or to other involved parties, or to accept the blame grudgingly.

Poor

Dear Mr. Gerst:

Your letter about the poor service you received in our
store comes as a great disappointment to us because it
clearly indicates the need to supervise our salespeople
more carefully.

We have spoken to Mr. Cross about the incident and have
warned him that a repetition will cost him his job. We
have also used your letter as a subject for a meeting
with all our salespeople in the Fur Department to im-
press upon them the effect of a careless and disinterested attitude.

We regret the incident, but we feel that there is nothing more we can do.

                                        Very truly yours,

Better

Dear Mr. Gerst:

We sincerely regret the inattentive service you received
at our store during a recent visit.

As a regular patron of our store, you probably know that
such service is not customary with us. Through careful
selection, training, and supervision of our employees,
we try to see that our customers are at all times waited
upon promptly and courteously. When such is not the
case, we do appreciate having our customers call the
matter to our attention, as you have done.

In return for your favor, we can only say that we shall
try even harder to give you the kind of service we ourselves should want if we were in your place. Thank you
again for taking the time to write.

                                        Sincerely yours,

BE DIPLOMATIC. The writer of the adjustment letter, and all
types of business letters, should be aware of the reader's feelings
and use words that conciliate, mollify, or placate—never words
that upset or irritate. Negative expressions like *you claim, your*

complaint, mistake, inconvenience, delay, unfortunate, recurrence, must refuse, not entitled to, you forgot, and *you failed* should be either considerably modified or avoided altogether by the correspondent.

Poor

Dear Mr. Fritz:

We are sorry to have your complaint about the poor performance of our Monay batteries. You claim your flashlight was damaged. Under separate cover we are sending you a new flashlight which we hope is not inferior to the one you submitted to us under our guarantee. Monay batteries are included. They were tested beforehand for any obvious defects.

Less than ½ per cent of our total proudction is unsatisfactory, and we are usually inclined to feel that the user of the flashlight is at fault, not the batteries. Since it is possible for some defective batteries to slip by our rigid inspection process, we follow the practice of replacing any damaged flashlights that are called to our attention.

It is unfortunate that you have had this inconvenience. We trust you will experience no further difficulties with our product.

Very truly yours,

Better

Dear Mr. Fritz:

We are sorry to learn of your recent experience with a set of Monay flashlight batteries. Under separate cover we are sending you a new flashlight of comparable value with the one you submitted to us under our guarantee. Fresh Monay batteries are included.

Far more than 99½ per cent of our entire Monay battery production is satisfactory. It would be nice if this record were 100 per cent, but in the absence of a perfect record, we do appreciate it when a customer brings an unsatisfactory experience to our attention.

We are sure that the fresh Monay batteries we are sending you will give you the same dependable service that
has made Monay batteries so famous all over the world.

                              Very truly yours,

ORGANIZATION OF THE ADJUSTMENT LETTER

The ideas in adjustment letters are ordinarily arranged as follows: (1) conciliatory statement, (2) explanation of facts, (3)
statement of action, and (4) expression of goodwill or assurance,
or both. Through this order of ideas the writer recognizes that
the reader's feelings come first. After the reader has been placated
(usually by a simple expression of regret), it is desirable to explain the facts before attempting to make or to refuse reparation.
In this way, the reader understands the basis of the decision before
he learns what the decision is. Even if the adjustment is granted,
the reader understands it better after following the writer's reasoning step-by-step.

The four steps of the adjustment letter are evident in the good
example that follows:

Dear Mr. Bard:

Conciliatory statement

I am sorry that service on your Modern Journal subscription has not been satisfactory.

Explanation of facts

To give you each week's up-to-the-minute news, the Modern Journal is published on a carefully co-ordinated
schedule which must be met exactly if copies are to
reach you promptly. Notwithstanding, in recent weeks
production difficulties and transportation delays have
caused a few shipments to reach New York late, thus
affecting delivery by the local post office.

Statement of action

We have given this matter our closest attention, and we
believe that during the coming months, dispatch sched-
ules will be met with greater regularity. Also, transportation facilities are being reviewed, and we have

every reason to expect that deliveries will soon be as
desired by all concerned.

We realize that this explanation is no substitute for
good service, and so we shall extend your subscription
term one month.

Expression of goodwill and assurance

We appreciate the interest in our publication which
prompted you to write, and we assure you that every effort will be made to provide you with the kind of service you have the right to expect.

Sincerely yours,

CONCILIATORY STATEMENT. Regardless of whether the seller or
the purchaser is at fault, the majority of adjustment letters begin
with an expression of regret.

Good

We are sorry to learn from your letter of April 27 that
the robe you ordered two weeks ago has not yet arrived.

We take such pride in our reputation for high quality
foods that you can imagine how sorry we were to learn
of your recent experience with our Ark-tik Fresh Frozen
Green Peas.

We regret that it is necessary for you to write to us
again about the performance of your Centrifugal Washing
Machine.

Another way the correspondent may win over the complainant
is to begin by showing appreciation for having been informed of
the error or other fault.

Good

Thank you for notifying us so promptly of the treatment
you received in our store last Thursday.

We appreciate your taking the time to write us about the
condition of your Co-zee Foam Rubber Mattress.

In answering a complaint, the writer occasionally makes an
exception to the usual pattern by beginning the letter with the

adjustment itself. This course of action is especially desirable
when the reason for the adjustment is so obvious that it needs
little or no explanation.

Good

```
We are pleased to send you with this letter a copy of
the Car Owner's Guide to replace the catalogue that we
sent you in error.

If you will stop in at our store at your first oppor-
tunity, I am sure we can adjust your bracelet to fit
perfectly.
```

```
Enclosed you will find our check for $5.50, representing
a refund on the shirt you recently returned to us.
```

EXPLANATION OF FACTS. Except when the circumstances leading
to a complaint are self-evident, the writer needs to explain the
facts in some detail.

Good

```
Your order was received on March 9 and shipped by ex-
press from our Altoona plant on March 12.  Under normal
circumstances you should have received the goods by
March 16.  Apparently the shipment has been delayed in
transit.

If you will consult the back of your credit card, you
will note that we frankly state our limited distribution
in Maryland, Virginia, West Virginia, North Carolina,
and South Carolina.  You will also note that we have re-
ciprocal credit arrangements with all of the stations of
the Kentucky Oil Company, which operates in Georgia,
Florida, Alabama, Mississippi, and Kentucky.  Similar
arrangements are in effect with various companies
throughout Canada and are explained also on the re-
verse side of your credit card.
```

When the customer has misunderstood company policy, the
correspondent should also explain the policy.

Good

As you know from your own experience with our store, we sell only fresh, clean merchandise. We could not long maintain this policy if we accepted for return articles of personal apparel that showed signs of wear.

We can understand your disappointment in learning that no dealership for our products is at this time available in your city. On the other hand, we are sure that you can appreciate the advantages of our exclusive agency policy and that you yourself will welcome its benefits when eventually an opening for which you qualify occurs.

When the complaint is caused by possible misuse of the product, the explanation should include instructions for correct use or care.

Good

Dear Mr. Groves:

We are very sorry that you are having difficulty with your Spencer pen and assure you that we want to be of assistance.

No doubt you have been filling your pen according to the attached instructions. The correct filling is very important for the good performance of the pen.

After it has been filled as instructed, a wiping tissue or soft cloth should be held to the point for a few seconds until a blot of ink about the size of a quarter has been extracted. If this is not done, the excess ink in the pen will give a false appearance of leakage.

Perhaps you are already aware of the fact that even the most costly pen of every manufacture will flow a bit more freely when the ink supply is low. When the volume of air in the reservoir is greater than the volume of ink, the sudden jolt or even the warmth of the hands can cause an upset in the molecular attraction, expelling the ink at the point.

As a special safeguard against leakage, we recommend

carrying a pen in an upright position (pen point up),
whether in a coat pocket or in a woman's purse. Ladies
may clip the pen to the inner lining or coin pocket of
the purse.

Before returning the pen to us, please dry out the metal
cap by putting a tissue over a pencil and inserting it
in the cap. Then, fill the pen according to the instructions and try using it for a few days.

If the results are not improved, please return the pen
to us by insured mail, marked for the attention of Mr.
B. R. Gaines, so that the matter will receive prompt
handling and personal supervision.

                                        Sincerely yours,

STATEMENT OF ACTION. When all the facts related to the complaint have been explained, the writer has to inform the reader of
what adjustment, if any, will be made; he must also give specific
instructions for carrying out the terms of the adjustment.

Good

We deeply regret your experience and are sending you
another toothbrush which we hope you will find completely satisfactory.

If you will present the enclosed credit slip to your
grocer, he will redeem it for one full-size package of
Malto.

We suggest that you take or send your shaver directly to
our Service Branch located at 456 East Fourth Street in
your city and explain the difficulty you have been having. Adjustments to the shaver will be made and the
shearing head will be checked. If the shearing head is
defective, it will be replaced at no charge.

When an adjustment is refused because the complaint is unjust,
the reason for refusal should be evident from the facts given earlier
in the letter. Here, it is especially important to avoid bluntness or
crudeness. It is occasionally possible to offer a suggestion or additional service as a substitute for the adjustment asked.

Good

Since inspection shows that the fault is due neither to
the construction of the article nor to the quality of
the materials used, we feel that we can not make the
adjustment you request.

Under the circumstances we are sorry that we can not
accept the dress for a refund. Our delivery service
will return the garment to you within a few days.

Should we be correct in assuming that some slight al-
terations will enable you to wear the dress with greater
satisfaction, we should be glad to have our expert
dressmaker alter it in accordance with your wishes. We
suggest that you drop in personally with the garment and
ask for Mrs. Coyne on the fifth floor.

If the complaint is one about poor service, the most the writer
can do, in the majority of circumstances, is to apologize and promise better service in the future.

Good

Please accept our apologies and the assurance that an
investigation will be made, so that we will give you
more courteous service in the future.

We assure you that your experience in this instance is
not at all typical. We do hope you will give us another
opportunity soon to demonstrate the high standard of
service that has won us countless friends.

STATEMENT OF GOODWILL. If the statement of reparation does
not already include reassurance or an apology, the writer usually
adds a final paragraph which is intended to cement the relationship with the customer.

Good

Your interest in bringing this matter to our attention
is very much appreciated.

We are certain that when your shaver is again in your

possession, you will enjoy complete shaving satisfaction.

Needless to say, we trust you will continue to use Clyde
products with the enjoyment and satisfaction you expect
from them.

It helps us to know of any question which arises about
one of our products, and we appreciate your reporting
this matter to us.

Review Problems

1. Which of the following statements are correct?
    a. Complaints are a nuisance, but they have to be answered.
    b. It is good business to give the customer the benefit of any doubt.
    c. When the fault is yours, avoid a direct admission.
    d. When the facts are self-evident, there is no need to explain them.
    e. Always give the facts before you refuse an adjustment.
2. Rewrite the following sentences for better tone:
    a. You must have misunderstood the assembly instructions that came with
the table.
    b. If you had specified the correct size in the first place, you could have
avoided the inconvenience of sending the stockings back for exchange.
    c. Because we want to keep you as a customer, we will make the adjust-
ment in this case.
    d. We are sorry to have your complaint of March 12 about the non-
delivery of the electric toaster you ordered two weeks ago.
    e. You may be sure that we shall do our best to prevent such an unfortu-
nate error from holding up delivery again.
3. Assume that you have received the following answer to a complaint. Rewrite the letter so that it will be more in accord with the principles stated
in this chapter.

Dear _____.

Inspection of your loveseats by our representative failed to disclose any
cause for dissatisfaction. Careful examination of the cushions reveals that
they fit the loveseats perfectly and could not be made to fit any better.

In reference to the slight fraying of the material on the back of the seats,
this condition is due to service factors. After all, you have had this furniture for almost a year.

Since inspection shows that the loveseats are well-constructed and are
made of good quality material, we feel that you do not have any basis for
complaint.

We regret your disappointment.

                                                    Very truly yours,

12
Sales Letters

Sales letters are a convenient and effective way of securing business. A single letter is often duplicated and sent out by the thousands or the tens of thousands. No other type of letter influences so many people or brings a greater return in actual dollars and cents. More so than other letters, the sales letter is highly specialized, and its writing requires exceptional ability and experience.

USES OF SALES LETTERS

Sales letters have five principal uses: (1) to sell by mail, (2) to produce sales inquiries, (3) to follow up sales inquiries, (4) to induce people to visit the store to buy, and (5) to build goodwill.

SELLING BY MAIL. Among the products sold directly to the consumer by means of letters are books and magazines; furniture, rugs, and clothing; and, thanks to modern methods of transportation, even perishable foods like fresh fruit, fish, and poultry. The letters are sent to carefully selected lists and are complete sales presentations, usually including illustrated circulars and reply cards, or order blanks and reply envelopes. Letters are also used to sell directly to manufacturers and to retail and wholesale outlets.

PRODUCING SALES INQUIRIES. Instead of trying to do the entire selling job by mail, sales letters may be confined to soliciting inquiries, which may be followed up by letter, telephone, or personal call.

FOLLOWING UP SALES INQUIRIES.[1] Many inquiries are unsought. Many more, however, are the result of sales letters and advertising in newspapers and magazines. Some inquiries can be handled by means of form letters and printed matter; others must be answered by personally dictated letters, sometimes with printed matter enclosed.

INDUCING PEOPLE TO VISIT THE STORE. Sales letters may be used to arouse customers' and prospective customers' interest, so that they will visit the retail store to buy. Individual stores may circularize their own customers, or their suppliers may provide the incentive with letters and, perhaps, coupons to be redeemed.

BUILDING GOODWILL.[2] Letters may be used to thank customers for their patronage, to extend the season's greetings, to announce new conveniences or services, and in other ways to cultivate relationships that lead *indirectly* to sales.

FACTORS IN PLANNING SUCCESSFUL SALES LETTERS

The success of the sales letter depends on many factors in addition to the actual composition. Thus, before he puts a single word on paper, the writer should know the answers to five pertinent questions relating to sales strategy.

TO WHOM AM I WRITING? A letter that is to be duplicated and sent to many people will have to be general in appeal, yet consonant with the common interests of the group; a letter to a single person may be individualized. In the former case, if the interests of the group are too varied for a single approach, the mailing list may be broken up into several smaller lists and a sales letter adapted to each. In any case, the correspondent must know to whom he is writing: One person? Fifty people? Ten thousand people? He must also know the sex, age, occupation or business of the individual or group to whom he is writing.

WHY AM I WRITING? The purpose of the sales letter will determine the amount and force of the copy. Thus, the writer will have to know: Is the purpose of this letter to sell directly? Is it to induce the reader to visit the store? Is it to produce inquiries?

---

[1] For the principles affecting replies to inquiries, see Chapter 7.
[2] For a discussion of sales letters that build goodwill, see Chapter 13.

A letter in which the correspondent makes only an attempt to secure inquiries or to induce people to visit the store will require less detail and less persuasion than a letter in which the writer tries to obtain an order. If goodwill is his primary aim, the correspondent will make his letter shorter and less insistent than he would if he were trying to produce a direct sale.

WHAT IS THE PRINCIPAL APPEAL OF THE PRODUCT? Since his appeal depends as much on a knowledge of *what* he is selling as it does on a knowledge of *to whom* he is selling, the writer should make a thorough study of the product or service he is offering. In this way, he will discover what features of the product will most influence the reader to buy. Knowing the reader's motives for buying the product will also furnish the writer with an effective appeal or approach. The correspondent may find it useful to know for example, that readers of a news magazine buy it principally to be well-informed, that users of a particular electric iron purchase it because it does not have to be lifted, and that buyers of blowout-proof tires are influenced by the fear of accident and injury.

IS PROOF OF SATISFACTION AVAILABLE? To make a sales letter convincing, the writer must often know the facts relating to the reputation of the company, the construction of the product, the records of product performance, and the like. Research of this type will pay dividends in making the sales letter more effective.

WHAT ENCLOSURES ARE AVAILABLE? Although the sales letter must be complete in itself, it may be supplemented by other sales aids. An effective combination is a good sales letter plus enclosures. Enclosures range from order blanks and reply cards and envelopes to illustrated folders and samples of merchandise.

FUNCTIONS OF THE SALES LETTER

The majority of sales letters perform, in varying degrees, four functions. These are (1) attracting attention, (2) arousing desire, (3) implanting conviction, and (4) stimulating action.

In the following letter, designed to obtain an order by mail or telephone, the four sales functions are distinctly developed. The first paragraph attracts the reader's attention; the second and third paragraphs arouse his desire; the fourth paragraph attempts to convince him; and the last two paragraphs stimulate him to act.

Dear AEA member:

No doubt you will want to see Washington, D. C. and vi-
cinity when you are attending the convention of the
American Economic Association during the week of April
25.

This is an especially good time of year to visit Mount
Vernon, Alexandria, and Williamsburg and to enjoy the
lovely countryside. With a Tripper rented car, which
you drive yourself, you can see all of these sights in
addition to many points of interest in Washington--
pleasantly, conveniently, and inexpensively. You can
actually turn your business trip into a relaxing vacation with your family and friends.

Our fleet consists of Chevrolets, Fords, Pontiacs, and
Buicks. You can rent a new model Chevrolet or Ford for
$14.00 a day plus 14¢ a mile, or $70.00 a week plus 14¢ a
mile. These rates include all gas, oil, and insurance.
Every car is equipped with a radio.

As an illustration of the value and pleasure you can
get out of a Tripper rented car, you may be interested
in the experience of Mr. Allen Taylor of Dallas, Texas,
who was here several weeks ago for the convention of the
National Association of Manufacturers. With his wife
and three children he toured all the important points of
interest in and around Washington, including Arlington,
the Pentagon, Alexandria, and Mount Vernon. Total traveling cost for three days: $50.00. He would have had to
pay $45.00 for the Mount Vernon trip alone if he and
his family had taken a regular, arranged tour.

As a member of AEA, you will not be required to post the
usual deposit and you will receive a special discount
of 5 per cent.

Please send us your reservation on the enclosed card or
telephone us at NAtional 2-1234.

                                        Very truly yours,

The letter below, intended to induce the customer to visit the retail store, is somewhat shorter. The illustrated booklet mentioned in the letter does a large part of the work of arousing desire.

Dear Mr. Kane:

You've heard a lot about quality . . . read a lot about economy . . . but let us explain just what these two words mean when you buy Florsheim Shoes . . .

> . . . they mean that, in addition to the finest materials and workmanship, the most authentic style, and the most comfortable fit, they give you "the extra wear of a second pair."

That's why Florsheim Shoes cost less per day of wear-- why Florsheim wearers keep coming back year after year -- why Florsheim has built the largest fine shoe business in the world.

This spring, we're ready with the widest variety of leathers and styles in our history. The enclosed booklet shows you just a few of scores of equally smart styles. . . . Won't you stop in soon and see them?

                                        Very truly yours,

ATTRACTING ATTENTION. Since a sales letter is not usually of pressing personal importance to the reader, it requires a special quality or device to draw the reader to it. The factors that engage attention are (1) the mechanical details of the letter, (2) the headline and subheadings, and (3) the opening sentence or sentences.

Mechanical Details. If cost prohibits the use of first-class postage and the individual typing of letters, favorable attention can still be secured by means of well-designed stationery, good printing or processing of the body of the letter, the use of color, and novel attachments or enclosures. If his letter is to be effective, the writer must consider how the letter will look. Examples of "visual" salesletter ideas follow:

A letter printed on sandpaper. (Headline: "Purchasing is a rough job.")

A letter postmarked London, England. (Purpose: to advertise British-imported overcoat fabrics.)

A letter imprinted over a facsimile federal income tax blank. (Theme: "Now—when every penny counts.")

A letter beginning with illegible facsimile handwriting. (Purpose: to emphasize the student's need for a typewriter.)

Headlines and Subheadings. Letters intended for mass circularization are usually processed without a personal inside address and salutation. In such instances, a provocative headline, placed in the same position as the inside address or running across the page, may be used to attract attention. See the following examples:

```
Will Coming Tax Changes Catch You Unprepared?

There Is Money
In Greeting Cards
Get Your Share

        Reserve Your Free Copy Now!
```

Opening Sentences. Although headlines and mechanical devices may catch the eye, they can not *hold* the attention of the reader. A good opening is needed to carry the reader's attention into the main substance of the letter. Good openings have two characteristics: (1) they are adapted to the reader's interests. And (2) they are relevant to the subject of the letter. If, in addition, openings are dramatic, original, concise, and expressed in short sentences and paragraphs, they have an even better chance of being read.

The sales-letter openings below are faulty.

Unoriginal

```
Spring is just around the corner.
```

Irrelevant

```
Are you a tea drinker?  We happen to like coffee.  No
matter what your taste, however, we think you'll like
the new Sportsman's Gazette.
```

Wordy and unoriginal

At this time we should like to announce to all our friends and customers who have patronized us over the past many years that we have opened a new children's wear department where you will find all the clothes you need for your boy or girl.

The sales-letter openings below are more effective.

To accountants

I should like to talk with you for a moment about the new tax bill now before Congress.

To housewives

Whenever Madeline Laundry inaugurates a new service, we invite a group of women--representing specially selected families--to try the service with our compliments and tell us frankly what they think.

To magazine readers

An ancient poet said, "If thou hast two pennies, spend one for bread. With the other, buy hyacinths for thy soul."

Poetry, perhaps; but hard sense as well.

To buy hyacinths for the soul, to become informed, alert, interesting in what you say to others, is just as important as progress in your business or social life.

To prospective brides

The happiest day of your life is at hand--your wedding day.

May we serve you by making that day one of exquisite beauty and correctness?

To business executives

Charles Lamb called work "that dry drudgery at the desk's dead wood."

Ever feel like that? Then the time has come to discover that desk drudgery today is inexcusable.

AROUSING DESIRE. Arousing the reader's desire for the product or service that the letter advertises involves two factors: (1) The reader must be made to recognize that he has a need for the product or service. And (2) he must be satisfied that the advertiser's product can fill that need.

Showing the Need. The writer emphasizes a need by appealing to a basic buying motive. If the writer is selling the idea of rewiring electrical circuits in old homes, he may wish to call attention to the danger and inadequacy of the old wiring (appeal to fear). If the writer is selling a room air-conditioner in hot climates, he may take for granted that the need for an air-conditioner is already obvious to the reader and, instead, relate his appeal to a competitive feature of the product. Thus, he may indicate the desirability of quiet operation (appeal to comfort), or low cost (appeal to thrift), or attractive appearance (appeal to domestic pride). The necessity for the product or service can be at least hinted at in the opening sentences of the letter, as the last five examples above demonstrate. In many instances, however, additional explanation is necessary to sharpen the reader's desire. Here, for example, is a fuller development of the idea in the fifth letter opening above.

Good

Dear Sir:

Charles Lamb called work "that dry drudgery at the desk's dead wood."

Ever feel like that? Then the time has come for you to discover that desk drudgery today is inexcusable.

Consider just what you <u>do</u> at your desk.

Mostly you read and think and talk and write. The meaningful part of desk work is <u>communication</u>--getting things <u>out</u> of your mind <u>into</u> other minds. It's a businessman's essential function. It usually takes a lot of time--and costs more than we realize.

Few of us in business communicate by longhand or by operating a typewriter. Most of us <u>dictate</u>--many to a

stenographer or secretary. No one considers this a perfect method but many executives and professional people
still put up with its inconvenience and delays and expense. You would much prefer, I am sure, a faster, more
convenient, more productive, and more economical method
of work. And that's precisely what the Dictaphone
method is.

Describing the Product. In showing how the product or service
fills the need, the writer employs description. The amount of
description necessary will depend on what the letter must do. In
a letter designed to sell by mail, the description must be exceedingly detailed, and much of it will often be printed in an accompanying circular. In a letter that is to be followed by a salesman's
call, it is necessary only to describe the highlights of a product or
a service.

Several types of description are used in sales letters. In one case,
the correspondent may describe the physical attributes of the product: its construction, origin, or content; in another, he may concentrate on describing the benefits of the product or its emotional
effect upon the reader. The following paragraphs from a subscription letter combine description of the contents with description
of the source and description of the benefit to the reader.

Good

Why do millions like it? Because the Reader's Digest is
not merely another publication, but a time-saving dis-
tillation, once every month, of all that's best and
newest and most vital in the world of print.

Seventy-one skillful editors read more than 500 publications each month: the general magazines, periodicals
in special fields, the chief newspapers of this and
other countries, and all the current books as well.
These watchful editors select everything that's interesting and important, and then use only the very best
of that!

And so the double cream of what is being written and
thought today appears in the 35 articles compressed each
month into the 176 pages of the Reader's Digest. In a
single issue is the condensation of material which one
person could not cover in two years' reading time. To

buy <u>the</u> <u>books</u> <u>and</u> <u>magazines</u> <u>quoted</u> <u>in</u> <u>the</u> <u>last</u> <u>12</u> <u>issues</u>
<u>would</u> <u>cost</u> <u>you</u> <u>more</u> <u>than</u> <u>$200.00.</u>

Was there ever so small a ship with so rich and great a
cargo?

The short paragraphs that follow continue the Dictaphone letter
begun on page 162. They describe the result of using the product.

Good

Dictaphone makes it easy for you to <u>communicate.</u>

Wherever, whenever you want to get something off your
mind, it's simply said and <u>done.</u> Your secretary, too,
finds it easy to do a better job in less time and with
less effort.

This method certainly should help you in your work.

A good product description is enthusiastic, interesting, and
specific. Contrast the next examples.

Too general

Manhattan Perfectos are well made to give you a better
smoke. You'll be agreeably surprised to find how en-
joyable they are--the best you ever smoked.

Better

Examine these Manhattan Perfectos closely. Note how
fragrant and mellow they are--how slowly yet evenly they
burn with a clinging white ash down to the very last
inch. Observe how expertly fine, imported Havana and
rich, full flavored domestic are superbly blended into
a cool, mellow-mild perfect Perfecto. Mark the new,
reinforced needle-punched head--no bother to clip or
bite when you light up--no shreds or bits of tobacco
to break off in your mouth--a free-drawing, even-burn-
ing, cooler smoke. Your only regret will come when the
last cigar in the box is gone--but you can always get
more.

IMPLANTING CONVICTION. Even when he recognizes his need,
the reader may still doubt the advertiser's claims for his product.
Actually, the description of the advertiser's product shows only one

way to satisfy the need. In many cases, the reader may be convinced if he has an opportunity to visit the store to examine the product and to talk with a salesman, who can answer his questions. In other cases, where customers must order by mail, the reader must rely on the letter alone to resolve his doubts. Thus, in a letter with a mail-order or similar purpose, the reader must be convinced by the writer that the advertiser's product is not only an acceptable way to satisfy his need, but also the best way.

The major factors in implanting conviction in a sales letter are: (1) making moderate claims, (2) using logical reasoning, and (3) proving satisfaction.

Making Moderate Claims. To present a convincing argument, the writer should use moderation and even understatement in claiming advantages for a product or a service. Generally speaking, the less fact and reason the writer has on his side, the more he is tempted to indulge in extravagant and refutable claims.

Unconvincing—extravagant claim

```
Don't let the low price fool you.  These watches at
$15.95 are comparable to many now selling up to $100.00
at Fifth Avenue jewelers.
```

Convincing—moderate claim

```
I believe you would find our Tax Letter particularly
useful during the coming year because it will bring you
news of so many important tax developments.  I am con-
fident that you--like so many other Tax Letter subscrib-
ers--would find the service worth many times its modest
cost of $15.00 per year.
```

Using Logical Reasoning. Specious arguments may satisfy the writer, but they do not convince the intelligent reader. To be convincing, reasoning should be based on facts and should be developed logically.

Unconvincing—specious reasoning

```
We have written to you three times about the set we have
reserved for you.  Holding your books in our storeroom
for two months has caused them to become slightly soiled
by dust.  Now these books are as good as new, but of
course they can not be sold as such.  Hence this 40 per
cent reduction in price.
```

Convincing—logical reasoning

Correct spraying of trees with modern equipment at the
proper time and with the right materials, accurately
mixed and applied, is true economy and protection.

The cost of protection is relatively small, but the cost
of neglect is great. Where the attacks of insects are
not combatted, serious and, perhaps, irreparable injury
may be done.

Proving Satisfaction. Description does not in itself constitute
proof nor does it always convince the reader. However, the more
specific the writer is about the attributes of the product or service,
the more effective and convincing the letter will be. (See the
Reader's Digest description, p. 163, and the contrasting descriptions of Manhattan Perfectos, p. 164.) The correspondent may try
also to convince the reader that the advertiser's product is the best
solution to his need by introducing various forms of proof. He
may report, for example, the results of a test of the product; or, if
it is feasible, he may enclose a sample of the product, which the
reader may examine or test himself. Also, the writer may include
the names of satisfied users and may quote their testimonials; he
may cite facts and figures in support of his claims of performance
or may guarantee acceptable performance with a money-back offer.
Examples of various types of proof are given below.

Test

The Twintex suit was made to a rigid set of specifications; then it was tested and approved by the Industrial
Testing Institute of Philadelphia. Here are a few of
the facts that the laboratory reports: cold-water shrunk
fabrics; strong linings; hand tailoring to fit every
curve of the body; careful off-pressing and under-press-
ing to hold that smoothness.

Testimonial

Letters from thousands of readers reveal how deeply
they feel about Current Reading. Writes General David
Geist: "Current Reading is an important part of the
'must-kit' of information of every thoughtful person."
Ambassador Nathan C. West writes: "Current Reading introduced a remarkably effective method of presenting interesting articles to the general public. It brought

millions of readers to a better understanding of our times." Governor William Groves writes: "In one neat time-saving package, Current Reading hands us the wisdom of the world."

Sample

Try the sample Regal Mimeograph Stencil enclosed. See what sharp, clear, clean-cut characters it produces. Note how strong and durable it is with its extra-long fibers--and how the absence of surface wax prevents clogging of typewriter keys and does away with fuzzy or chopped letters. It's a stencil you can keep because it's unaffected by hot or cold temperatures.

Facts and figures

In the 34 years of our existence we have insured more than $950,000,000 worth or automobiles and, after paying all losses and expenses, have returned as dividends to our policyholders 49 per cent of the premiums received on fire and theft insurance and an average of 31 per cent on liability coverage.

By actual count the 48 best-selling books abridged in Omnibook last year cost $288.00 in regular editions--yet Omnibook readers got the vital content of these books for only $15.00.

Guarantee

Examine the Public Speaker's Treasure Chest in your own home, without any obligation. If, after reading it, you do not agree that it will pay for itself many times over in giving you sound and practical guidance, simply return it and pay nothing.

With your Hi-Fidelity unit you receive a written guarantee providing for unlimited free service for a full year from date of purchase, and you also get a warranty providing for free replacement of any defective part within five years.

STIMULATING ACTION. Even if the reader is convinced of the soundness of a proposition, he may still put off action. Perhaps he does not know how he is expected to respond, or he lacks stationery or a stamp, or he does not have enough incentive to take decisive action, or he merely procrastinates.

The correspondent should anticipate all circumstances which might deter the reader's action and should take steps to prevent them. He may (1) specify the action he desires, (2) provide reply forms and postage, or (3) offer special terms and inducements. The extent to which these methods are applied depends in each case on the difficulty of the job the letter must do. There is likely to be, for example, more resistance to a letter designed to sell dinnerware by mail to "cold" prospects than to a letter inviting old customers to the retail store to see a preview of spring fashions. Hence the pressure on the reader to act will be stronger in the former case than in the latter.

Specifying Action. The most elementary way to produce action is to tell the reader what he should do. The clearer and more specific the instructions, the better. With few exceptions, the instructions are put in the form of a rhetorical question or a direct command.

Good

Won't you drop in today or tomorrow.

Call Plaza 8-4326 and our deliveryman will pick up your rug at your convenience.

Come and see the new patterns this evening, and let us tell you how little it will cost to have new linoleum in any room in your home.

Providing Reply Forms. In nearly all sales letters requiring action by mail, the correspondent encloses a return card, or an order blank and an envelope. The card and envelope are usually of the "business reply" variety, for which a post-office permit is required.[3] Reference to the order blank, card, or envelope should always be made in the letter.

Good

Just mark and mail the return card today. No stamp is required.

---

[3] Postage on these cards and envelopes is paid by the advertiser at the regular rate, plus a one-cent service charge for each piece returned. There is no postage charge for cards and envelopes not returned.

Good

The special order blank enclosed is for your convenience.

The air-mail card will speed your subscription order to
us at our expense.

Offering Special Terms and Inducements. To overcome the
reader's hesitancy or inertia, the writer may state that it is not
necessary to send money with the order. Usually, the customer
pays the postman when the goods are delivered; or he may be permitted to use the goods on trial (for ten days or so) without payment, after which he either returns the goods or pays the charge.
As added inducement for sending the order, the advertiser may
offer a gift—a pen, a wallet, a book, an additional unit of the article
being sold—if the order is received before a specified time. In
other instances, the advertiser may press for immediate action on
the ground that the quantity is limited or that the price at which
the article is being sold will be raised.

The close, reprinted below, employs a combination of methods
to provide an especially strong stimulus to action. It not only
specifies the action desired and refers to the return post card, but
also offers a discount, a free trial, low down-payment and easy
terms, and a gift which the reader may keep even if he decides not
to go through with the purchase.

Good—strong stimulus

To get the New Continental Encyclopedia established
quickly we are offering it at a liberal discount--just
at first! You get 20 per cent off on your copy if you
decide after inspection you want to keep it.

We will mail it to you for a week's free examination,
carriage charges prepaid. At the end of the week, send
it back if you like--or keep it and pay only $3.00 a
month until the special price of only $9.00 (not $10.00)
has been paid.

The enclosed reservation postcard needs no stamp. We
pay the postage at this end. Sign and mail it today!

                                    Very truly yours,

P.S. If you mail the enclosed postcard reservation
AT ONCE you will receive FREE, with the book, a gift
copy of a new <u>Gazetteer</u> <u>Atlas</u> <u>of</u> <u>the</u> <u>World</u> which you
may keep even if you return the book! It contains 32
pages of new four-color maps and is bound in attractive
flexible bristol board covers.

SALES LETTER SYSTEMS

Few sales letters are "all-or-nothing" ventures. Sales letters are usually planned in series, and a number of the letters are sent to the same mailing lists. At least three types of systems are observable: (1) the wear-out system, (2) the continuous system, and (3) the campaign system.

WEAR-OUT SYSTEM. The *wear-out system* is used to sell low-priced products by mail. Each letter is a complete sales presentation, with or without reference to other letters in the system. The letters are sent to a selected list of prospects several weeks or months apart until the point is reached where a letter fails to produce a satisfactory profit. The sender then turns his attention to another mailing list, using the same letters or devising new ones. Magazine and book-club subscriptions are obtained from new prospects largely through the wear-out system.

The following example may seem quite long, but in both length and content it is typical of letters in the wear-out system. The letter was accompanied by a lavishly illustrated folder and a business reply order card.

Dear Reader:

Last spring when I wrote you that we were planning to
publish in book form our fabulously illustrated series
on "The World We Live In," you and other readers of
LIFE were given the opportunity of reserving a copy of
this extraordinary book <u>in</u> <u>advance</u> at a special pre-
publication price.

The response to this offer has been overwhelming. During the past few months we have received orders for
<u>more</u> <u>than</u> <u>a</u> <u>quarter</u> <u>of</u> <u>a</u> <u>million</u> <u>copies</u>--and advance
reservations are still coming in.

Because my original letter might have arrived at an in-
convenient time, or been mislaid, I am writing again to
remind you that publication of this book will take place
in a very short time--and orders thereafter will have to
be accepted at the retail bookstore price.

For the intellectually curious, or for those to whom the
whole world is full of wonder, this extraordinarily
beautiful book will provide an exciting and eloquent
account of how the earth, the life upon it and the air
around it came to be. It will be browsed through, ex-
claimed over, and cherished for many years to come.

Very shortly this 318-page volume will be available in
bookstores for $13.50.   The public demand, together with
our already reserved copies, may well exhaust our one
printing--and we can not go back to press.

> If you missed my original prepublication
> offer, or for some reason overlooked it, this
> is your last opportunity before publication to
> reserve a copy of THE WORLD WE LIVE IN for
> only $9.95--$3.55 under the bookstore price.

Once the book is published, this special rate will no
longer be valid. If you wish to own this book, or order
it as a gift, you can save $3.55 by reserving your copy
now. When the book is published it will be mailed to
you together with a bill for only $9.95. If for any
reason you are not completely satisfied, you may return
it at no cost whatsoever.

For your convenience, a postage-paid reservation card is
enclosed. You need only check the edition (for those
who prefer, there will be a deluxe edition for only
$2.00 more) and sign your name and drop it in the mail.

I sincerely believe that when you see this magnificent
book, you'll find it even more rewarding than you had
imagined.

                              Very truly yours,

If you followed "The World We Live In" in LIFE, you can
visualize what it will mean to own the complete thir-
teen-part series in book form. I am enclosing a brochure which may recall for you some of the remarkable
illustrations and brilliant color of "The World We Live
In". But it can only partially describe what was probably the most acclaimed and widely-read series of articles ever to appear in LIFE--and what will soon become
a magnificent 318-page volume.

> Here will be an unparalleled physical history
> of our world--from its very beginning to its
> probable end. You will see how our planet was
> formed . . . how the seas were born . . . and
> life emerged to populate the land. You will
> see how life developed--and now abounds in
> every region of the earth's varied surface.
> Here will be five-billion years of natural
> history in a treasury of magnificent paint-
> ings, photographs and drawings.

Since I last wrote you, the editors have been working
to put this book together--and right now it is being
printed and made ready for the bindery. The press
sheets I have seen are incredibly beautiful. Because
virtually the entire 318-page volume is made up of full-
color illustrations, the printing is being done on a
high quality, enameled paper--giving a new brilliance to
the color reproduction.

This will be a large book--LIFE-size--handsomely bound
in simulated leather and buckram, with the title stamped
in gold. We have even included in its pages the ten
panoramic fold-out illustrations which originally appeared in the magazine.

I feel sure that this is the kind of book you will want
to own--for yourself--for your children. It will be
read and reread. It will be referred to and looked
through again and again.

> Walt Disney said, "To own 'The World We Live
> In' in book form is a not-to-be-missed oppor-
> tunity for any family--it's a wonderful and
> exciting adventure in learning" . . . and New
> York's Superintendent of Schools, Dr. William

Jansen, wrote, "In presenting 'The World We
Live In' in popular form, LIFE performs a
great service both to the specializing schol-
ars and to all the rest of us."

CONTINUOUS SYSTEM. The purpose of letters in the *continuous
system* is mainly to keep in touch with present customers or prospective customers of a product or service which is high in price or
for which there is a recurrent demand. The letters in this system
may be used to sell directly, to solicit inquiries, to invite the reader
into the store, to make an announcement, to extend greetings, and
in other ways to promote business relationships. Usually, the letters
continue to be sent at regular or irregular intervals as long as the
relationship is valued.

The kinds of businesses that employ the continuous system include department and specialty stores, banks, insurance companies,
wholesale institutions, and manufacturing firms. The following
letters are part of the continuous system of a large insurance company.

Dear Mr. Lomax:

I was thinking the other day how few people really have
complete protection for their household furniture and
effects, even though they have been renewing their policies from year to year. Suppose you should have a fire
tomorrow. Would your insurance be enough to cover the
losses?

Since you took out your policy, you have probably ac-
quired some new furniture and electrical equipment, to
say nothing of new linens, silverware, etc. Why not let
us help you check your home in detail? You will be surprised at the variance between the amount of your policy
and the value of your household possessions.

The enclosed card will put us on the job immediately.
No obligation, of course.

                                Sincerely,

Dear Mr. Lomax:

Whether you go North or South for your winter vacation,

you will want to get the full benefit of the change.
You will want to leave worry behind.

If you've ever lost a suitcase, trunk, or bag, or ever
had a pair of shoes or a suit stolen, you'll appreciate
more than ever knowing that it is possible to secure
the protection of our Tourist Baggage Policy.

In the Tourist Baggage Policy you have a bell boy who
works for you every hour of the day for less than you
would think of giving in a single tip. Protection
starts the minute you leave your doorstep.

The enclosed folder, "Protection Going and Coming,"
tells the whole story. Read it carefully. Then mail
the card, which is part of it, or, better still, use the
telephone to obtain complete details. You'll be under
no obligation.

                                        Sincerely,

Dear Mr. Lomax:

Of course we could talk about Aircraft Damage Insurance
to protect your roof in case Santa's plane lands heav-
ily, or Riot and Civil Commotion Insurance to cover
Christmas festivities. But selling insurance is not the
object of our letter.

We want to tell you that we do appreciate your patronage
and wish you a joyous old-fashioned Christmas.

                                        Sincerely,

CAMPAIGN SYSTEM. Letters of the *campaign system* are used to
pursue sales inquiries, to secure renewal of orders by mail, and to
produce any other type of sales action requiring the application of
pressure over a period of time. Often the follow-up letters in this
system make reference to the response received from others or to
the failure of the reader to have responded. As the series continues, increasing emphasis is placed on the functions of implanting conviction (p. 164) and of stimulating action (p. 167).

Because there is often a target date, timing is probably more important in this system than in the others. The series must be

started well ahead of the date that final action is required, and the letters must be carefully spaced. Occasionally, terms are eased or special inducements are offered as the series progresses. Enough time must be allowed between letters to reduce to a minimum the possibility that the reader's order at the old price will cross the letter offering a lower price or other inducement.

Unlike the wear-out system, which continues only as long as each mailing in the series pays its own way, the campaign system consists of a specified number of letters planned in the aggregate to do a sales job, and the series is not concluded until the last letter is mailed or until a favorable response has been received.

These are the first and second letters in a campaign system designed to obtain a contract renewal.

Dear RCA Television Owner:

For nearly a year, you have enjoyed protection and service for fine television reception . . . assured by your RCA Victor Factory Service Maintenance Contract. Within a few weeks, this contract will expire, but . . . here is good news . . . you can arrange for an RCA Victor Factory Service Maintenance Contract for another full year.

Even if you had little occasion to need service during the past year, remember that this service protection can prove doubly valuable in the months ahead. Your set is now a year older. The replacement and adjustment of a single part--the picture tube, for example--can cost as much as a Maintenance Contract, in many cases considerably more. Yet under its provisions, any parts of your set that fail in normal use will be replaced at no extra expense to you, and your set kept in good working order.

The enclosed application describes the many benefits and advantages of three popular contracts. Surely, you will find one to suit your need. No matter which contract you choose, you are always assured prompt, courteous, and expert attention by RCA's own television specialists.

Why not protect your investment in continued television

pleasure for many months to come. Simply sign the
application NOW and mail it, together with your check
or money order, in the enclosed postage-paid envelope.

                              Very truly yours,

Dear RCA Television Owner:

Our offer to provide service and parts protection for
another year has brought an overwhelming response from
owners of RCA Victor television sets.

You'll be interested in a letter accompanying one of the
applications for a Maintenance Contract:

> "Sign me up again," it says in part, "for your
> Factory Service Contract. Last year, your
> service kept my RCA Victor set in top condi-
> tion, and I want to be sure it stays that way.
> I think a service contract is a 'must' for
> every television fan."

Perhaps your application crossed this letter in the
mails. If not, the Factory Service Maintenance Contract
advantages you now enjoy on your set will expire soon.

Remember, you have now been using your set for a long
time. Should things go seriously wrong--worn-out tubes
or other parts fail--you want to be sure of getting experienced, reliable service, and genuine replacement
parts from the factory--quickly.

The enclosed folders describe the many benefits and advantages of several popular contracts. Surely, you will
find a Maintenance Contract to suit your need.

One way to be sure of this protection is to fill out the
application and mail it with your check. Don't take the
chance of disappointing guests when good programs are
coming along.

                              Very truly yours,

    The following is the third letter in a campaign system designed
to obtain permission for a salesman to call:

Dear Mr. Payne:

As we have suggested in our previous letters, our representative, Mr. Joseph Ray, is prepared to show you how
an up-to-date Universal Cash Register can substantially
increase your profits.

Only last month Mr. Ray demonstrated the Universal System to Mr. George Vincent of Vincent's Market in your
town. Now the system is installed, and Mr. Vincent
writes, "With your Universal Cash Register in my store
for only a few days, I have already served more customers in less time than I thought was possible. In a
few months the Universal will already have paid for itself in saved time and increased volume. I'm glad I
took Mr. Ray's advice."

It will put you under no obligation whatever to let Mr.
Ray put all the facts before you. You can then make
your own decision. But first--get those facts.

Just fill out and mail the enclosed card now.

                                    Very truly yours,

Review Problems

   1. State the following with relation to the sales letter:
      a. Four main uses.
      b. Two ways of attracting attention.
      c. Two ways of creating desire.
      d. Three ways of implanting conviction.
      e. Three ways of stimulating action.
   2. Write two different openings for a sales letter designed to sell this book
by mail to college students who are studying business writing. Assume that
examination time is approaching.
   3. Write the descriptive portion of a letter designed to sell a box of 100 as-
sorted greeting cards (for all occasions) by mail to a list of housewives. Assume
any necessary details.
   4. To a list of owners of new cars write a letter designed to sell by mail the
MiraKleer Cloth. Assume that an order blank and business reply envelope are
enclosed.
   MiraKleer Cloth is chemically treated to put an invisible coat on any glass
surface. This coat prevents fog, mist, or frost from forming. MiraKleer Cloth
makes driving safer by keeping windshield and rear window clear in nasty
weather. It is also useful when applied to bathroom mirrors and eyeglasses. One
wipe lasts for days. The cloth is guaranteed for a year.

The price is five cloths for $6.00 payable on delivery. Complete satisfaction is guaranteed or money will be refunded in ten days. Offer free with the $6.00 order an 8-ounce can of Glazo, the new combination cleaner and paste wax for all car finishes—easy to apply, needs no rubbing. The purchaser may keep the can of Glazo even if he decides to return the wax for a refund.

5. Assume that the following letter is the last letter in a campaign system designed to obtain a subscription renewal for a weekly news magazine:

Dear Subscriber:

Last week we sent you your last copy of *Current Facts* under the terms of your subscription. If you wish to continue to receive the magazine, please mail us your check for $8.50 to cover the next 52 issues. A return card and envelope are enclosed for your convenience.

                                                                    Very truly yours,

Rewrite the letter, making it more effective. Assume any facts within reason.

13
Sales Promotion Letters

Sales promotion letters are used to sell indirectly. In a letter of this type, the writer induces the reader to buy, but does not urge him. By not emphasizing his selling mission, the correspondent meets with lowered sales resistance from many readers, who have learned to be wary of the direct sales appeal.

CHARACTERISTICS OF SALES PROMOTION LETTERS

Several characteristics distinguish the sales promotion letter from other types of business letters. The correspondent uses it (1) to capitalize on a timely circumstance or event, (2) to express goodwill or to perform (or to offer to perform) a service of value to the reader,[1] and (3) to connote a personal and friendly attitude. The last is accomplished mainly through the style in which the sales promotion letter is generally written.

TIMELINESS. Sales promotion letters are prompted by a special occasion. An anniversary, a holiday, the arrival of new merchandise, the beginning of a season, or another event or circumstance may be seized upon to draw together the sender and the reader of the message.

The letter below was written by a correspondent at a large Texas store to a customer temporarily living in New York City. The event, the winning of an advertising award, is not in itself impor-

---

[1] See "The You Attitude," pp. 43–44.

tant to the reader, but it makes possible a friendly communication
between the firm and a distant customer.

Good

Dear Mrs. Anderson:

Although Texas is 1200 miles away--a long way even with
the crow flying it--we often think of you and wish there
were some way to send you our morning ads and snatches
of Neiman-Marcus news. But you can be sure whenever
anything particularly "New Yorker" or special comes
along we do think of you.

Recently our advertising won the Art Director's award
as the best work in the country and now our advertising
is being exhibited in your city at the Museum of Modern
Art. What a good way for you to see a bit of Neiman-
Marcus--and a winning bit at that!

One of the winners, an advertisement on a series of
iridescent denim playclothes, would be of particular
interest to New Yorkers who like to garden on weekends
in the country, go to Connecticut or to the Sound to
dig clams and to swim. The nicest part of this is that
you can receive these playclothes before your Long Is-
land sun begins to warm up.

Another ad, through which we could be of service to you,
showed our green and blue guest room, now being exhibited in our Decorative Galleries here in Dallas.
The room combines provincial furniture and modern--cold,
austere colors with warm effects. It's typical of the
fine decorating our staff does all over the country.

The Art Director's Show will be exhibited at the Museum
of Modern Art until April 15. Won't you stop in and see
it?

                                    Sincerely yours,

GOODWILL AND SERVICE. Sales promotion letters sell indirectly.
Whereas the sales letter says in effect, "Buy," the sales promotion
letter says, "Let us serve you." Whereas the sales letter says, "Be
a customer," the sales promotion letter says, "Be a friend."

In the letter below, which was written by the correspondent of a moving company, the sales message is effectively tempered by the writer's expressions of goodwill and his desire to serve.

Dear Mr. Schaeffer:

Your moving is finished and we are glad you are in your new home. It was a pleasure to work for you.

Perhaps the completion of your moving can be the beginning rather than the end of a pleasant business relationship, because we can do so much more for your home than move your furniture.

At the top of this letter is a listing of our home services. In addition, we invite you to ask the help of our interior decorator in solving any of your decorating problems.

Please call our representative any time.

We wish you happiness in your new home.

                              Sincerely yours,

INFORMAL STYLE. Because the writer of sales promotion letters is free of the necessity to obtain immediate business, his style of writing is usually informal, friendly, and personal. In each letter he may suggest, but he does not press the sale. The following message, which was sent to prospective customers by a printer of circular letters, is a good example of the relaxed style of sales promotion letters. It was printed in green ink.

                              March 16, 19--

Is your shamrock showing . . .?

You'll need it for the parade, you know. It won't be Saint Patrick's Day and it won't be Fifth Avenue, without the sight of shamrocks in the crowd.

They'll be coming from everywhere to watch the parade. Green will be the color of the day . . . and we won't mind it a bit!

Of course, we <u>do</u> wish more people knew it was <u>our</u> anniversary, too. We wouldn't expect a parade of course.
Just some quiet little affair . . . say a stroll down
our side of Forty-fifth Street.

Twenty-nine years! That is not very old, as time goes.
But it does seem, well, somewhat substantial. Anyway,
we don't really need a parade to feel good. Just remembering the splendid people we've worked for over the
years is enough.

We'd like to work for you, too.

                                         Sincerely,

USES OF SALES PROMOTION LETTERS

Sales promotion letters have almost as many uses as there are
opportunities to create good business relations. The majority of
these uses fall into four major categories: (1) maintaining contact
with customers, (2) awakening inactive accounts, (3) welcoming
new customers, and (4) inviting business from new sources.

MAINTAINING CONTACT WITH CUSTOMERS. In sales promotion
letters, the correspondent may announce the arrival of seasonal
lines, describe new services, suggest the opening or extended use of
credit accounts, offer the advantage of "private sales," send birthday and other personal greetings, and so on.

Offer of seasonal service

Dear Mr. Baker:

Nowadays, in spring, a man's fancy (and a woman's, too)
turns to open roads and highways . . . to a desire to
see the other side of the mountain . . . and, quite
logically, it turns also to his Cadillac.

For your Cadillac is your magic carpet . . . your key
to excitement, adventure and new experience . . . your
passport to hours of summer motoring.

But whether you stay at home or seek out new places, we
should like to make one simple and sensible suggestion
that will increase tenfold your motoring pleasure.

Let us remove all traces of winter from your Cadillac.
For wonderful as your Cadillac is, the winter months
take their toll. Perhaps the finish has lost some of
its original sheen . . . or the engine could be improved
with a minor tune-up . . . or perhaps it's simply a
matter of changing lubricants. In any case, we can
quickly have your Cadillac looking, sounding, and performing the way it should. Our master mechanics are
schooled in factory methods of service. They will have
your car ready for those wonderful miles ahead in just
a short time.

So why not drive in to see us tomorrow and ask for a
"Cadillac Spring Conditioning."

                              Very truly yours,

Announcement of private sale

Dear Madam:

We are about to announce in the newspapers one of the
greatest linen sales in years--with reductions ranging
from 40 per cent to 70 per cent. The advertisement will
appear on Sunday, June 1. Since you are one of a special list of customers who, we feel, would know and
love fine linens, we want to give you the opportunity
to make your selections on Tuesday, Wednesday, and
Thursday, May 27, 28, and 29.

From Italy, France, and Spain we have assembled a co-
lossal collection of hand-embroidered dinner sets.
There are mosaics, Italian-type embroideries, lavish
Appenzelles, Richelieus, Perugian or shadow embroideries, flat Venice or Tombole inserts, filets and cut-
work, and hand appliques . . . all exquisitely wrought
and phenomenally low-priced at $25.95 to $100.00 (regularly $35.95 to $185.00).

You will treasure these luxurious pieces yourself or
give them proudly to June brides. These linens are
mainly one-of-a-kind. Consequently, we advise your
earliest attention and selection.

                              Very truly yours,

AWAKENING INACTIVE ACCOUNTS. Customers stop buying for
many reasons. A few may have moved away, others were enticed
away by competition, still others were dissatisfied with the goods
or service. In the case of customers who have moved away, letters
may be used to offer mail-order service. In other instances, letters
may be used to invite former customers to tell why they have
stopped buying and to offer to correct the cause of any grievance.[2]
Sales promotion letters may also be employed for special merchandise or service announcements designed to entice the customer back into the fold.

Sale announcement to inactive account

Dear Sir:

Miracle Day, the famous Stanton one-day sale, takes
place on Wednesday, May 16. Through a personal inspection, I feel that the values are of extraordinary importance.

The enclosed circular will give you a few more details--
the values are too many to mention--and include everything you would possibly want for spring and summer for
your home, your family, and yourself.

This is an opportune time to remind you that you still
have a charge account with us, although it has been inactive.

We have missed you as one would miss an old friend and
hope for a renewal of our friendly relations.

                                        Cordially yours,

WELCOMING NEW CUSTOMERS. One of the best opportunities to
build goodwill is afforded when a customer makes his first purchase. A letter that says, "Thank you," and asks that the company be allowed to be of further service is sure to strike a responsive
note.

---

[2] For an example of a letter designed to bring back lost business, see Chapter 11.

Welcome to new patron

Dear Mr. Gates:

It is good news that you have opened a savings account
at our bank. As you continue to add to it, I hope it
will help bring you happiness and security.

In welcoming you as a depositor, I invite you to make
use of our many services designed for your convenience.
Some of these services are described in the little
folder enclosed.

This is now your bank. Please feel free to call on us
at any time for additional information that may assist
you in planning your savings program.

                              Very truly yours,

INVITING BUSINESS FROM NEW SOURCES. The writer who wishes
to bid for new business with sales promotion letters must first find
a good service approach. He may welcome a new resident to the
community, offer good wishes to a new business establishment,
congratulate a winner of honors, announce a new service, or suggest a way of solving a personal or business problem. The following letter was written by an employee of a children's shoe store.

Welcome to new resident

Dear Mrs. Glen:

May we extend you our hearty and most cordial welcome to
Suburbanville.

Mrs. Ballard, the Welcome Wagon hostess, told us of her
pleasant visit with you. Consequently, it is a genuine
privilege to include you and your family among our community shoppers.

Our extensive experience as specialists in fitting children's footwear gives assurance that we are eminently
qualified to answer all your questions.

We hope you will give us the opportunity to be of service.

                              Cordially yours,

Announcement of a new service

Dear Mr. Simmons:

Planned for your convenience is the enlarged reservation
service we have installed at the Metropolitan House for
all hotels in the Glidden chain.

For example, if you wish to secure a New York reservation, or if you are going to Chicago or any other point
where we have a hotel, just phone CIrcle 8-6350. Say,
"I wish a New York reservation," or "I wish an out-of-
town reservation." In the majority of cases, you will
receive an immediate confirmation.

The list of hotels at the bottom of this letter shows
where we can serve you for vacation or business trips.
We hope to have the privilege of making a reservation
for you at an early date.

                                        Very truly yours,

Review Problems

1. Which of the following statements are correct?
   a. Sales promotion letters are not as effective as sales letters.
   b. The emphasis in sales promotion letters is mainly on service.
   c. Sales promotion letters may be used to offer mail-order service to
former customers who have moved out of the trading area.
   d. Persuasiveness is characteristic of the style of sales promotion letters.
   e. A businessman should be able to send a sales promotion letter at any
time with equal effect.

2. Assume that you are the circulation manager of *Reader's Digest, Holiday,
Life,* or *Newsweek.* Write a letter to thank subscribers who have just renewed
their subscriptions for another year.

3. Assume that you are the branch manager of a large chain store dealing
in moderate-priced clothing for every member of the family. Easter is approaching. Write a sales promotion letter to residents of your community suggesting
that they fill their Easter clothing needs at your shop. You may assume any
necessary details.

4. Assume that you are working for a local hardware store. It is January 2
and you are about to mail to all of your customers a wall calendar illustrated
by works of famous artists. Write a letter to go with the calendar.

5. Assume that you are working in the customer relations department of a
local business bank. Write a sales promotion letter to be mailed to customers on
the occasion of the tenth anniversary of the opening of their accounts.

14
Letters of Application

Many a talented worker is employed in an inferior position because he is unable to present effectively the facts about his fine character, ability, and experience when applying for a position by letter. No other correspondence is of such direct and personal importance to the writer. Here the essentials of the successful letter of application and résumé (data sheet) will be explained.

PURPOSE AND ADVANTAGES OF A WRITTEN APPLICATION

Although there are other ways of seeking a position—such as by telephone or by a personal visit to a company—writing a letter is the most usual method of applying for one of the better openings. Provided that the applicant's qualifications for a particular job are satisfactory, his letter of application will probably be the deciding factor in securing an interview. The immediate purpose of the application is to secure an interview, for the applicant hopes that by means of personal contact (with the personnel manager or department supervisor), he will eventually obtain the job he wants.

The written application has two advantages over other means of requesting employment: (1) It provides a permanent record to which the employer may refer as often as necessary. And (2) it enables the employer to determine the value (to his firm) of an interview with the applicant.

TYPES OF APPLICATION LETTERS

Letters of application fall into two principal categories: (1) so-

187

licited and (2) unsolicited. Ordinarily, the person seeking a position may use both types.

SOLICITED LETTERS. A solicited letter of application is written in response to an invitation, usually in the form of an advertisement, from the employer.

The primary advantage to the applicant in writing a solicited letter of application is the certainty that an opening exists and that the employer is anxious to fill it. Furthermore, the writer is aided considerably by the employer's statement, however brief, of the qualifications required for the job.

The main disadvantage of a solicited letter of application is that in most instances it is just one of many written in response to the same advertisement. If it is to be read, it must be better than average; if it is to be regarded favorably, it must be one of the best received.

The following are a newspaper advertisement for a part-time shoe salesman and a good letter which one young man wrote in answer to it:

SALESMAN. Young college student to work part time as shoe salesman for high quality local chain. Prefer man with merchandising education and practical experience. Opportunity for managerial position during summer months. Box 205.

                                        105 Burton Place
                                        Ann Arbor, Michigan 48104
                                        February 16, 19--

Box 205
Ann Arbor Dispatch
Ann Arbor, Michigan 48107

Gentlemen:

Your advertisement for a part-time shoe salesman emphasizes your need for a thoroughly competent person with merchandising education and practical experience. Will you take a moment to consider my qualifications?

I am 23 years of age and a graduate of Fairleigh Dickinson College, East Rutherford, New Jersey, where I re-

ceived my Associate of Arts degree in Merchandising.   In
addition to the regular business administration courses,
my curriculum included specialized courses in retail
buying and control, retail organization and management,
merchandise control, and the psychology of salesmanship.
At present I am majoring in economics at the University
of Michigan at Ann Arbor.

For the past three years I have been working part time
for the Ann Arbor branch of a national shoe chain.   In
addition to my usual duties as shoe salesman, I have
been responsible for stock co-ordination and the checking of inventories.   I know shoes and shoe styles and
attribute my success as a salesman to my ability to influence people by using that knowledge.   I take great
pride in the fact that my sales have averaged $300.00
a day.

I have for a long time had the desire to sell a better
quality shoe.   Your store would afford me the opportunity to advance on my own merits.   Conditions at my
place of employment are pleasant, but the opportunities
for promotion are limited.   I know I can handle greater
responsibilities.

If my qualifications interest you, I should appreciate
the opportunity of meeting you in person.   My telephone
number is ARbor 3-5816.

May I hear from you?

Respectfully yours,

Marvin D. Brown

Marvin D. Brown

UNSOLICITED LETTERS. An unsolicited letter of application is
written to a prospective employer who has *not* advertised a job
opening.

The primary advantage of writing an unsolicited letter is the
likelihood that it will not have to compete with other applications.
Also, the writer is able to send a similar, if not the same, letter to
a number of prospective employers at the same time.

The chief disadvantages of the unsolicited letter are: (1) There is a possibility that no job is available. And (2) the writer must determine for himself the qualifications in which the employer will be most interested.

This is a good example of an unsolicited letter of application.

                                              4932 Frederick Street
                                              Philadelphia, Pa. 19054
                                              March 15, 19--

Mr. William Traebert, Director
Camp Fenimore
Shawnee, Pennsylvania 18356

Dear Mr. Traebert:

From my friends I have heard so many good things about your camp that I wish you would consider me for your counseling staff this summer.

I am eighteen years of age and a graduate of Benjamin Franklin High School in Philadelphia. At present I am completing my first year at Temple University, where I am studying business administration.

During the past seven summers I have gained invaluable experience through my dealings with children of all ages. For five of these summers I was a camper at Camp Walden, Palmer, Massachusetts. I participated in all the camp activities and I was able to discover what qualities campers want most in their counselors. For the last two seasons I was a junior counselor at the same camp.

For several years I was a member of the camp varsity baseball and varsity basketball teams which won the championship in our intercamp league. In addition, I was an active participant in tennis, football, handball, squash, volleyball, and softball. I also became adept at water activities. Besides being able to handle a rowboat and a canoe, I successfully completed the courses in junior and senior life saving.

My record at Benjamin Franklin High School was equally

good. I participated extensively in dramatics and club
and sports activities. I was president of the Glee
Club in my junior year and carried my varsity letter as
a member of the basketball and baseball teams.

Although I have been happy at Camp Walden, their policy
required that full-fledged counselors be nineteen, and
I do not wish to serve as a junior counselor again.
Hence my desire for a change. I am sure that Mr. William Sampson, the Director of Camp Walden, will be glad
to vouch for my character and ability.

If you feel that I measure up to your qualifications for
counselor, I shall greatly appreciate it if you will let
me know when and where I may meet you. I am sure my
father would drive me out to see you at Shawnee any
weekend.

My home telephone number is INdependence 4-6532. I can
be reached there any time after 6 p. m.

Very truly yours,

Samuel Fogarty

Samuel Fogarty

FUNCTIONS OF APPLICATION LETTERS

Since all letters of application are intended to "sell" the writer's
attributes and qualifications to the reader, they should be organized in a fashion similar to sales letters. Specifically, the functions
of application letters should be: (1) to establish favorable attention, (2) to create desire, (3) to convince, and (4) to stimulate
action.

ESTABLISHING FAVORABLE ATTENTION. A letter of application
ordinarily faces considerable competition from other letters written by applicants for the same job. Its chances of being read, therefore, depend greatly on the extent to which it establishes a favorable impression or attracts attention. In order for his letter to
perform this initial function, the applicant must be particularly
careful of (1) the physical appearance of his letter and (2) the
manner in which he begins it.

Physical Appearance.[1] The letter should be as businesslike in appearance as possible. It should be neatly written or typewritten on good quality white bond paper, 8½ x 11 inches in size. Typewriting is preferred in all cases except where the advertisement specifically states, "Reply in own handwriting." Many businessmen prefer a one-page letter. The applicant should try to write enough to fill at least three-quarters of a sheet. If the letter is briefer, it may give the impression that the applicant is inadequately qualified. The applicant should resist the temptation to use tricky devices to attract attention.

Letter Opening. The applicant should give a good deal of thought to the phrasing of the opening sentence of his letter. He should especially try to avoid the stereotyped introductions characteristic of so many of the other applications the employer receives.

Perhaps the best way for the applicant to open a solicited letter is to state what he consider to be one of his important qualifications for the job. This qualification should be related to the requirements stated in the advertisement, and it should be worded in an original or at least an unhackneyed way. The reference to the advertisement itself should be subordinated; it may even be omitted, for the box (newspaper, magazine, etc.) to which the letter is normally required to be addressed tells the employer that the letter is an answer to his advertisement.

Stereotyped	*Good*
Replying to your advertisement in this morning's <u>Gazette</u>, I am listing my qualifications below.	After three years of experience in marketing research, I feel that I am qualified to fill the position of market analyst advertised in this morning's <u>Gazette.</u>
This is in reply to your advertisement in yesterday's <u>Times.</u>	Your advertisement appeals to me because it offers the opportunity to accept responsibility, a task for which I believe I am qualified.

---

[1] See Chapter 3, "The Physical Form of the Letter."

Stereotyped	Good
Being interested in the accounting position advertised in today's <u>Herald</u> I thought I would write.	Because I have had two years of formal training in accounting at Pace College, I feel well qualified to work as a junior accountant with your firm.
I would like to be considered a candidate for the stenographer's position which you advertised in yesterday's <u>News.</u>	When I graduated from the Devoe Secretarial School last June, I was third in my class in stenographic and typewriting proficiency. I believe you will find me an accurate and efficient worker.

Unlike the writer of the solicited letter, who usually has a description before him of the job for which he is applying and can adjust his reply accordingly, the writer of the unsolicited letter must name the position he wants. He should be as specific as possible. "I am looking for a clerical job" and "I should like to work in your advertising department" are too vague to enable the reader to visualize the kind of job the applicant is seeking. More specific statements, such as the following, clarify the writer's goal in the reader's mind:

Two years' experience as a typist and clerk in the personnel department of a large industrial firm, qualify me, I believe, for a similar position with your firm.

As a college student specializing in marketing, I should like to obtain supplementary experience this summer as a field investigator in your advertising department.

The writer of an unsolicited letter of application has an advantage in that he knows the name of the company to which he is writing. He may capitalize on this knowledge by relating why he would like to work for the company or by otherwise demonstrating familiarity with the company's operations.

Good

Your athletic staff has gained such an enviable reputation over the years that I would consider it a privilege to be associated with it.

In addressing the national convention of the American
Statistical Association in Detroit last June, Mr. Jason
Kamm, the president of your company said:

> "There is a need today, as never before, for
> young men with business training and scien-
> tific minds to explore the many new opportu-
> nities that have been opened up in the field
> of statistical quality control."

If you have room in your business research division for
a young man with the qualifications mentioned by Mr.
Kamm, please consider me as a candidate for employment.

Through my instructors I have learned that yours is the
fastest growing company in the field of industrial design. As one who intends to make her career in industrial design, I am therefore anxious to start with your
company as a junior stenographer.

CREATING DESIRE. A letter of application should create desire
in the reader's mind for the writer's services. An applicant accom-
plishes this objective by (1) an orderly plan of presentation and
(2) a description of his qualifications for the job.

Plan of the Letter. The applicant who wishes to insure an
orderly presentation of his qualifications should outline them
briefly before he writes his letter. Such an outline may read:

Age
Education
Experience
Special qualifications

The choice and arrangement of topics and the extent to which
they are developed will depend on the position and the qualifications of the applicant. The young man or woman who has recently completed high school or college may have no experience to
write about. Thus, the young person may dwell at some length
on the training he received in school. The more mature person,
on the other hand, may emphasize his experience by moving it to
the top of his outline; he may also find it sufficient, in writing about
his education, to mention only the last school he attended and his
specialization and graduation date.

Description of Qualifications. The reader's desire to meet the writer is increased when the writer describes his qualifications from the reader's point of view. Since, by its very nature, the letter of application must concentrate on the writer's background and personal characteristics, adaptation to the reader is not easy. Nevertheless, the reader's viewpoint can be emphasized in many ways.

The writer should be certain to emphasize the manner in which his qualifications meet the requirements in the employer's advertisement. If "at least five years of experience in industrial advertising" is mentioned in the advertisement, the applicant obviously captures the reader's point of view when he writes of his experience in that field. When "must be willing to travel" is stated in the advertisement, the applicant impresses the reader favorably when he writes that one of his primary aims is to find a job which will allow him to travel.

It is evident that an employer will naturally prefer workers whose interests are likely to make them more enthusiastic about their jobs. The writer, therefore, may state his reasons for desiring to work in the particular field or industry.

Good

Having worked in both government and private industry, I feel from experience that my best opportunity for achievement in personnel management lies with private industry.

Wherever possible, I have chosen those electives in my college course that would most definitely lead to a position in the chemical industry.

It has always been my desire to work for a small concern.

All my job experience proves that I am best suited to do administrative work.

The applicant should lend emphasis to his qualifications by stating them in concrete terms. The one who writes, "I am well-educated," or "I am tactful," or "I am ambitious," does not give the employer an opportunity to make his own estimate of the applicant's ability. Furthermore, the writer gives the impression of making the very judgment which is the prerogative of the employer to make. A description of qualifications is considerably more effective when it is stated so that the employer may draw his own conclusion.

Good

After graduating from the Wharton School of the University of Pennsylvania, I came to New York City where I was admitted to the New York University Graduate School of Business Administration. I have now completed all of my course work for the Ph.D. degree, and I am writing my thesis.

(Rather than: "I have a good business education.")

For more than two years I was assigned as trouble-shooter to adjust service complaints from industrial customers in the New England territory. This position required more than ordinary patience, tact, and understanding.

The writer should, of course, state his qualifications in an original and interesting way. Qualifications stated too matter-of-factly not only make dull reading, but also tend to convey the image of a lackadaisical person. Contrast the statements below.

Dull	Improved
(Rather than: "I am tactful.")	
My major subject is accounting.	Because I feel that as a credit man I should be able to analyze financial statements, in order to determine the credit risk involved, I chose accounting as my major subject.
I am a veteran.	I regard many of my experiences as a supply sergeant in World War II as valuable training for this job.

Dull

I also wrote advertisements
for this firm.

Improved

After doing production work
for a year, I began to submit my own copy for some of
the advertisements called
for in my production sched-
ules. As time went on,
more and more of my copy
was accepted for publica-
tion.

CONVINCING THE EMPLOYER. The applicant strengthens his
case when he backs up his own appraisal of his qualifications with
evidence to support it. Among the types of convincing evidence
used in letters of application are (1) specific details, (2) letters of
recommendation, (3) names of references, (4) samples of work,
and (5) results of aptitude tests.

Specific Details. Whenever the applicant describes his qualifications in detail—providing actual names, dates, and other facts
about his education and experience—he arouses desire for his services and he also convinces the reader of the truth of his statements.
Compare the examples below.

Vague

I have a high school education.

Specific

I was graduated from Hamilton High School in this
city in June 19--. In my
last two years, I specialized in commercial sub-
jects, including shorthand,
typing, and bookkeeping.
I was fifth in my class in
scholastic attainment.

For several years I worked
as assistant to the advertising manager.

For three years I worked as
assistant to Mr. John
Kirby, the advertising manager. In this capacity, I
wrote copy; placed orders
for art work, typography,
and plates; read proof; and
kept production records.
My experience included both
newspaper and direct-mail
advertising.

Letters of Recommendation. The applicant may obtain letters of recommendation from his former employers, his school principal, his instructors, or other persons of good standing in the community. He may then enclose a copy of one or more of these letters with his letter of application, or he may indicate that he has such letters and will be glad to present them at the interview. He should not send the original letters, for few employers like to be bothered with returning them.

Letters of recommendation are effective and convincing because, through them, the word of a third party is added to the claims of the applicant. Furthermore, these letters may stress the applicant's ability in a way which modesty would normally prevent. Such expressions as "showed unusual skill" or "did a magnificent job" constitute effective and appropriate endorsements when written by a third party, but they would create the impression of extraordinary conceit if they came from the applicant himself.

Names of References. The prospective employer often prefers the names of references to letters of recommendation, because he may check for himself the references' opinions of the applicant. In some cases, the names themselves may influence the employer in the applicant's favor. On the other hand, most employers are aware that an applicant usually names as references only those persons who approve of him and his work.

In naming references, the applicant should be sure to spell the names correctly and to give business addresses and telephone numbers. He should secure permission from the references to use their names in his letters, except when he uses the names of former employers.

Good

My direct superior at Jones & Co. was Mr. Robert Gross. I am sure that Mr. Gross will be glad to tell you about the caliber of my work if you will write to him at 475 Shetland Avenue, Greenstone, Pa. 17227, or telephone him at GReenstone 6-5000, Extension 231.

For additional information regarding my personal qualities, I refer you to Mr. George E. Kidd, pastor of the Greenwood Reformed Church. His telephone number is GReenwood 2-1345.

Samples of Work. In effect, the letter of application is always taken as a sample of the applicant's ability to use the English language and to write by hand or to typewrite. In many instances, however, additional opportunities are afforded the applicant to present samples of his work. The would-be copywriter, for example, can offer samples of advertisements he has written. In other circumstances, a blueprint, a pattern, or a sketch may help to prove the applicant's ability.

Unless the applicant can send a sample that can be kept by the prospective employer, he should not include samples with his letter. Rather, he should state in his letter that he has samples to show and that he will bring them with him to the interview.

Results of Tests. Employers are attaching increasing importance to aptitude and intelligence tests as means of indicating a prospective employee's ability. Consequently, the results of such tests, administered by reputable agencies, constitute valuable evidence in the letter of application.

Good

```
Aptitude tests taken at the Placement Bureau of Trenton
College showed I am best fitted for contact work (sales
and personnel activity).

In a test taken early this year under the auspices of
the Association of National Advertising Agencies, I
scored 93.7 per cent in copy effectiveness and 89.5 per
cent in knowledge of marketing theory.  Should you care
to see it, I shall be glad to show you my official rat-
ing card at a personal interview.
```

STIMULATING ACTION. The ultimate aim of the letter of application is, of course, to secure a position, but few jobs are obtained without a preliminary talk between employer and applicant. Therefore, it is expedient that the letter close with a request for an interview. This request should be designed to stimulate action on the employer's part and should be courteous and definite. If the applicant is available for interviews only at certain times, he should say so. He should also include his telephone number, if he has one.

OTHER CONSIDERATIONS

In the course of writing a letter for a job, the applicant will undoubtedly meet problems not already covered in this chapter. These problems include such matters as tone, salary, and previous employment.

TONE. By the tone he uses in his letter, the applicant provides the prospective employer with a clue to his personality and character. Since the employer is usually more particular about these qualifications than about any others, the applicant will be wise to give great care to expressing attitudes. To put the best complexion on his ability and experience, he should concentrate on his strong points and should avoid calling attention to his deficiencies. The applicant who is timid or apologetic or is boastful or overconfident makes an unfavorable impression. The tone of the ideal application is modest and confident, but not cocksure.

Poor	*Better*
My knowledge of credit is limited, but I suppose I can learn.	Because of my study of credit problems in college, I have acquired a keen interest in the subject and am sure I can convert my knowledge and interest to practical use.
Although I have no actual experience, I did take shorthand and typing for two years in high school.	In high school I studied shorthand and typing for two years. My grades were excellent.
If there is a better salesman in this town, I'd like to meet him.	I should certainly welcome the opportunity to demonstrate my selling ability in the field.

Occasionally, the applicant is apprehensive about the frequent use of *I* in his letters and wonders if this practice is a violation of the "you" attitude (Chapter 4). Perhaps it would help him to remember that *I* stands for the "product" he is selling and that, as in a sales letter, there is an advantage in referring to the product often, if the benefits to the reader are clearly stated or implied.

SALARY. The subject of salary is rather delicate. Therefore, the applicant would be wise not to mention it unless the advertisement specifically asks that salary be stated.

When salary is mentioned in the letter, its statement may be hedged by certain qualifications; but the applicant should be careful of the attitude he expresses. The employer will not approve of the applicant who either overvalues or undervalues his services.

Poor	*Better*
I must receive $120.00 a week.	I would consider a starting salary of $120.00 a week satisfactory.
I received $100.00 a week in my last job, but I know I am worth much more.	I received $100.00 a week in my last job but in view of the additional responsibilities in the new position, I feel that I should start at $115.00.
I will work for anything just to get the experience.	After you have had the opportunity to judge my qualifications personally, I should be pleased to discuss the subject of salary with you.
Salary does not mean very much to me. I just want the opportunity to show what I can do.	Because salary is secondary to opportunity with me, I should be willing to start at whatever figure you consider right for the job.

PREVIOUS EMPLOYMENT. If the applicant has a job at present, he should state why he wants to make a change. If he has had a job in the past, but is not now employed, he should explain why he left his last position. Since certain reasons are more acceptable than others to prospective employers, the applicant should exercise extreme caution in this part of the letter.

Poor	*Better*
I am really on a dead-end street in my present job.	Although I enjoy the work I am now doing, it does not offer an opportunity for advancement in my chosen field.

My reason for desiring a
change is that I do not get
along with my present
supervisor.

I am particularly inter-
ested in becoming associ-
ated with your company because of its widely re-
spected personnel policies
with regard to placement
and promotion.

THE RESUME

It is customary for an employer to ask a job applicant to submit a résumé. The résumé, or data sheet, is an organized summary of the applicant's background which ordinarily includes his age, marital status, business experience, education, and references. It differs from the application letter in that it is generally in outline form and does not carry an inside address, salutation, complimentary close, or signature. The résumé is not a substitute for an application letter, but a supplement to it.

Employers like the résumé because it provides in convenient form a complete documentation of the applicant's qualifications. It is helpful to the applicant, too, because it can be Xeroxed or otherwise duplicated for enclosure with any job letters the applicant writes. Résumés also make it possible to shorten one's letters, for many of the details in the résumé do not have to be repeated. The letter accompanying a résumé serves the function of making a direct appeal for the job by highlighting the main qualifications and referring the reader to the résumé for the full record.

PHYSICAL APPEARANCE. The résumé is typewritten on 8½- by 11-inch white bond paper. With good planning and arrangement, only a single sheet should be necessary, but that sheet should be reasonably well filled. The use of headings, indentions, and other typographic devices add to the attractiveness of the page. A title like "Résumé," "Data Sheet," or something more personal—for instance, "Personal Record of James Smith"—is optional.

CONTENT. The topics treated in the résumé include the following, though the order may be varied to suit the particular tastes and qualifications of the applicant.

1. Name, mailing address, and telephone number.
2. Position desired or job objective.
3. Education, including major courses, honors, and extracurricular activities.

4. Positions held, with inclusive dates, title of position, name of employer, and duties.

5. Military experience, if any.

6. Hobbies, interests, special skills and achievements.

7. Personal data, which may include age, height and weight, draft status, marital status.

8. References (optional).

COMPOSITION. Many of the same suggestions already given for emphasis and proportion in the letter apply as well to the writing of the résumé. The idea is to play up one's strong points, such as education or job experience, by giving them the most space. It is not necessary under any circumstances, however, to list all schools attended. The last may be sufficient if it provides the only record the applicant wishes to present as an asset for the job. However, there is often some advantage in listing all jobs held, so that a complete or continuous record will be provided. In the absence of job experience, emphasis should be put on educational achievements and special skills and interests. Schools and jobs should be listed in inverse chronological order, that is, the last first. All the data in the résumé should be highly specific and stated very tersely in phrases rather than complete sentences.

Examples of résumés are shown in Figs. 9 and 10.

RÉSUMÉ

```
JOSEPH E. HARMON                      Telephone
52 West 85th Street                   (212) 495-7668
New York, N.Y. 10009

JOB OBJECTIVE

    Management Trainee:   General Management or Office
        Management

EDUCATION

    19-- - 19--.   New York University School of
                   Commerce
                   Bachelor of Science in Management.

    Major Courses:  Management and Organizational
                    Analysis, Behavioral Science,
```

Fig. 9. A job résumé

> Foundations in Management, Manage-
> ment Science, Management Information
> Systems, Office Management and
> Systems Analysis.

Minor Program: Courses in domestic marketing and
foreign trade; labor legislation,
labor economics, statistics.

EXTRACURRICULAR ACTIVITIES

Management Club: Chairman of the Advisory
  Committee, member of Management Training Program
  Committee
American Management Association, student member
Canterbury Club: Social Chairman and member of the
  Executive Board
Vice President, Senior Class

BUSINESS EXPERIENCE

September 19-- - Present. Assistant in registration,
New York University School of Commerce,
Washington Square, N.Y.

Summer 19--. Stockroom manager and assistant order
fulfillment manager, Stokeley's, Inc., 470 Park
Avenue, New York, N.Y. 10003.

Summer 19--. Clerk in Accounting Department, Saks
Fifth Avenue, New York, N.Y. 10022

MILITARY EXPERIENCE

September 26, 19-- - August 5, 19--. U.S. Army;
served as communications supervisor and Post
Exchange NCO in Saigon, Vietnam, handling employment and supervision of 36 indigenous personnel.

PERSONAL DATA

Age: 24   Marital Status: Single   Weight: 180 lbs.
          Height: 6'4"   Health: Excellent
       Willing to travel and relocate

WORK QUALIFICATIONS OF

Jeffrey Paramenter
1050 Park Terrace
Chicago, Illinois 60675

<u>Position Desired</u>: Auditing Department, analysis of
financial statements

EDUCATION

Northwestern University, Chicago, Illinois, Sept.
19-- - Present. Expected date of graduation:
June 19--.

University of Illinois, Urbana, Illinois, Sept.
19-- - June 19--.

Wayne Country School, Chicago, Illinois, 19-- -
19--.

<u>Major Course Study</u>	<u>Related Course Studies</u>
Principles of Accounting	Business Finance
Management Accounting	Corporate Financial Management
Auditing and Financial Statements	Law and Business Enterprise
Computer-Based Information Systems	Business Communication

WORK EXPERIENCE

Chicago Financial Corporation, summers 19-- and
19--. Financial research and miscellaneous
clerical duties

Tampa Cigar Company, Chicago Office, part-time
work, Sept. 19-- to June 19--. Salesman,
survey taker, and warehouse supervisor.

ACTIVITIES AND ORGANIZATIONS

<u>College</u>	<u>High School</u>
Bridge Team; Varsity Baseball	Newspaper; Yearbook; Math Club

Fig. 10. Another arrangement of a job résumé

Phi Epsilon (social   Varsity Sports: Key
   fraternity)   Society
   One-time member, All-America Bike Team sponsored by
              American Bicycle Manufacturers

PERSONAL INFORMATION

Age: 20   Height: 5 feet 8 inches   Weight: 155
     Military Status: 2S   Special Interests: Outdoor
     sports, bridge, mathematics

REFERENCES

Mr. Walter M. Wildenberg, partner, Chicago Financial
     Corporation, 250 State Street, Chicago, Ill. 60608

Mr. John Sanders, manager, Tampa Cigar Company, 2560
     Dearborn Street, Chicago, Ill. 60623

FOLLOW-UP EMPLOYMENT LETTERS

Often it is to the applicant's advantage to get in touch with a firm shortly following (1) the original application, (2) the employer's acknowledgment of the application, or (3) the interview. Effective results may be secured by means of follow-up letters.

FOLLOWING UP THE ORIGINAL APPLICATION. When the employer does not acknowledge the original letter of application, the applicant may send an inquiry concerning its status. A courteous and brief follow-up letter may achieve the purpose of obtaining a statement from the employer regarding the applicant's chances. Furthermore, since follow-up letters are less frequently received, the second message may attract more attention than the first.

Good

Gentlemen:

On August 20, in response to your advertisement of August 19 in the Herald, I submitted a letter of application for the position of assistant controller.

I am still quite hopeful that my application is being considered because I believe my qualifications fit the requirements you stated. Inasmuch as the position is an

important and a responsible one, it is possible that a
candidate has not yet been chosen.

Would it be convenient for you to let me know the status
of my application?

Very truly yours,

FOLLOWING UP THE EMPLOYER'S ACKNOWLEDGMENT. In those
instances where the employer has acknowledged the application
but indicated that there is no vacancy, the applicant may nevertheless express his appreciation for the consideration given his request. Such a letter makes a favorable impression on the employer.
More important, it may wield some influence in the event of a
future vacancy.

Good

Gentlemen:

I want to express my appreciation for the careful consideration you gave to my letter of application dated
October 11.

Your reference to a possible upturn in production in the
spring encourages me to believe that a vacancy in my
field may occur then. If so, I want to emphasize my
continuing interest in working for your firm.

May I take the liberty of writing you once again several
months from now. I should like to send at that time an
up-to-date résumé which would include my most recent
business experience.

Very truly yours,

FOLLOWING UP THE INTERVIEW. Where an interview is granted
—and no matter what the outcome—it is worth while for the applicant to thank the employer (or interviewer) for the opportunity
to talk with him.

The interview usually provides the applicant with several specific clues as to the employer's main interests; consequently, the

letter following up an interview can be effectively adapted to the reader.

Good

Dear Mr. Jones:

Thank you very much for affording me the opportunity to discuss with you my qualifications for the job of administrative assistant in your purchasing department.

The fact that you expect the man in this position to assume great responsibility during the purchasing manager's frequent trips to the warehouse makes the position even more appealing to me. One of my aims is to exercise greater responsibility than the job I now hold permits.

You indicated that you intended to interview several other applicants. I hope that you will conclude that my past business and educational experience qualify me for the position.

In any event, may I take this opportunity to express my appreciation for your interest in my application.

                                        Very truly yours,

Review Problems

1. Answer the following questions with respect to letters of application:

   a. What is the difference between a solicited letter and an unsolicited letter?

   b. The solicited letter is most like what other type of letter?

   c. How can the applicant consider the reader's point of view even while writing about himself?

   d. Principally, what two functions of the application letter are accomplished by giving specific details?

   e. How does the résumé differ from the letter of application?

2. From the classified advertisement columns of your local newspaper select an advertisement that describes a job you believe you can fill. Write a letter applying for the job. Use facts only.

3. Write a follow-up letter for Problem 2.

4. Write to a company of your choice a letter of application for full-time, part-time, or summer employment. Use facts only.

5. Prepare a résumé which you may enclose with a letter of application or leave with an employer at the time of the interview. Use facts only.

PART 3
BUSINESS REPORTS

PART 3
BUSINESS REPORTS

A business report is an orderly presentation of information about some specific aspect of business activity. It may also include the writer's interpretation of the information, including his conclusions and recommendations. Although some reports are given orally, the written report is traditional in business because it saves the receiver's time, makes reference convenient, and leaves no room for later disagreement as to what the reporter said.

Reports are a very important part of a company's communication network. Directed chiefly upward, they serve as a permanent record of performance in every sphere of the organization's activities. They also help management see how previous decisions are working and provide the basis for new decisions. As the decision-making process becomes more rational, business reports grow in number and sophistication. Many use data processed by the computer as well as the latest mathematical techniques of problem-solving. Yet the basic requirements of reports remain fairly simple: (1) begin with the reader's need for information or guidance in making a decision; (2) research the problem thoroughly; (3) organize the data effectively; (4) write the report; and (5) show concern for the mechanics of the report and the final impression it will make. In the end, the report must be judged by the following criteria:

1. *Utility.* The report must serve the purpose for which it was written. It should provide needed information in convenient form and, if the report objective permits, it should reach conclusions and make recommendations that will be helpful to the reader.

2. *Reliability.* The information must be accurate, specific, and dependable. It must also be unbiased in the sense that no data should be omitted that may affect the conclusion and unimportant data should not be given undue weight.

3. *Persuasiveness.* All conclusions and recommendations must be adequately supported by the evidence, and arguments for them should be logical and reasonable without resort to emotive or prejudicial language. At the same time adequate consideration should be given to any contrary evidence.

4. *Readability.* The report must be organized and written for maximum comprehension. Questions to be answered affirmatively are, "Is the language free of ambiguity and as simple as the subject permits?" "Are ideas expressed in the most concise way?" "Have headings, tables, charts, and other visual devices been used for optimum clarity and interest?"

15
Conceiving the Report:
Planning and Research

The most important decisions about a report are made in the early stages. These decisions relate to the purpose and kind of report to be written, the kind of research to be done, and the specific sources of the data to be used. Hand in hand with these preliminaries is the over-all concern for the course of the investigation and the probable results. Although the formal organization and interpretation of data come later, the writer must make certain assumptions, or hypotheses, at the beginning in order to direct his search into the proper channels. This chapter deals with options of several kinds that confront the report writer intially and yet strongly influence the finished product.

CLASSIFICATION OF REPORTS

Probably the best overview of reports can be obtained by grouping and describing them according to (1) purpose and (2) format and style.

PURPOSE. On the basis of purpose, a business report is either *informational* or *analytical*.

Informational Report. The informational report is designed only to communicate factual data. Such data may include figures, personal observations, and the results of interviews and other investigations. The inferences from these data, however, are left to the reader. Examples of informational reports are a foreman's weekly report of production in his section; a salesman's expense sheet; a management consultant's report on employees' daily work habits; and a buyer's report of coat styles being shown in Paris.

Such reports are valuable for their facts alone, but they may also form the basis—perhaps in conjunction with other reports—for certain conclusions and decisions by the managements to which they are submitted.

Analytical Report. Like an informational report, an analytical report contains facts, but it is also characterized by the writer's conclusions or recommendations based on an analysis of the facts. The analytical report is overtly designed to guide management decisions and therefore puts more than ordinary responsibility on the writer. An analytical report might, for example, weigh alternative plans for reimbursing employees for tuition fees, pointing out the advantages and disadvantages of each plan. The same report may also—though not necessarily—recommend a plan for adoption. Other analytical reports may provide the data and recommendations on how a new product could be marketed successfully, how a company's cafeteria service could be speeded up, or how hiring and firing provisions should be altered to meet current conditions.

FORMAT AND LANGUAGE. On the basis of format and language, reports are either *formal* or *informal*.

Informal Report. The informal report may range from a short, almost fragmentary, statement on a single page to a more developed presentation taking several pages. Usually, the informal report is submitted in the form of a letter or memorandum (Fig. 11). Irrespective of length, the informal report rarely, if ever,

August 27, 19--

Memorandum to Mr. Norton:

I have been in touch with L. M. Crewes Associates about the terms under which they will revise our form letters. The fee is a flat $10,000.00 for one year's service, including the following:

1. Reviewing and rewriting where necessary the form letters of all departments.

2. Preparation of a Correspondence Manual for use by all those who dictate. (The cost of printing is not included in the fee.)

Fig. 11. Short informational report in memorandum style

3. A series of six one-hour discussion meetings
   for all letter-writing personnel.

4. Distribution of the <u>Crewes Better Letters Bul-
   letin</u> every two weeks to all persons included
   in the program. A sample is attached.

After one year, continued service will be provided for
$2,000.00 per year. This fee will include review of all
new form letters, three group meetings, and continued
distribution of the <u>Crewes Better Letters Bulletin</u> every
two weeks.

Mr. Draper, with whom I spoke, said his company could
begin at any time upon one month's notice. He mentioned
the Standard Bank and Trust Company, the Amalgamated Oil
Company, and the Universal Mining Company as recent
clients.

Robert Griswold

Robert Griswold:WF
Enclosure

carries a cover, table of contents, or similar editorial trappings,
though it frequently includes statistical tables and charts.

The language of the informal report is like that of a letter—
natural, relaxed, and more or less personal, depending on the
subject and the reader. The first person—*I* or *we*—is regularly
used, and contractions are acceptable.

Formal Report. The formal report is usually identified by the
fact that it has a cover and binding and other features that might
include a covering letter, title page, table of contents, and index.
Tables and charts, sometimes in bulky appendixes, are other
characteristic features. When it is to have wide distribution, the
formal report is often printed and bound like a book. As may be
surmised from this description, the body of the formal report generally consists of more than a few pages and may run into hundreds
of pages. In fact, reports of several volumes are not unusual. When
reports are long, it is customary to provide summaries of the main
points, usually at the beginning.

The language of the formal report is relatively impersonal and
restrained. For the sake of objectivity the writer strives to subdue

his own personality and point of view. Thus where a memorandum might say, "I learned that," the formal report would say, "it was learned that."

OTHER CLASSIFICATIONS. There are many other ways in which companies describe their reports: *routine, operational, inspection, periodic, annual, sales, statistical, record, progress, special, examination,* and so on. Actually, the name applied to the report is less important than the writer's complete understanding of what is wanted and needed for the particular circumstance. Even where the same term of reference is used for a report, there is often great disparity in treatment from company to company and department to department.

DETERMINING THE TYPE OF REPORT

Before he begins the necessary research and writing, the reporter needs to know what kind of report the situation requires. Otherwise he may not provide enough data or the right kind of data, or he may put the data in the wrong form. Equally bad, he may collect a great deal of unwanted data and thus waste time and effort that could have been expended more profitably on other projects. Guides for determining the type of report do exist; they involve principally four factors: (1) the precedents already established, (2) the time allowed for completion of the report, (3) the importance of the report, and (4) the intended audience.

PRECEDENTS. In most instances, a business report is requested or authorized by a particular person in the organization. If he does not give specific instructions for the kind of report he wants, it may be possible to find in the files similar reports that have been written for the same individual. With a precedent already established, in the form of an earlier report, it is very likely that a report along similar lines will be acceptable. If no precedent or example is available, it may be possible for the writer to talk with the person authorizing the report, should there be some questions as to the type of report desired.

TIME ALLOWED. The length of time the writer is given to prepare the report has a strong influence on the kind of report eventually produced. A report that must be produced in a few hours will be necessarily short, probably in the form of a hastily dictated memorandum. A report project that allows weeks or months, however, will certainly suggest a long document with data thoroughly researched and analyzed. To provide an example, an office manager who is requested to do an on-the-spot report on absenteeism will just about be able to compile some figures for the past weeks or months. If he were given more time, however, he could include a comparison with similar periods in past years and analyze the reasons for differences in the absentee rate. He might also wish to make suggestions for controlling absenteeism.

IMPORTANCE. Some reports require deeper investigation and more formal treatments than others because their subjects are more important. A report that may eventually lead to the introduction of a new product line or the merger of two firms should receive all the research and writing talent that can be commanded. If, on the other hand, management wants to know the advantages of one office copier over another, inquiries among a few manufacturers, a little experimentation, and a report of a few pages would probably be sufficient. Similarly, a salesman writing the report of a trip would probably meet all expectations if he listed the customers he visited, noted the orders they gave him, and estimated the prospects for future orders. If a marketing report of broader significance were wanted, it would probably be assigned to a marketing expert trained in using government statistics and spotting trends.

AUDIENCE. A report intended for a single reader is, of course, adapted to that reader. If he is an associate or co-worker, the report is very likely to be quite informal. If he is a superior, a longer or more formal report is probably in order. When a report is intended for a number of readers on several levels of authority and different levels of knowledge, many more details must be included and much explanation must take place that would be unnecessary under other circumstances. A report intended for public distribution is usually formal in format and language.

ANALYZING THE PROBLEM

Apart from the ordinary questions relating to the kind of report to be prepared, there are the broader questions relating to the objectives of the report and the best ways of fulfilling those objectives.

REPORT OBJECTIVES. Unless the report-writing task is very simple or routine, it will challenge the resources of the writer in a number of ways. In all probability, it will present a problem requiring solution; it will test the writer's ability to get the data he needs to study the problem; it will force him to study alternative solutions; and it may give him the responsibility of recommending the most desirable course of action.

The task is complicated by the fact that the assumptions one normally makes about a problem are often wrong, and that if one is not willing to open his mind to other possibilities, the solution he arrives at will be ineffective and short-lived. To cite an example: an analyst was asked to report on the ways of improving the personnel recruitment rate among female high school graduates at Company X. Investigation showed that in a comparison with competing employers, all factors were about equal. An obvious way to improve recruitment seemed to be to raise wages or increase benefits above the going standards. The analyst, however, was not satisfied that this solution would work; it would also be very costly, perhaps prohibitive. On an impulse, he checked the written applications filled out by the applicants at the time of the initial job interview. One of the questions was, "Why did you apply to Company X?" In over 40 per cent of the applications the reason checked was, "A friend works here." Further inquiries among young girls working for the company showed that mothers worried about their daughters working in strange places and preferred to have them working, and traveling to and from work, with friends. A test campaign at a local high school, using the theme, "Meet your friends at Company X," proved very effective. The result was a recommendation to enlarge the campaign to include all the city's high schools and to make a greater effort to recruit friends of present employees.

As the example demonstrates, the analysis of a report problem may extend well beyond matters of composition. The writer must be prepared to leave the obvious paths of inquiry for new areas of research, to reason logically, and to think creatively and objectively about the real needs of the organization for which he writes.

INVESTIGATIVE TECHNIQUES. The value of a report usually bears a direct relation to the research performed by the writer. A report written "off the top of one's head" may have some interest for the reader, but it cannot guide him with any degree of assurance to informed and effective action. The writer must not only know what information he needs; he must also know what methods of investigation are available to him and be able to conduct his research in such ways that he will obtain valid results. At the same time, he must be both thorough and systematic so that no information will be lost to him because of carelessness in the search or in note-taking and record-keeping. These basic aspects of report preparation will now be discussed.

PRIMARY SOURCES OF INFORMATION

After the writer has a clear idea of the kind of report he is going to prepare and has done considerable thinking about the problem and its possible solution, he is ready to gather the information he needs. The sources he will use are of two kinds, *primary* and *secondary*. *Primary sources* provide first-hand information which has not been altered, abstracted, or interpreted. They include (1) company records, (2) observation, (3) experimentation, and (4) interrogation by means of interviews, letters, and questionnaires. *Secondary sources* consist chiefly of books, periodicals, and similar library materials which represent, in fact, the research of others and are borrowed for the reporter's immediate purpose. This section will deal with the primary sources, and the treatment of secondary sources will follow.

COMPANY RECORDS. Much or all of the information the reporter needs may already be in the company's possession. It may be in the form of letters, reports, or records of sales, financial transactions, personnel administration, purchases, or factory operations. Current or recent data may be readily available in the files, but older information may have to be sought in warehouse archives or microfilmed records. Examples of information that would be obtained from a company's records are (1) the company's contributions to charitable organizations over the past ten years, (2) the ratio of workers in various age categories, (3) the effects of a change in the company's marketing policy on sales and profit, (4) the estimated cost of a program of periodic replacement of light bulbs in the company's headquarters building, and (5) the reasons for the dismissal of employees.

OBSERVATION. Many types of information can be obtained only by personal observation. A study of the movement of store traffic, for example, would place the investigator at doors, stairways, escalators, and elevators to note directional flow, crowding, and other factors that might have a bearing on sales, display of merchandise, safety, and the like. An internal auditor will actually go into the teller's cage and observe his procedures in order to determine how well the rules governing transactions are being carried out. In other instances, an office manager will witness a demonstration of a new calculator before recommending purchase, and a restaurant chain will have its investigators regularly make observations regarding décor, cleanliness, and food service.

Observation is costly in time and often in travel expense. It requires a sharp use of the senses and the ability to record the results accurately. The objectivity of the process is very much in its favor, but this factor can be negated by a prejudiced or careless observer. However, at a time when so much communication is mediated through the eyes and ears of others, it becomes especially important for business to be able to get some data regarding physical phenomena through its own experienced and trusted analysts.

EXPERIMENTATION. Whereas observation entails the reporting of phenomena exactly as they are found, experimentation requires some alteration of the phenomena so that the results can be studied and applied to the solution of a business problem. For example, a mail-order advertiser may wish to know whether the color of the return envelope makes any difference in the number of orders received. For purposes of the experiment, the mailing list is divided so that every other name receives a blue return envelope instead of the white one sent to the others. All other conditions remain the same: both groups are sent the same advertisement on the same day by the same class of mail. When the returns are counted, any difference between the two groups may be attributed to the color of the envelope. The experiment can be repeated for verification of the results, and a number of different colors may be tested in the same way.

The particular way in which an experimental problem is solved is called "the design of the experiment." The design of the experiment cited above is graphically shown in Fig. 12.

Another type of experiment employs a control group to verify results. Some years ago, for example, the General Services Administration was interested to learn what effect air conditioning would have on work production. To measure results before and after the installation would not have given valid results because

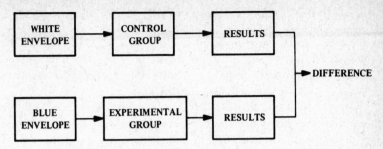

Fig. 12. Design of experiment described on pp. 220–222

an increase in production might be due to factors other than the air conditioning. To meet this objection a second office was set aside for control purposes. This office had the same general characteristics as the first and employed the same number of persons equally distributed as to sex and age. In both the first (experimental) and second (control) offices, new, brighter lighting was installed and the walls were painted. Only in the first, however, was the air conditioning installed. When the results showed production in the first office better by 10 per cent as well as a significant decline in absenteeism, the air conditioning was credited, and the broader use of air conditioning in government offices was recommended.

It should be observed that two variables (lighting and painting) were introduced into both groups, but that the third (air conditioning) was introduced only into the experimental group. The purpose was to avoid the "Hawthorne effect," [1] under which improvement in morale or production may take place not because of the introduction of the experimental factor, but because the participants have been singled out for special attention. By introducing new lighting and painting into both offices, the General Services Administration sought to insure that any difference in performance would be attributable to the air conditioning alone.

It should be further observed that other factors—like matching the size of the office, the kind of work, and the characteristics of

---

[1] So named after Western Electric's Hawthorne Works, near Chicago. There in 1927, Harvard sociologist Elton Mayo discovered the phenomenon when both an experimental and a control group responded equally well to the introduction of new lighting for the first group only.

the personnel—were equally important to the result. In this and other instances, the size of the sample chosen for the experiment, the selection of the sample, and the methods used to evaluate the results are also significant. It goes without saying that this method of investigation often employs the aid of the computer and requires some sophistication in mathematical skills.

INTERROGATION. When it becomes necessary to canvass a large number of people a questionnaire may be the only feasible method of research. Other methods of interrogation include the use of interviews and letters.

Letters. Letters serve well when they are sent to responsible parties and ask for specific information which can be given from the respondent's experience or records. A credit inquiry falls into this category, as does an inquiry asking for a company's experience with some business practice or policy that the inquirer is considering for his own organization. (See also "General Inquiries," pp. 80–81.)

Interviews. Interviews serve the same purpose as letters. They take more time; but they are more flexible, because the answers to the planned questions may lead to other questions and important but unforeseen avenues of knowledge. Interviews are also less inhibiting than correspondence and may elicit information that the interviewee would be reluctant to put in writing. In many instances of modern research, interviews are conducted on a large scale by professional interviewers using prepared questionnaires. "Open-end," or in-depth, interviews are also used to elicit information of a less organized sort, but the interviewers need to be especially well trained and perceptive if the results are to be meaningful. In some instances, the telephone is used, but considerable resistance has developed toward this method of inquiry and extreme care is necessary to avoid resentment.

Like persons receiving mailed questionnaires, interviewees must be selected to provide a valid sampling of the whole group when it is not feasible to interview everyone. In this respect interviewing has an advantage over the questionnaire in that, while the sample may be equally good in each instance, the interviews will bring more representative answers. The reason is that the questionnaire will be ignored by many people to whom it is sent, with the result that the sample will be altered. An interviewer, on the other hand, can get an answer from almost everyone or at least, through proper selection, insure that the sample will remain valid.

Questionnaires. Apart from the disadvantage previously cited, questionnaires have a great advantage over interviews in that the questions can be carefully controlled and are the same for everyone. The subjectivity of an interviewer, so often the cause of distortion—or his lack of diligence—cannot affect the results of the questionnaire. Also, the questionnaire can be answered at leisure and often evokes more accurate and more thoughtful answers. An example of a questionnaire that can be sent to everyone affected is that used by a business organization to check on the effectiveness of a course in its training program. All participants in the course are asked to answer questions about the strengths and weaknesses of the course and the performance of the instructor. A tabulation of the results goes into a report which makes recommendations for improvement. An example of a questionnaire employing a small sample is that used by an electrical appliance manufacturer to determine consumer preferences. Since canvassing all prospective users would be prohibitive, a small sample is selected to reflect the income, family status, and mode of living of the whole group. An analysis of the answers is used in planning the company's advertising and in making improvements in the design and performance of its products.

Questionnaires have a strong appeal for many researchers because they seem to put the burden of work on the recipients. The fact is that questionnaires can be worse than useless if great care is not taken in their construction and phrasing.

Types of Questions. The researcher contemplating the use of questionnaires should be familiar with the several types of questions he can ask.

1. The yes and no type. *Example:*

Are you married: Yes____   No____

2. Question asking for a single fact. *Example:*

How many people now live in your home?____

3. Multiple-choice question. This calls for either a factual or a qualitative answer.

Examples of factual multiple-choice questions:

(a) Check your approximate age group:
                                   ____Under 20
                                   ____20-29
                                   ____30-39
                                   ____40-49
                                   ____50-59
                                   ____59 or over

(b) Do you use bleach in your washing machine?

____Every time   ____Occasionally   ____Never

Examples of qualitative multiple-choice questions:

Examples of qualitative multiple-choice questions:

       (c) In general, how much influence do you feel the department head has in setting personnel policies?

           ____Much   ____Little   ____None

       (d) Evaluate the following aspects of your job by circling the number beside each question which most nearly expresses your evaluation:

             1 - Very poor
             2 - Poor
             3 - Average
             4 - Good
             5 - Very good
          NO - No opinion or question does not apply.

IBM Codes	Poor Good		
	←—— 1 2 3 4 5 NO ——→		
(76)	1 2 3 4 5 NO	7a.	Your office facilities
(77)	1 2 3 4 5 NO	7b.	Your present annual salary
Etc.			

4. Open-end question. This permits the respondent considerable freedom in his answer. Since numerical tabulation of such answers is not feasible, the answers are classified and summarized in capsule form. *Examples of open-end questions are:*

(a)   What is your "pet peeve" about the washing
      machine you now use?

(b)   What aspect of the training program did
      you find most helpful to you on the job?

Some Guiding Principles. For best results in phrasing and arranging questions, the following suggestions should be followed:

1. Be considerate of the reader's time. Limit the questions to those that are directly relevant to the purpose of the questionnaire, and make it possible to answer with the use of as few symbols as possible.

2. Avoid confusing questions. Confusion results from questions that sound alike, or don't apply to the particular respondent, or are open to a number of interpretations. For example, the owner of an air-conditionad car who has already answered a question about the "comfort" provided by the air conditioning system may later be confused when he comes across a question about its "cooling power."

3. Avoid leading questions. A leading question is one that suggests a particular answer as, for example, "Do you serve tasty Miracle Bread in your home?" This question is biased in favor of a "yes" answer. A question that would get more truthful, if less flattering, results would be, "What brand of packaged bread do you customarily use in your home?"

4. Avoid blanket questions. A blanket question is too general to elicit a classifiable or meaningful response. Thus, "Have you bought a washing machine *recently?*" could be interpreted to mean in the last few weeks, months, or years. A better question would be phrased:

Have you bought a washing machine:

_____in the last 3 months?
_____in the last 3 years?
_____more than 3 years ago?
_____I don't own a washing machine.

5. Ask personal questions with care. Questions about salary, religion, and personal habits are offensive to many respondents, and the answers are often distorted to conform to the image they would like to project rather than to the facts. Questionnaires that do not require the respondent to reveal his identity are, of course, less subject to these disadvantages.

6. Arrange the questions in some systematic or progressive order. As an example, the questions in a consumer preference survey may follow this arrangement:

(a) Questions intended to fix the relative social and family position of the respondent

(b) Short-answer questions about considerations that led to acquiring a particular possession

(c) Short-answer questions relating to considerations that will control a replacement of the possession

(d) Open-end questions asking for general comments, sugges- .tions, or complaints

Systematic order also requires the numbering or coding of answers to make tabulation easy either manually or by computer.

A postpaid envelope should always be included with the questionnaire. Sometimes, as an inducement to answer a questionnaire, the receiver is offered a copy of the tabulated results, or of the report based on the results. The letter accompanying the questionnaire should, in any case, state the reason for the questionnaire, assure the reader that its confidences will be kept, and win the reader's co-operation by its courtesy. Naturally, the reader is more willing to give up his time to answer the questionnaire if he is made to believe it will serve a valuable social purpose. As a final suggestion to the report writer, a copy of the questionnaire should always be included, preferably as an appendix, in the report which uses its findings.

SECONDARY SOURCES OF INFORMATION

A good reporter tries to benefit from the experience of others. It is certainly wasteful to investigate matters that others have already thoroughly investigated with perhaps greater resources than the present researcher has at his command. Thus the use of library

or "secondary" sources has very practical value. Some examples of
the kinds of information that can be obtained most conveniently
and perhaps exclusively from printed sources are stock exchange
records, economic indices, government statistics, statements of government and business leaders, editorial comment, biographical and
historical data, legislative and judicial proceedings, and the decisions of regulatory bodies.

Where to find such information is a real test of the investigator's
resourcefulness. The principal types of publications, with some
representative titles, are given in the following list. Additional
titles can be obtained from the sourcebooks named and from the
catalogs and reference books that are a feature of all well-stocked
libraries. But a word of caution: No matter how reliable and complete the facts, they must also be up-to-date. The user of printed
sources must therefore use great care to ascertain the date of his
facts and figures and to get the latest information available.

Selected References

STANDARD REFERENCE WORKS

Business Periodicals Index
Economic Almanac
Encyclopaedia Britannica
New York Times Index
Rand McNally Commercial Atlas and Marketing Guide
Reader's Guide to Periodical Literature
Wall Street Journal Index
Webster's Third New International Dictionary
Who's Who in America
World Almanac and Book of Facts

BIBLIOGRAPHIC GUIDES TO BUSINESS INFORMATION

Comans, Edward T., Jr. *Sources of Business Information.* Rev. ed. Berkeley:
University of California Press, 1964.
Johnson, H. Webster. *How to Use the Business Library, with Sources of Busi-
ness Information.* 3d ed. Cincinnati: South-Western Publishing Co., 1963.
Management Information Guide Series. Detroit: Gate Publishing Co., 1963.
Public Affairs Information Service Bulletin

BIBLIOGRAPHIES OF GOVERNMENT PUBLICATIONS

Andriot, John L. *U.S. Government Serials and Periodicals.* McLean, Va.: Documents Index, 1964.

Checklist of State Publications. Washington, D.C.: Library of Congress.
Monthly Catalog of U.S. Government Publications
Schmeckebier, Lawrence F. and Roy B. Eastin. *Government Publications and Their Use.* Rev. ed. Washington, D.C.: The Brookings Institution, 1969.
U.S. Department of Commerce Publications

STATISTICAL SOURCES

Handbook of Basic Economic Statistics. Washington, D.C.: Economics Statistics Bureau. Monthly.
U.S. Board of Governors of the Federal Reserve System. *Federal Reserve Bulletin.* Monthly.
U.S. Bureau of the Census. *Business Cycle Developments.* Monthly.
————. *Statistical Abstract of the United States.* Annually.
U.S. Bureau of Labor Statistics. *Monthly Labor Review.*
U.S. Department of Commerce. *Survey of Current Business.* Monthly.
Wasserman, Paul, *Statistics Sources.* 3rd ed. Detroit: Gale Research Co., 1970.

CORPORATE INFORMATION

The Fortune Directory
Moody's Manual of Investments
Standard Corporation Records
Thomas Register of American Manufacturers

BUSINESS AND FINANCIAL SERVICES

A number of services specialize in reporting and interpreting statutes and administrative decisions relating to labor, industrial relations, securities, banking, taxes, etc. The most prominent names in this field are Commerce Clearing House (CCH), Prentice-Hall (P-H), and the Bureau of National Affairs (BNA). Some representative publications:
  BNA Antitrust and Trade Regulation Reports
  BNA Tax Management
  CCH Standard Federal Tax Reporter
  CCH Labor Law Reports
  P-H Federal Tax Service
  P-H Industrial Relations

NOTE-TAKING

As he conducts his research activities, the writer should take notes in such a way that they will be useful to him in drafting the report. Notes must be legible, logically classified, and easily accessible. Slovenly notes on odd scraps of paper are likely to lead to waste of time in arranging and deciphering them and to lack of thoroughness in the report.

   To serve most efficiently, notes should be written on cards of uniform size, preferably 4 by 6 inches or larger. The names of books and other sources of information composing the bibliography should be kept on one set of cards, one entry to a card; and notes or quotations from these sources should be kept on other cards, one topic to a card. An exception to this rule may be made when lengthy notes are made from only one or several sources in some orderly arrangement. These notes may be most conveniently put on a legal size pad ($8\frac{1}{2}$ by 14 inches), with careful annotations of the sources, including page numbers.

   BIBLIOGRAPHY CARD. The bibliography card should include all the information needed for the footnotes and bibliography that will be part of the report. It should be complete enough to permit the writer or the reader to go to the original source without difficulty. The bibliography card for a book should contain the author's name (last name first), the title of the book, date and place of publication, and publisher's name. It should also include the volume number or number of volumes in the whole work, the edition, and the name of the series of which it may be a part. The library call number, placed in the upper right hand corner of the card, will make it easy to call for the book again, should it be necessary. (Fig. 13.)

```
                                             HF5549
                                             .5C6
        Bassett, Glenn A.                    .B3



        The New Face of Communication

        New York:  American Management Association, 1968

        204 pp.
```

Fig. 13. Bibliography card (book)

The bibliography card for an article should bear the name of the author, title of the article, the name of the book or magazine in which the article appears, the volume number and date of the publication, and the inclusive page numbers. (Fig. 14.)

Janis, J. Harold

"The Writing Behavior of Businessmen"

Journal of Communication, vol. 15 (June 1965)
pp.81-88

Fig. 14. Bibliography card (article)

NOTE CARD. The note card should have the name of the topic at the top, and the researcher's notes or direct quotations from the source directly below. At the end, the notes should be identified by the last name of the author, the title (or shortened title) of the book or article, and the page reference. Only one side of the card should be used. Direct quotations should be copied carefully within quotation marks and the exact spelling and punctuation of the source should be observed. If the reporter wishes to omit any part of the quoted passage, he should use ellipses (see Part 4, Section IX, "Punctuation") to show the omission. (Fig. 15.)

The use of underlining for the names of books and periodicals and quotation marks for the names of articles and chapters will help the writer separate the two types of sources. A single alphabetical file of the bibliography cards by name of author (or title of the work, if no author is indicated) and another file of the note cards by subject will make reference easy. Records and notes of interviews, lectures, and speeches experienced first-hand by the

```
Employer-employee communication

     "The subordinate who brings to his manager
bad news . . . may well be doing the manager a
service by mentioning the trouble before it
becomes any more severe, but he may also have
to bear the brunt of the manager's ire for
being the bearer of bad news. . . .

Bassett, Communication, p. 95
```

Fig. 15. Note card

reporter, may be entered on cards in much the same fashion as the
bibliographical entries and notes.

Review Problems

1. Name and explain the criteria by which a business report is judged.
(This question relates to the introduction to Part 3, "Business Reports.")

2. What are the differences between an informational report and an analytical
report? Between an informal report and a formal report?

3. Name and discuss briefly the factors that determine the type of report.

4. Distinguish between primary and secondary sources of information and
name the principal types of each.

5. Design an experiment for a study of the relative effects of window display and newspaper advertising on the sales of a retail store. Explain the
design in words and graphics.

6. Develop a questionnaire to elicit from fellow classmates information about
their educational and career goals. Assume that this information will eventually
be passed on to the Curriculum Committee of your school for their guidance.

7. Name a specific business topic in which you have a special interest, and
develop a bibliography of at least a dozen books and articles that would serve
as a preliminary guide in the study of the subject.

16
Organizing Report Data

During the course of his investigation and note-taking, the writer has little time to reflect on the way each fragment of information will ultimately serve him in the finished report. When the preliminary work is done, however, he needs a period of assimilation during which he may again give careful thought to the purpose of his report and attempt to establish a logical relationship between his seemingly scattered facts. Although much of this thinking will be lacking in definite form, he should—after a while—take overt steps toward the realization of the report. These steps will consist of, first, classifying the data and, second, arranging the data in the most effective order. The third step, the construction of an outline, is a logical accompaniment of the first two steps and a necessary prelude to the actual writing.

CLASSIFICATION OF DATA

Classification is the sorting of data into homogeneous groups. The aim, in essence, is to keep like data together so that they may be more easily dealt with and their relationship established. The alternative is an undigested and disorganized mass of material that represents the writer's confusion and eventually leads to the reader's. Fortunately, the writer comes to his task with some ready notions of the main classes or divisions into which his data will fall. He probably had some ideas about the organization of the report before he began his research; he also had the opportunity to examine his information while gathering it and to make trial classifications in the process. In the end, it is not unlikely that his general plan, at least, will bear a resemblance to that of other reports. The reason is that, over-all, most report data fall into a few broad classes, and the organization of a report is therefore never completely unique.

A SIMPLE CLASSIFICATION. The simplest division of material is a familiar one, for it is applicable not only to business reports, but to other forms of business composition as well:

```
  I. Introduction
 II. Body
III. Conclusion
```

Although the parts of a business report may not bear these names, the names do describe the three kinds of material found in most reports.

Introduction. The introduction tells the reader what he has to know in order to understand the significance of the data that follow. Depending on the length and nature of the report, any or all of the following points may be treated:

1. Authorization for the report
2. Purpose of the report
3. Scope and limits of the report
4. Statement of the problem
5. Organization of the report
6. History or background of the subject
7. Method of investigation
8. Sources of information
9. Definition of terms
10. Acknowledgments
11. Abstract, or summary, of the report
12. Summary of conclusions and recommendations

Body. The body is usually the main part of the report, containing the research data and the discussion. Here is the support for whatever conclusions are drawn. The specific contents are suggested by the following kinds of information, only a few of which would probably be used in a single report:

1. Analysis of present conditions; strengths and weaknesses

2. Details of structure, functions, methods
3. Proposals
4. Evidence, reasoning, testimony, and other forms of proof
5. Use of "models," mathematical or graphic
6. Narrative or chronology
7. Procedures: past, present, proposed
8. Causes and effects
9. Comparison of data
10. Alternatives
11. Advantages and disadvantages
12. Summary tables and charts

Conclusion. Many short informational reports are complete without conclusions. When conclusions are used in any report, however, they may treat information in these categories:
1. Summary of purpose and main points
2. Significance of the data
3. Inferences to be drawn from the data
4. Recommendations
5. Anticipated results

SOME OTHER CLASSIFICATIONS. The division of material into introduction, body, and conclusion is a good starting point for the study of the organization of reports, but it has its limitations. For one thing, the names are too general. In the instance of the term *body* especially, not enough guidance is given as to the kinds of data that will be found. Another limitation is that the order suggested is not always the order best suited to the writer's purpose. A common variation of the classification is:

```
  I. Statement of problem
 II. Recommendations
III. Supporting data
```

Here the nature of the contents is more clearly defined by the names of the topics. Furthermore, there is a radical departure in the order, in that the recommendations (conclusion) follow the data instead of preceding them as in the earlier classification. More

detailed divisions of material and further variations in the order
are evident in the classifications that follow:

A	B
I. Introduction	I. Background
II. Analysis of problem	II. Faults of present system
III. Proposed solution	III. Alternatives
IV. Anticipated results	IV. Recommendations
V. Recommendations	V. Conclusion

C

```
  I. Introduction
 II. Recommendations
III. Background
 IV. Present procedure
  V. Proposed procedure
 VI. Conclusions
```

ARRANGEMENT OF DATA

As the preceding examples show, the mere fact of classifying
data may automatically suggest the best sequence to be followed.
However, the samples deal with the main divisions of the report
only, and even these provide some choice with respect to order.
Furthermore, as the main divisions are subdivided, new classifications become necessary and additional questions arise as to the
best arrangement to follow.

GENERAL SEQUENCE. The choice that has the broadest implica-
tions for the finished report is that relating to the juxtaposition of
data and conclusions. In the interests of objectivity, a good report
is developed inductively. That is, the writer forms his conclusions
after he has made his investigation and studied the results. True,
he will begin with certain hypotheses or tentative conclusions
which the evidence will either support or reject. But that is quite
different from forming one's conclusions first and then searching
for evidence to support them. This last method can only lead to
serious omissions and biased results.

Having developed his conclusions inductively, however, the
writer still has the choice of presenting his conclusions at the beginning or at the end of his report. There is something to be said

on both sides. Conclusions are usually more convincing when they follow the supporting data, and this order is certainly more effective when the reader has an initial bias against the conclusions. However, an important quality of reports is convenience to the reader, and when the solution to a business problem is uppermost in an executive's mind, it is annoying to have to wade through page after page of dry data before discovering what the writer's recommendations are. For that reason there is a definite preference in organizations for an initial statement of conclusions and recommendations. Even when it seems desirable to hold the full details of these parts for the end, summaries may be presented in the introduction.

SEQUENCE IN THE PARTS. Quite independently of the decision regarding the position of the conclusions, other decisions must be made with regard to the order to be followed in both the larger and smaller units of the report. Fortunately, the writer can choose from a number of standard patterns or arrangements, the exact choice in each case depending on the nature of the material treated. These patterns include the order of (1) time, (2) space, (3) importance, (4) interest or familiarity, (5) comparison and contrast, and (6) support.

Time. In a narrative report or the narrative parts of a report, events may be arranged in the order of their occurrence, or chronological order. Thus a transaction may be traced from the placing of the order, through acceptance, shipment, and payment. In other instances, inverse chronological order is preferred. In this order, the last event is described first, and the others are related backward in time. A job résumé uses this order in the parts dealing with education and work experience, where the last school attended and the last job held are presumably more pertinent and hold more interest for the employer than the earlier experiences.

A time sequence is used in many reports dealing with business operations. The before-after and present-future techniques are especially valuable. Examples of these orders in outline form are shown below:

```
 I.  Conditions before installation of X machine
II.  Conditions after installation of X machine

 I.  Present method
II.  Proposed method
```

Space. Some parts of reports lend themselves to the arrangement of data according to space, position, or geography. If a number of different plant sites are being considered, they may be taken up in some geographical order as uptown-downtown, city-suburbs, east-west, north-south. A company's study of cafeteria operations might include a description of the flow of traffic, from the entrance to the various parts of the serving line, to the cashier, the table area, and the exit. The description of a factory or company's head-quarters might similarly take the reader to the outside, then the inside, stopping at the various floors in a sequence designed to reveal the company's operations most clearly. Other spatial orders are clockwise and counterclockwise, from left to right and vice versa, and from the center to the periphery and vice versa.

Importance. When a number of parallel ideas are to be treated as, for example, reasons, points, proposals, or advantages, the arrangement is usually that of the most important to the least important. Thus the reader's interest is captured at the start. When the points are to lead to the conclusion, however, there is the danger that the reader's interest will be lost before the conclusion is reached. In such an instance, the ideas may be arranged climactically. Another plan is to put the conclusion (or summary of the conclusion) first, followed by the supporting data in anticlimactic order (most important point first).

Interest or Familiarity. Data are often arranged to capture the interest of the reader, regardless of other reasons. For example, telling the reader in the beginning how the report came to be written and what it proposes to do is necessary not only to aid the reader's understanding, but to involve his curiosity and interest, so that he will read further. Similarly, ideas that evoke recognition are more likely to capture interest than those that are new or strange. Thus the reader will be led from the familiar to the unfamiliar, and from the known to the unknown. For example, a survey of a company's duplicating machine requirements will probably move from such standbys as the Ditto and Mimeograph to the more expensive and sophisticated photo-offset and electro-static machines. The report will probably also take up the familiar uses of the duplicating machines before going into the possibilities for professional print-shop work.

Comparison and Contrast. Similarities and differences are

pointed up by means of comparison and contrast. The before-after technique already mentioned is one form of comparison. Other examples might include:

```
I.   Advantages
II.  Disadvantages

I.   Analysis of incoming orders
II.  Analysis of outgoing orders

I.   Panic of 1907
II.  Wall Street crash of 1929

I.   Features of Machine A
II.  Features of Machine B
```

Such arrangements conveniently group a great many details and make for an easy and orderly progression. They also suggest the possibility of alternation, or the rotation or matching of points, as the following example shows:

```
I.   Features of Machine A
         A. Space requirements
         B. Performance
         C. Cost

II.  Features of Machine B
         A. Space requirements
         B. Performance
         C. Cost
```

Support. Any data leading to a conclusion may be arranged in one of two patterns, called the orders of support. These are the *inductive* and *deductive* orders. The *inductive order*, as an earlier reference in this chapter indicated, proceeds from an examination of the facts, reasons, or evidence (the specific), to the conclusion derived from those data (the general). The *deductive order* proceeds from the conclusion (the general) to the supporting data (the specific). Like the report as a whole, the individual parts may follow either order, though some consistency should be observed. In a series of parallel sections, for example, all the sections should be either inductively or deductively arranged. Within each section, however, individual paragraphs may be developed one way or the other. This often means simply that the topic sentence may come at the end or the beginning of the paragraph. There is some preference for putting the topic sentences at the beginning because they aid comprehension. In the larger units of the report, consideration should be given not only to the reader's convenience, but also to his feelings about the subject: the less likely that the reader will accept the conclusion, the more reason for using the inductive order, that is, withholding the conclusion until the supporting evidence has been given.

A comparison of the inductive and deductive orders in a report context may be made with the help of the following examples:

Inductive Order

According to the Unit's manual of procedures, bids on meat and poultry are to be obtained on a quarterly basis. The temporary Chief improved on this system and shopped for meats on a weekly basis. When the cook prepared the weekly menus to determine the quantities of the various items needed, she submitted the list to the Chief. He then telephoned three vendors to receive quotations on the items. After a comparison of prices, he placed orders for the items at the best price. Although this is not the usual procedure of sending out regular quarterly requests for bids, it is apparently feasible and has made reductions in cost possible. It is therefore recommended that the Service Division continue the practice of obtaining weekly bids on food purchases.

Deductive Order

The system of obtaining food bids on a weekly basis has reduced food costs and should be continued. According to the Unit's manual of procedures, bids on meat and poultry are to be obtained on a quarterly basis. The temporary Chief improved on this system and shopped for meats on a weekly basis. When the cook prepared the weekly menu to determine the quantities of the various items needed, she submitted the list to the Chief. He then telephoned three vendors and received quotations on the items. After a comparison of prices, he placed orders for the items

at the best price. Although this is not the usual
procedure of sending out regular quarterly requests
for bids, it is apparently effective.

MAKING THE OUTLINE

Probably the best aid to good organization in the report is a
carefully constructed outline. Although the outline for a short
report is easily contained in one's head, the relationships in a
longer report are usually so involved that only a written outline
can serve the writer's purpose. Such an outline should provide a
place for at least every *class* of data and thus give the reporter an
opportunity to see the relevance of his material and the connection
between the parts. In the outlining process, he may find that some
of the collected data will have to be thrown out, that some new
data are needed, and that his preliminary ideas about the form of
the report and its content will have to undergo some change.

A written outline may be useful for other reasons as well. It may
be called for by a superior to satisfy himself that a report in process
conforms to his wishes, or it may be submitted to any other interested party for evaluation before time is spent (or wasted) in
writing up the finished report. If the outline is done well, it will
also serve as the basis for the table of contents, and the topics may
be transferred to the report itself to serve as headings and subheadings, often without change in phrasing. When a report is prepared
by a team, outlines for each share of the work are necessary, so
that the parts may be brought into consistent and proportionate
relationship.

KINDS OF OUTLINES. Outlines may be classified as formal or
informal. An informal outline is one that exists only in the mind
of the user or consists of a few scratches on paper as reminders of
the topics to be covered and the order to be followed. A formal
outline is always written, with the parts carefully numbered to
show their relation. The formal outline is of two kinds: (1) sentence outline and (2) topic outline. The sentence outline is
constructed of full sentences so that the outline constitutes an
abbreviated narrative report (Fig. 16). The topic outline consists
of short phrases only (Fig. 17). When an outline is required to be

A STUDY OF THE POST OFFICE BOX COLLECTION PLAN

I. The present method of handling cash receipts is far from
   efficient.
   A. Handling incoming checks used to take 3-5 days.
   B. Steps taken to shorten time have not succeeded.
   C. The Post Office Collection Box Plan offers a possible
      solution.

II. The present method has been in use for the past 8 years.
   A. Mail is picked up by the company's trucks at local post
      offices.
   B. A cash report is prepared for the cashier by the Mail
      Department.
   C. The cashier examines each check for
      1. Post-dating
      2. Name of payee
      3. Signature
      4. Agreement of written and figure amounts
   D. Verified checks are deposited, with each check listed on
      deposit slip.

Fig. 16. Part of a sentence outline

submitted for approval before a report is written or spoken, preference is sometimes shown for the sentence outline, for it provides
better understanding of the report than the topic outline. However, the topic outline is by far the favorite of report writers because it is easier to construct, takes less time, and makes the parts
of the report stand out more prominently for examination and
possible rearrangement.

REPORT ON THE ADVISABILITY OF OPENING A WAREHOUSE
IN CHICAGO

I. Present warehouse facilities
   A. Historical background
   B. Locations of present warehouses
      1. Areas served by present warehouses
      2. Distances from present warehouses to new mar-
         kets in Middle West
   C. Evaluation of services of present warehouses
      1. Condition of materials after shipment to
         Middle West
      2. Routing problems

Fig. 17. A topical outline

```
        3. Time factors
           a. Mail communication
           b. Rail, truck, and air schedules
 II. New markets in Middle West
     A. Results of market survey
        1. Areas of greatest potential profit
        2. Other areas of possible concern
     B. Experiences of competitors in Middle West
        1. Alton Company
        2. Bryson Brothers, Inc.
        3. The Fairlawn Services Company
III. Effects of new warehouse in Chicago
     A. Advantages to those who wholesale our products
        1. Proximity to warehouse
        2. Increase in diversity of products available
        3. Lower delivery costs
     B. Advantages to those who retail our products
        1. Assurance of stocks when needed
        2. Increase in diversity of products available
        3. Lower wholesale costs
     C. Advantages to our company
        1. Proximity to new and expanding markets
        2. Diversification of markets
        3. Increase in storage space
        4. Stabilization of production
     D. Disadvantages to our company
        1. Keen competition
        2. Increase in shipping costs
        3. Acceptance or regional economic risks
 IV. Conclusion:  Evidence weighted in favor of estab-
     lishment of new warehouse
  V. Recommendations
     A. That the president submit a favorable report on
        the proposal to the Board of Directors
     B. That a company representative be assigned to
        locate several possible sites for the new ware-
        house
```

NUMBERING SCHEMES. Part of the value of an outline is the identification of each point in such a way as to show its relation to all other points. The numbering scheme used in the outline in Fig. 17 provides such identification. If further subdivisions of material are required, they may be represented by arabic numbers in parentheses and small letters in parentheses as in the following skeleton. However, it is seldom necessary and usually undesirable, to have so many subdivisions.

```
 I. First degree division
    A. Second degree division
       1. Third degree division
       2. Third degree division
    B. Second degree division
       1. Third degree division
          a. Fourth degree division
          b. Fourth degree division
             (1) Fifth degree division
             (2) Fifth degree division
                 (a) Sixth degree division
                 (b) Sixth degree division
       2. Third degree division.
II. First degree division
```

In scientific work, a preference is shown for a decimal system of numbering; the following is an example:

```
1.   First degree division
     1.1  Second degree division
          1.1.1  Third degree division
          1.1.2  Third degree division
     1.2  Second degree division
          1.2.1 Third degree division
              1.2.1.1  Fourth degree division
              1.2.1.2  Fourth degree division
          1.2.2 Third degree division
          1.2.3 Third degree division
2.   First degree division
     2.1  Second degree division
          2.1.1 Third degree division
          2.1.2 Third degree division
```

PRINCIPLES OF CONSTRUCTION. In addition to having a consistent numbering scheme, the outline should follow certain other principles concerned with clarifying the relationship between the parts:

1. The number of main topics should be few—several, perhaps a half dozen, in a report of up to twenty pages or so; more, in a longer report. The number of subdivisions and the number of topics listed under the subdivision should also be limited.

2. The relationship between topics should be shown by their ranking in the outline. Topics should not be given equal rank when, in fact, some are subordinate to others. One should be suspicious of an outline that consists, for example, of all main topics or has, at best, very little subordination. Compare the confusing welter of topics in the first outline below with the more manageable classification in the second.

IMPROVING CONTROL OF COLLECTION FEES

I. Billing procedure	I. Billing procedure
II. Requirements of good internal control	A. Requirements of good internal control
III. Present billing procedure	B. Present procedure
IV. Modifications needed to meet requirements	C. Modifications needed to meet requirements
V. Accounting for fees received	II. Accounting for fees received
VI. Recommendations for improvement	A. Present method
VII. Forms for filling and recording fees	B. Recommendations for improvement
	III. Forms for billing recording fees

3. Single subheadings should be avoided because any division of a topic normally presumes at least two subtopics. If a second topic cannot be created, the single subtopic can be absorbed into the topic to which it belongs. An exception to this rule can be made when the single subtopic marks the use of an example.

Illogical   *Logical*

III. Extent of damage   III. Extent of damage
     A. Upper three floors   A. Upper three floors gutted
         gutted   B. Roof destroyed

                               III. Damage to upper three floors only

Acceptable

```
II.   Public service advertising
      A.  Ex.:  Mobil Oil Company
```

4. The phrasing of topics should be reasonably consistent. If a topical outline is used, full sentences should be avoided. In other respects, too, the phrasing of topics of the same rank should generally follow the same grammatical pattern.

Poor

```
II.   Qualities of Yarn 4Y
      A.  High tensile strength        (noun phrase)
      B.  Won't lose its color         (verb phrase)
      C.  Moisture resistant           (adjective phrase)
```

Better

```
II.   Qualities of Yarn 4Y
      A.  High tensile strength        (noun phrase)
      B.  Color fastness               (noun phrase)
      C.  Resistance to moisture       (noun phrase)
```

Review Problems

1. What is the purpose of classifying data when preparing to write a report?

2. Name a simple classification of data for reports and tell what each category may include.

3. Discuss the overall organization of an analytical report. What alternatives does the writer have? What factors influence his choice?

4. Name and describe the principal ways of arranging data within specific parts of the report.

5. What is the difference between the inductive and the deductive order, and when is one to be preferred over the other?

6. After an investigation of the subject, write a topic outline for the report mentioned in Chapter 15, Problem 7.

17
Report Language

Following the investigation of the topic and the organization of the data, the writer is ready to compose the report. This is a crucial step, for even the most diligent preparation will have been for nothing if the writer cannot put his thoughts into words. An initial responsibility in this respect is that of observing the ordinary requirements of good English. Businessmen have very strong feelings on this subject and are inclined to regard grammatical errors, misspelling, and improper word use by a subordinate as a serious reflection on the organization and a stain on the writer's record. But in addition to the need to write correctly, there is the need to write effectively, that is, clearly, interestingly, and persuasively. Such a result depends largely on the way the writer deals with three major problems. The first relates to the objectivity he maintains. The second relates to the degree of formality the language reflects. The third relates to the writer's efforts to make the report easy to read.

OBJECTIVITY

Objectivity, or the lack of bias, is an important quality in a report because it is the measure of the trust the reader can place in the document. Objectivity can be upset by leaving out significant data that run contrary to the writer's desired conclusions or by giving a disproportionate amount of space to data favoring his prejudices. This technique, called "slanting," is avoided by the conscientious reporter. For the most part, however, the degree of objectivity is controlled by the writer's use of language, particularly his ability to distinguish among *facts, value judgments,* and *conclusions.*

FACTS. Facts are statements about the things the writer has observed or experienced. They can be verified and carry the weight of evidence. No matter how bad judgments or conclusions may be, a report will still have considerable value if it gives the reader factual data from which he can form his own judgments and reach his own conclusions. Most reports abound in facts; some consist only of facts. Examples of factual statements follow:

Four out of the eleven banks studied do not have an educational loan program.

The Traffic Payment Department currently consists of a department head and sixteen clerks.

The operator runs a tape of the cards, simultaneously punching the dollar amount into the keysort card.

Monday is the heaviest cash receipt day.

VALUE JUDGMENTS. Value judgments are expressions of the writer's approval or disapproval. Since value judgments are personal and biased, and also usually vague, they do not contribute materially to the report except when they are offered as the opinions of experts. The following statements are examples of value judgments:

The fees charged for these services are excessive.

The offices are attractively furnished and provide a pleasant atmosphere for work.

Mr. Smith proved himself to be thoroughly incompetent in the new job.

Ways of improving these statements are shown in the discussion that follows.

CONCLUSIONS. Conclusions are inferences the writer makes from the information presented; their strength depends on the validity of the information and the logic with which they are drawn. Value judgments may qualify as conclusions if they are

supported by concrete evidence. Extreme or intemperate statements, however, should always be avoided. In the following re-
visions of the examples above, the value judgment has been elimi-
nated from the first example, retained in the second, and modified
in the third. The conclusions in all three examples (shown by
underlining) are now supported by facts.

<u>The fees charged for these services appear to be in-
consistent with those charged by other companies.</u>
Estimates received indicate . . . .

The offices are completely carpeted and furnished with
new double pedestal walnut desks. Flush ceiling
illumination, central air conditioning, and walls hung
with contemporary art complete the setting and <u>provide
a pleasant atmosphere for work.</u>

Mr. Smith was charged with four errors last month. One
of them involved a difference of $2,800. In another
instance . . . . <u>All in all, Mr. Smith's performance
is well below that which we expect of an employee in
his position</u>.

Even when a value judgment seems amply supported by facts, it
is often better not to express it. For instance, in the last example
immediately above, the writer could still be charged with bias,
especially if the report did not examine the records of other employees in similar positions. Such a charge would more easily be
avoided if the final sentence were omitted and the reader were
permitted to draw any conclusion he wished.

A weakness of many conclusions is known in logic as "the hasty
generalization." This is a sweeping statement not supported by the
evidence. For example, a writer reports that a prospective employee
has a degree in mathematics. "This proves," the writer states,
"that he is qualified for the position of systems analyst." The fact
proves nothing of the sort. It would be fairer, and more convincing, to say that the applicant "has the educational background in
mathematics for the job." The second statement can be supported;
the first cannot.

As this discussion has attempted to show, good report style is
even-tempered, rational, and free of prejudice. It does not always
shirk judgments, but it leans to fair conclusions amply supported

by facts. In any case, the writer is well advised to cultivate caution and, when prudence suggests, to seek protection from over-statements in such terms as "the facts suggest," "it seems likely that," and "probably."

FORMALITY

A question that every report writer must resolve is the degree of formality to observe in the language of the report. Two styles can be identified. The *personal style* is characterized by the use of *I* and *we* and a direct, sometimes conversational, manner. The *impersonal style*, on the other hand, avoids personal pronouns and, instead, refers to the writer, if at all, as "the writer," "the analyst," "the investigator," etc. In other instances the reference to the writer is avoided by the use of the passive voice and other circumlocutions. For example, he may say, "A bid was obtained," instead of "I obtained a bid"; "the evidence shows," instead of "I believe"; and "it is recommended," instead of "I recommend." The effect ranges from natural (but not colloquial) to fairly stiff. The following examples are representative:

Personal Style (Informal):

For the first half of 19--, my preliminary data on cooperative advertising for the New England Division shows that seven District Offices ordered 3,956 mats for bulk distribution to wholesalers. During the same period we paid $36,920 to 163 wholesalers as our share of their advertising. From the information we have, I'd be inclined to conclude that here in the East at least one-half of our wholesalers are using some part of our advertising and promotion program.

Personal Style (Formal):

We recommend a reduction of five men from the maintenance way gang. We are of the opinion that the reduction of five should comprise two track walkers and three laborers. The lack of specific unit and cost performance data on the total program makes it virtually impossible to measure current efficiencies. We suggest, however, that extending the maintenance cycle in the following areas will produce these reductions.

Impersonal Style (Natural):

Invoices applying to deliveries and shipments received
are audited by the field units and any errors in
quantity billed, prices, or computation are corrected
before the invoices are forwarded to the central office
for payment. Because delivery men cannot be kept
waiting while these invoices are checked and because
some shipments are received from out-of-town vendors,
the vendors' copy of an invoice cannot be corrected at
the time of delivery. In order to reduce clerical work
at the field units, the handling of adjustment notifi-
cation is assigned to the Accounts Payable Department.

Impersonal Style (Formal):

Tabulation I also shows that there are 176.59 excess
hours per month in the night file clerk position. It
is therefore suggested that in addition to work from
peak periods, work from the day force be assigned to
the night force. Perhaps some of the pulling for vault
papers, treasury bills, and/or bond maturities could
be delegated to them . . . . The analyst will be glad
to work with the Supervisor in determining the hours
required for each of the suggested jobs and the
possibilities for redistribution to the night force.

It is hard to issue any flat rules for the choice of style. The tendency is to use the personal style (informal or formal) in a report
that takes the form of a letter or memorandum. In a long or formal
report the writer will use any style except the informal personal
style. In the parts of many reports, the question of using personal pronouns is academic because the writer must concentrate
on things and processes rather than on his reaction to them. In
other reports the *I* must give way to *we* because the report is issued
by a group or represents the collective efforts of several persons.

In general, it may be said that the impersonal style is regarded as
more objective than the personal style, but that the personal style
is quite acceptable in situations in which the writer has considerable authority or expertness, or is intimately connected with the
decision-making process. Even then, however, restraint in using
the pronoun *I* is advised.

READING EASE

Making a report easy to read requires consideration for the reader's vocabulary, his time, and his powers of concentration. In recent years a great deal of attention has been given to this phase of composition because of the increasing volume of reports and other reading matter that comes across the executive's desk. A pioneer in "readability" is Rudolf Flesch, whose research spawned a number of books on the subject.[1] Largely as a result of his efforts, there is now a strong awareness of the problem and of the techniques for treating it.

LEVELS OF DIFFICULTY. As might be expected, readability does not impose rigid standards of diction. What is easy for one reader may be difficult for another, and vice versa. A particularly important point relates to the use of jargon. In its favorable sense, jargon is the technical vocabulary used by those engaged in a particular calling. When it is commonly understood by the parties to a communication, it becomes a sort of shorthand that gets the message across quickly, authoritatively, and much more accurately than is possible with ordinary language.

Jargon is characteristic of most internal reports and is recommended when it performs the function just described. It is not recommended when the report is expected to reach individuals not familiar with the vocabulary. Since the reader's level of understanding is not always known, however, many writers take the practical course of defining technical terms or using a more general level of diction altogether. The following examples show vocabulary treatments on several different levels of difficulty:

Technical Level:
```
Data in core memory of the Honeywell 110 computer may
be in binary form as a six-bit character, or as a
signed decimal number.  Instructions are variable in
length.  Hardware interrupt is a standard feature of
the central processor, which enables automatic
branching between the main program and service
routines.  Simultaneous I/O operation with computing
is possible through two read/write channels, one of
which is optional.
```

[1] See, for example, Flesch, *The Art of Readable Writing* (New York: Harper & Row, 1949).

Management Level:

The Railroad's general practice is to use new material
in its replacement program. When high quality used
rail and used creosoted ties can be purchased at a
suitable price they are used in lieu of new material.
It should be pointed out that used creosoted ties
have a substantially longer life than new untreated oak
ties normally used. The General Transportation Company
manufactures the oak ties from used pilings and sells
the ties to the Railroad Company at labor cost
(carpenters' time).

General Level:

Our Borehole Televiewer was patented in 1968. This
instrument records the "fractures," or cracks, through
which an oil well is drilled, and indicates the
direction in which such fractures run. The Borehole
Televiewer works even when the well is filled with oil
or drilling mud, and can probe miles below the earth's
surface with such precision that fractures as fine as
1/32 of an inch can be detected. Locating fractures
is a key element in the discovery and production of oil
and gas.

TREATING UNDESIRABLE JARGON. A type of jargon not favorably
regarded in any circumstances is the stilted, pretentious, and obscure language often associated with business writing. This is an
example:

Poor

It is considered that the increased responsibility
assumed will be balanced by the diminished ineffectual
intelligence originating in the department activities
of the various subdivisions delegated under the new
setup. Each will be responsible for its own. Pending
the reissue of the organizational procedure to be
adopted, it will be deemed sufficient for our purposes
if unco-ordinated activity be confined to those
specific groups not immediately concerned and then only
on such matters as are not within the scope of the
above. Any retroactive action will be considered at
a later date.

The difficulties of reading and understanding this kind of writing are evident. Several remedies are suggested. They include (1) striving for conciseness, (2) keeping sentences and paragraphs within reasonable length, (3) avoiding stereotyped expressions, and (4) using the active voice wherever the style and sense permit. These techniques are discussed and demonstrated in Chapter 5, "Essentials of Style," so it is necessary to indicate here only their pertinence to reports.

Conciseness. Too often wordiness in the report is due to the writer's failure to assimilate his data and reduce it to its simplest and clearest terms. Apart from a thorough understanding of his subject and a logical organization of his thoughts, the writer must find the time and discipline to edit his work with a strong hand. The following examples show what such editing can accomplish:

Poor

```
I have surveyed the present rubbish disposal arrange-
ments and find that the utilization of metal bins
would satisfy the current requirements relative to
specific protection.
```

Improved

```
Putting the rubbish in metal bins would meet all
sanitary and safety requirements.
```

Poor

```
The Company recognizes that the success of the
organization is entirely dependent upon the competence
of the men and women who comprise its staff.
```

Improved

```
The Company's success depends on the competence and
character of its staff.
```

Sentence and Paragraph Length. Despite the desirability of short sentences and paragraphs, they are sometimes difficult to achieve in technical discussions. Some methods of treating the problem are, however, available. A long paragraph may be broken after the topic statement or before the conclusion. It may also be broken at some convenient transition in the middle. Paragraphs of twelve or fifteen lines are tolerable, but shorter ones should predominate, and an occasional paragraph of two to four lines provides emphasis and welcome variety. With a little editing, long sentences can also be broken up, as the following example shows:

Poor

The key factor in the plummeting injury rate lies in the steel industry's underlying belief that safety must be regarded as an integral element of operations because instead of just producing steel and adding safety as an afterthought, the companies plan the safe production of steel, and everything from engineering through education and enforcement is designed to that end.   (One sentence of 59 words.)

Improved

The plummeting injury rate did not just happen. Perhaps the key factor lies in the steel industry's underlying belief that safety must be regarded as an integral element of operations. Companies don't just produce steel and add safety as an afterthought. They plan the safe production of steel, and everything from engineering through education and enforcement is designed to that end.

(Four sentences of 8, 22, 11, and 20 words.)

Unstereotyped Language. Stale writing discourages interest and does an injustice to fresh data. The narrative portions of reports tend to discourage the use of stereotyped expressions, but a good deal of stiltedness may find its way into the beginning, the end, and the transitional parts.

Poor	*Improved*
Pursuant to your request, I am submitting herewith a report on	Here is the report you asked for on
as per company policy	following company policy

Poor	*Improved*
the cost of said repairs	the cost of the repairs
the subject study	this study
in view of the above	for these reasons
we hereby recommend	we recommend

Active Voice. The directness of the active voice has much to commend it over the indirectness of the passive voice, as the following example indicates:

Passive (awkward)   *Active (better)*

In the survey, attention will be focused on areas that may not have been considered by the manufacturers before.

The survey will focus attention on areas the manufacturers may not have considered before.

Desirable as the active voice is, however, it is not always feasible when the style of the report is formal and the writer wishes to avoid reference to himself. The passive voice is also necessary whenever the writer wishes to put emphasis on acts performed rather than on the agent who performs them.

Passive (approved)

The investigation was made during the two-week period ending January 20.

Numeric codes can be supplied for all messages originating in the warehouses.

Three committees were organized to deal with the basic areas of interest.

The cost-estimating system should be replaced with a more efficient one.

CONNECTION BETWEEN IDEAS. When reports extend beyond several paragraphs, as they usually do, the connection between the parts presents a special readability problem. The reader—especially the hurried or harassed reader—must often be able to sense the meaning without concentrating on every word. But even if he were to read every word, he would appreciate any effort of the writer to make reading easy and meaning clear. Some of the techniques for achieving smooth transition are discussed in Chapter 6, "Plan and Construction of the Letter." They include the use of connecting words and phrases, connecting sentences, and the numbering of parallel ideas. Although these techniques apply as well to reports as to letters, the scale of their application is somewhat broader, as the following discussion will show:

Visual Reference. A report of more than a page or two is best broken up into smaller parts and sections which are labeled to show their content and relation to each other. The headings may often be transferred verbatim from the outline. Through this technique, the frame of the report becomes immediately visible to the reader. The display aids the appearance of the page, eases the tension of reading, and enables the busy reader to conveniently select the parts he wants for closer attention. (Figs. 21 and 22.) A related technique, the enumeration of parallel points (or reasons, steps, advantages, etc.) also provides visual reference and aids conciseness.

"Feedforward." The reading of a report is eased considerably when the writer makes frequent use of topic statements that sum up the content of the following paragraph or paragraphs. The technique is sometimes referred to as "feedforward." Here, for example, is a statement made early in a memorandum:

```
This memorandum will attempt an analysis of factors
contributing to the delay and offer suggestions for
avoiding this condition in the future.
```

The key words *analysis* and *suggestions* reveal the plan of the memorandum. Presumably the discussion will follow in the order indicated.

In the following example, enumeration is used to mark the development of the report even more clearly, and the key words are repeated at the beginning of the respective parts of the discussion:

Topic statement

Enumeration

| Topic statement | The application of electronics in banking falls into two distinct areas: (1) deposit |
| Enumeration | accounting, and (2) all other bank record-keeping functions, including general account, loans, trusts, and mortgage activities. |

*First point repeated
and developed*

| First point repeated and developed | The problems involved in deposit accounting . . . . |

*Second point repeated
and developed*

| Second point repeated and developed | The problems incident to all other bank record-keeping functions . . . . |

The feed forward statement can also incorporate a phrase or two that give the sense of the discussion that has already taken place. Thus the reader is told, in a single sentence or paragraph, both where the discussion has taken him and where it is leading. The example below demonstrates the technique:

(Reference to point already discussed)

In addition to <u>a decrease in telegraphic traffic volume</u>, the new system will also require <u>a substantial reduction in clerical time</u>.

(Reference to point about to be discussed)

It is hard for the reader to lose his way when the writer is so explicit in his directional signals.

Review Problems

1. What is the importance of objectivity in the report and how is it maintained?

2. Classify the following statements as facts or value judgments:

    a. The original cost of the machine was $249.75.

    b. The price they are now asking is much too high.

    c. If we accept this plan, success is certain.

    d. Over a two-year period, the plan will cost the company $24,000.

    e. The report predicts that the plan will be a huge success.

3. Support (or refute) the following conclusions. Use the inductive or deductive order (see Chapter 16), and tell which order you are using:

    a. The computer has taken over many clerical functions.

    b. A great deal of taste and art go into today's advertising.

    c. Generally, industry is far ahead of education in its use of the new communication media.

4. Recast the following statements to make them less personal (but avoid stiltedness):

    a. On the basis of the findings in my report, I suggest that we offer our salesmen a bonus plus commission, beginning January 1.

    b. In response to your request, I am happy to submit this report of my investigation into the need for additional filing space for our credit department.

    c. I am sure that a consideration of these facts will lead you to adopt the recommendation I make.

5. Recast the following statements to make them sound more natural:

    a. As mentioned elsewhere in this report, a new site cannot be selected because the funds available for same have not been determined.

    b. It will be recalled that a similar suggestion was made by this writer in March of last year.

    c. Herewith is enclosed the report based on the undersigned's personal selling experience. It is recommended that close attention be given especially to the part relating to telephone orders.

6. Rewrite the following statements to make them clearer and easier to read:

    a. Please note the following revisions in accounting for the cost of purchasing tickets for affairs sponsored by local civic or charitable organizations, advertising in programs of such affairs, or the cost of donations in lieu thereof, all of which were heretofore charged to entertainment expense.

    b. The source and use of funds available on January 1 (the date considered to be the approximate seasonal peak of loans and advances outstanding) of selected years, are shown in the following table.

    c. The improperly trained personnel, often inadequate to carry out their functions efficiently, coupled with a lackadaisical attitude toward enforcement policies, indicate the need for a complete reorganization of the office.

    d. The analyst will be glad to work with the supervisor in determining the hours required for each of the suggested jobs and consequently which can be distributed to the night force.

    e. If this programed instruction system for clerks is adopted, we should also arrange for some system of evaluation so that we can determine if this technique has sufficient value to our institution so as to be considered for other training courses.

18
Mechanical and Graphic Display

Unlike other types of writing, the report requires not only composition but assembly, for it consists of a number of elements that must be put together if the report is to be considered complete. Prefatory features, footnotes, and a bibliography may have to be included. In addition, more than usual attention must be given to the display of the text and the desirability of tables, graphs, and other forms of visual representation.[1]

PARTS OF THE REPORT

In the order of appearance, the parts of a report may be classified as (1) the preliminaries, (2) the text, and (3) the reference matter.

PRELIMINARIES. Before the text or discussion is reached, a long report may include all or several of the following features:

Cover. The cover attracts attention to the report and protects its appearance. It should bear at least the title of the report, typed a little above the center, but it may also include the name of the author, the date, and the name of the company.

Title Page. Whether or not the information appears on the cover, the title page should include the title of the report and the name of the author; it may also include the date and the company's name.

[1] For a fuller treatment of the mechanics of business reports, see J. Harold Janis, *The Business Research Paper: A Manual of Style* (New York: Hobbs, Dorman & Co., 1967).

Letter of Transmittal or Foreword. A long report prepared for a particular individual usually contains a letter of transmittal, which in effect conveys the report to the reader. It tells who authorized the report and, in some instances, states the purpose and scope, refers to the sources used, acknowledges the help of others, and highlights any special features of the report. This information may be divided between the letter of transmittal and a foreword, or—when the report is intended for circulation among a number of readers—a foreword or preface may take the place of the letter of transmittal.

Table of Contents. In a report of more than a few pages, a table of contents is needed. This consists essentially of a list of the first- and second-degree headings in the report, and the page numbers. It will list, in addition, any appended materials. A separate list (or lists) may be used for formally labeled tables, charts, and other exhibits. This may be called "List of Tables," "List of Illustrations," "Exhibits," or the like.

TEXT. The text contains the results of the research: the introduction, discussion, and conclusions.

Introduction. The contents of the introduction have already been described in Chapter 16. Since the options are many, the author will choose only those features essential to his needs. If it seems desirable, he may also separately label such parts of the introduction as "Definition of Terms," "Abstract," and "Summary of Conclusions and Recommendations."

Body of the Report. Here the writer includes his full discussion, well divided by headings and subheadings. Other physical aspects of the body are discussed in the next section, "The Display of the Report."

Conclusions and Recommendations. If the introduction does not already include a summary of the conclusions and recommendations, the full treatments may either precede the body or follow it. If it seems desirable, the conclusions and recommendations may be treated as separate consecutive divisions.

REFERENCE MATTER. The back of the report is used for those exhibits and details that support the findings but are too cumbersome to include with the text.

Appendix. One or several appendixes may be used. They will include tables, charts, maps, diagrams, pictures, and the like;

also, copies of original documents referred to in the report, questionnaires, and printed forms.

Bibliography. If many books and periodicals were used in the research, a bibliography should be included. The form of the bibliography is discussed on pp. 269–271.

Index. Except in a very long report in which reference to particular topics would otherwise be difficult, an index should not be included. However, the correct form of an index is demonstrated by the index to this book.

PAGE DISPLAY

Reports are conventionally typewritten on white bond paper of good weight (16 or 20 substance) and $8\frac{1}{2}$ by 11 inches in size.

TYPING. Either single-spacing or double-spacing may be used. Although double-spaced copy is easier to read, wide margins and space between paragraphs make single-spaced copy quite readable also. The layout of key sample pages is shown in Figs. 18–22.

The typing should give a crisp, black impression. If errors cannot be neatly erased or removed with whitening, the pages should be done over. Inexperienced typists are advised to use "erasable" paper, which permits neat corrections with a soft eraser.

HEADINGS. Major heads may be typed in all capital letters. Lesser heads may be typed in capital and small letters and underlined. The ranking of topics may also be shown by the use of centered heads, side heads, and run-in heads. (Figs. 21 and 22.)

LONG QUOTATIONS. Direct quotations of more than three or four lines should be indented five spaces, single-spaced, and set off from the text by a skipped line above and below the quotation. No quotation marks are necessary under this arrangement but, through a footnote or otherwise, the source of the quotation should be given.

PAGINATION. Beginning with the title page, a number is allotted to each page and the number is typewritten on each page except the title page. The page following the title page is numbered ii and all other pages up to the first page of the text are numbered in consecutive Roman numerals. All pages of the text, beginning with the first, are numbered in consecutive Arabic numbers, beginning with 1. The number on the first page of each major division (e.g.,

THE EMPLOYEE MERIT RATING SYSTEM

OF THE THIRD NATIONAL BANK

Prepared for

Mr. Charles F. Cordley
Vice President
Erie County Trust Company
Buffalo, New York

Prepared by

George E. Turner
Assistant Vice President
Third National Bank
Albany, New York

April 9, 19--

Fig. 18. Title page of a formal report

April 9, 19--

Mr. Charles F. Cordley
Vice President
Erie County Trust Company
Buffalo, New York 14202

Dear Mr. Cordley:

It's a pleasure to give you information about our Employee
Merit Rating System. The subject is very familiar to me
because as a Supervisor of a staff of twenty people, I have
important responsibilities in preparing this document annually.

The enclosed report includes a comprehensive description of
the benefits of the merit rating system to the company and
the employee. It also describes the rating operation, including rating preliminaries, preparation for rating, and
the mechanics of making a rating. Supplemental exhibits
include a work history of a fictitious employee, with a
sample Merit Rating Report completed on the basis of the
information supplied.   Another exhibit provides statistics
on a composite of ratings on this case as supplied by confer-
ees in a recent Supervisory Conference Program which I
attended.

The information for this report was obtained both from personal
experience and from the records of our Personnel Administration
Division. Please let me know if I can be of further assistance
to you after you have studied the report.

                                        Sincerely yours,

                                        George E. Turner

                                        George E. Turner
                                        Assistant Vice President

Fig. 19. Letter of transmittal

Preface, Introduction, Body, etc.) should be centered at the bottom. The number on all other pages should be typed at the upper
right margin two or three spaces above the first line of copy.

CONTENTS

Fig. 20. Table of contents

I.   THE BENEFITS OF A MERIT RATING SYSTEM

A.   Benefits to the Bank

Merit rating provides the Bank with an annual record of
the supervisor's evaluations of each employee with comments
by senior supervision and by the Personnel Administration
Division where appropriate. This method permits an accumu-
lation of such annual evaluations and thus serves as a basic
index of the employee's past and potential value to the
company.

Merit rating also provides a sound basis for equitable
application of personnel policies by means of a uniform rating
procedure. It provides a valuable and permanent record of
the employee's skills, educational accomplishments, and
ambitions. It provides an excellent opportunity to ascertain
whether or not employees are properly assigned both in their
own interest and in that of the Bank. And, finally, it provides
a way of discovering the strengths as well as the weaknesses of
individual employees.

B.   Benefits to the Employee

The merit rating system is beneficial to the employee
because it serves as a means of observing his work and keeping
him informed about his job progress. It provides data for
making salary adjustments; it furhisnes an opportunity for an

Fig. 21. First page of a formal report showing use of centered and side heads

After assuring himself that the employee's statement
has been completed and signed, the supervisor should
prepare to make the rating.

B. The Recommended Approach
Supervisors are cautioned to be as objective as
possible in the completion of the merit rating forms.
They are urged to adopt a standardized approach which
reflects the general standards of the particular job
and of the Bank. The rating should be one on which most
detached observers would agree. It would then be a
valuable merit rating that deserves to be put in
writing and kept in the employee's personnel folder.

   Importance of Objectivity. Merit ratings often
determine how a request for a leave of absence or other
special consideration should be treated. The employee
deserves to have personnel policies applied fairly, and
this can be done only if the ratings have been
objective. If the ratings are based on the supervisor's
liking or disliking an individual, then all employees
will begin to feel that they are the victims of either
favoritism or discrimination.

   Relation to Job Performance. Ideally, the rating
should be related principally to the performance of the
individual on the job and to his possible future jobs
within the organization. This does not mean that
everything else is irrelevant and should be omitted,
but only that the performance on the job provides the
best opportunity for observation on the part of the
supervisor.

Fig. 22. An inside page of a formal report showing the use of side and run-in heads

FOOTNOTES

Footnotes are frequently found in formal business reports. They
are not used in informal reports, where any necessary references
are incorporated into the text. Footnotes are of two kinds: *explanatory footnotes* and *reference footnotes*.

Explanatory footnotes may give cross-references to other parts of the report or contain incidental intelligence not considered important enough to be included in the text. They should be used very sparingly. These are examples:

1 Compare with the figures given for urban transit on p. 36.

2 At the time the number of entries permitted by any individual or company was not limited.

Reference footnotes give specific credit for quotations and other borrowed material and establish authority for the researcher's own statements, where the need for support is indicated.

FIRST REFERENCE. A reference footnote is written as a single sentence, punctuated in the manner shown in the examples below. A first reference to a work consists of the following parts:

1. Name of author or authors as given in the book or article.

2. Name of the book or article. Names of books and other self-contained works are underlined. Names of articles, chapters, and other parts of longer works are put in quotation marks. The edition of a book, other than the first, should be shown by such abbreviations as "2nd ed." and "rev. ed.," following the title.

3. Facts of publication. In the instance of a book or chapter, these data include—in parentheses—the place of publication, the name of the publisher, and the date. In the instance of an article in a periodical, only the date of the issue is given, but when the source is a learned journal, the usual style consists of the volume number followed by the date in parentheses.

4. Page reference.

The style of footnotes is indicated in the following varied examples:

Book (Single Author)
  ¹ Herbert Simon, *The Shape of Automation* (New York: Harper & Row, 1965), pp. 109–111.

Revised Edition
  ² William V. Haney, *Communication and Behavior: Text and Cases,* rev. ed. (Homewood, Ill.: Richard D. Irwin, 1967), pp. 135–137.

Corporate Author
  ³ Association of the Bar of the City of New York, *Conflict of Interest and Federal Service* (Cambridge: Harvard University Press, 1960), p. 59.

Chapter in Edited Work

[4] Edward J. Kilduff, "On Appealing to Favorable Opinions," in J. Harold Janis, ed., *Business Communication Reader* (New York: Harper & Row, 1958), p. 120.

Work in Series

[5] Walter G. Barlow, "Measuring Effectiveness in Communication," in *Human Relations,* American Management Association General Management Series, No. 181 (New York: AMA, 1956), p. 24.

Article in Scholarly Journal (Two Authors)

[6] M. E. Baehr and R. Renck, "The Definition and Measurement of Employee Morale," *Administrative Science Quarterly,* Vol. 3 (September 1958), pp. 157–158.

Signed Magazine Article

[7] John Tebbel, "Television: The View from Europe," *Saturday Review,* August 9, 1969, p. 43.

Unsigned Magazine Article

[8] *Time,* February 6, 1970, p. 63.

Signed Newspaper Article

[9] Stacy V. Jones, "New Method Records TV Pictures on Film," *New York Times,* August 9, 1969, p. 31.

Unsigned Newspaper Article

[10] "Profits Decline Seen," *Chicago Tribune,* May 16, 1969, p. 44.

SUBSEQUENT REFERENCES. Additional references to a work already footnoted omit all but the most essential information. The following examples show a variety of styles. The Latin abbreviations—which should be used sparingly, if at all—are explained in the section immediately following the examples.

First References

[1] Jules Backman, *Advertising Effectiveness* (New York: New York University Press, 1967), p. 23.

[2] Charles S. Steinberg, *The Mass Communicators* (New York: Harper & Row, 1958), pp. 57–60.

Subsequent References

[3] *Ibid.,* p. 74.

[4] Backman, p. 27.

[5] Steinberg, *op. cit.,* pp. 88–92.

[6] Backman, *loc. cit.*

ABBREVIATIONS. Following is a list of abbreviations commonly used in footnote references:

ca. (circa)   about. Used where the date of a work is unknown, as in
                 "*ca.* 1876."

ch., chs.   chapter, chapters

ed.	edition, editor
et al.	and others. Used when a work has more than three authors, for example, "Carl I. Hovland *et al.*"
f., ff.	and the following page, pages, as in "pp. 28ff."
ibid. (*ibidem*)	in the same work. Used instead of the author's name to refer to the work in the immediately preceding footnote.
l., ll.	line, lines
loc. cit. (*loco citato*)	in the place cited. Used with the author's name, but without page number, to refer to the same place already cited in a preceding footnote.
n.d.	no date of publication given
op. cit. (*opere citato*)	in the work cited. Since this abbreviation does not aid identification, it is really not necessary.
p., pp.	page, pages
rev.	revised
vol., vols.	volume, volumes

ADDITIONAL SUGGESTIONS. The correct use of footnotes imposes these additional requirements:

1. Separate footnotes from the text page by a 10-space rule beginning at the left margin. See that footnotes do not extend below the bottom margin of the page.

2. Single space footnotes, but preferably double space between footnotes. Indent the first line of each footnote five spaces.

3. Number footnotes consecutively throughout the report or for each page or chapter.

4. Key footnotes to the text by raised arabic numbers (called superscripts or index numbers). The superscript in the text should preferably be placed at the end of the sentence or paragraph to which reference is made, but it may also be placed after a word or phrase in the sentence in order that the point referred to may be identified more easily.

BIBLIOGRAPHY

A bibliography is a list of source materials on a particular subject. In a formal report it shows what books and other library materials were consulted, and it includes all of the works mentioned in the footnotes. As part of the reference matter, it follows the appendix or appendixes.

The bibliography lists all works alphabetically by name of author, although a long list may be divided by type of material, as for example, books, articles, and miscellaneous sources. In these other respects, too, the bibliographical lists differ from the footnotes:

1. The last name of the author is given first. However, if there is more than one author, the names of the other authors may be written with the given name first.

2. The first line of each entry starts at the margin, but succeeding lines are indented five or ten spaces.

3. When an author is represented by more than one work, a line ten spaces long is used to denote the author's name in the second and succeeding references.

4. Periods instead of commas are used to divide the main parts of the entry and, except for dates of periodicals, the parentheses around the facts of publication are omitted.

5. In the instance of a corporate author, when no individuals are credited, the name of the sponsoring organization is listed as author in the correct alphabetical slot.

6. The number of pages of a whole work or the inclusive pages of an article or chapter may be given, but not the page reference to any particular point.

Sample entries in a bibliography follow:

BOOKS

Arensburg, Conrad M. *et al. Research in Industrial Human Relations: A Critical Appraisal.* New York: Harper & Row, 1957.

Chase, Stuart. *The Power of Words.* New York: Harcourt, Brace & World, 1954.
———. *Roads to Agreement.* New York: Harper & Row, 1951.

Dooher, M. Joseph and Vivienne Marquis. *Effective Communication on the Job.* Rev. ed. New York: American Management Association, 1963.

Gellerman, Saul W. *The Management of Human Relations.* New York: Holt, Rinehart & Winston, 1966.

PERIODICALS

Besco, R. O. and C. H. Lawshe. "Foreman Leadership as Perceived by Superiors and Subordinates." *Personnel Psychology,* Vol. 12 (Winter 1959), pp. 572–583.

Burnett, Verne. "Management's Tower of Babel." *Management Review* (June 1961), pp. 4–11.

"Committees: Their Role in Management Today." *Management Review* (October 1957), pp. 36–41.

Moser, George V. "Avoiding Pitfalls in Conference Leading." *Management Record*, Vol. 20 (November 1958), pp. 374–377.

MISCELLANEOUS

Bureau of Educational Research, Ohio State University. *Leadership and Supervision in Industry: An Evaluation of a Supervisory Program*. Monograph No. 33. Columbus: The Ohio State University, 1955.

General Electric Co., Schenectady, N.Y. Press release, Oct. 18, 1969.

Habbe, Stephen. *Communicating With Employees*. Studies in Personnel Policy, No. 129. New York: National Industrial Conference Board, 1952.

U.S. Department of the Air Force. *Preparation of Written Communications*. Air Force Manual No. 10–1. Washington, D.C.: U.S. Government Printing Office, 1959.

TABLES

Tables offer a concise and convenient way to present quantitative data. A *spot table* is one that is run into the text without a title or number (Fig. 23). A *reference table* is carried independently and

A survey of 127 typical plants and offices in the East
showed that companies paid their employees' tuition as follows:

	Plants	Offices
In advance	16.8%	26.9%
After completion of courses	71.2%	57.7%
In installments	12.0%	15.4%

Most companies (about two-thirds of the firms having percentage
formulas) specified a flat percentage for all reimbursements:
50 per cent is the most frequently mentioned figure; 75 per cent
is the next.

Fig. 23. Sample of text showing a spot table

bears a title and number (Fig. 24). A reference table should follow as closely as possible the text to which it applies. Typing of the report is easier if the table is placed on a separate sheet, though two or three short tables may occupy the same page. Long tables that have no close relation to the text should be put in the appendix. Some organizations prefer to have all tables in the appendix.

The parts of a table are shown in Fig. 25. Some pertinent comments follow:

TABLE 1

ANTICIPATED PERSONNEL REDUCTIONS

	Number of men		
	Present work force	Proposed work force	Reduction
Yard crews (five men	40	35	5
to a crew)	13	8	5
Track maintenance gang			
Locomotive maintenance	6	5	1
Shop men	3	1	2
Hostlers	62	49	11

TABLE NO.

TITLE OF TABLE

Stub Head	Caption		Caption	
	Subcaption	Subcaption	Subcaption	Subcaption
Stub	XXXX	XXXX	XXXX	XXXX
Stub	XXXX	XXXX[a]	XXXX	XXXX
Stub	XXXX	XXXX	XXXX	XXXX
Stub	XXXX	XXXX	XXXX	XXXX
Stub	XXXX	XXXX	XXXX[b]	XXXX
Total	XXXX	XXXX	XXXX	XXXX

[a]Footnote
[b]Footnote

Source:

Fig. 24, *above*. Example of reference table. Fig. 25, *below*. The parts of a table

1. When a reference table appears on the same page as the text, it should be set off by a ruled border. Horizontal and vertical rules should be used within tables whenever they are helpful for good display and reading ease.

2. The table number and title should be centered at the top. It is customary to use Roman numerals and all capitals. The title should specify the exact nature of the table, including such data as the subject, dates, place, etc. A title that runs beyond the width of the table should be broken into two or more lines, or a shorter title with a subtitle centered below it should be used. The units in which the data are given are also included below the title, usually in parentheses, for example, "Millions of Homes," "Workers in Thousands."

3. The column titles are called captions. A caption may also span several columns, each with its own subcaption. The stubs are the side heads that describe the content of each horizontal row. Column totals may appear at the bottom or, if more convenient, at the top.

4. Spaces in a table should not be left blank. If there are no figures to be supplied, the fact should be indicated by a dash or the abbreviation "n.a." (not available).

5. If footnotes are necessary, they may be indicated by asterisks, but since these are cumbersome, the letters a, b, c, etc. may be used as superscripts. The footnotes should be placed directly under the tabulated data.

6. When figures are obtained from other than primary sources, the source is indicated at the bottom, for example, "Source: Monthly Labor Review, January 1970."

CHARTS

Charts provide the most graphic way to compare different sets of data.

TYPES OF CHARTS. Common types of charts are shown in Figs. 26–29. They may be described as follows:

Pie Chart. The simplest type of chart, this is a circle that divides a whole quantity into its parts. Segments of the "pie" may be shown in color or by shading with black ink. Each segment should be clearly identified to show what it represents.

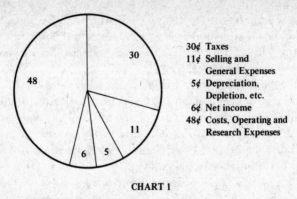

30¢ Taxes
11¢ Selling and
General Expenses
5¢ Depreciation,
Depletion, etc.
6¢ Net income
48¢ Costs, Operating and
Research Expenses

CHART 1

Distribution of Consolidated's
Revenue Dollar, 19--

Fig. 26. Pie chart

Bar Chart. The bar chart compares the magnitude of different things. A sequence of dates or amounts is distributed along the horizontal axis, while the things being compared are represented by the bars extending from the vertical axis. The bars may be subdivided to show their components.

Column Chart. The column chart is a "two-scale" chart in that it permits measuring both horizontally and vertically. The hori-

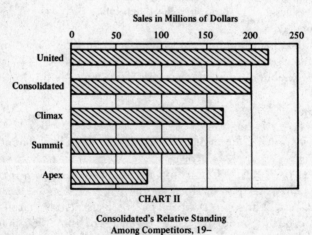

CHART II

Consolidated's Relative Standing
Among Competitors, 19--

Fig. 27. Bar chart

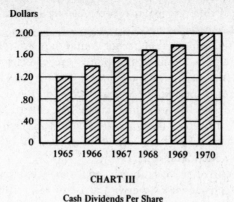

CHART III

Cash Dividends Per Share

Fig. 28. Column chart

zontal scale usually measures time values, while the vertical scale measures quantitative values. Thus columns strung along a base representing successive years, quarters, or decades may extend upward to indicate varying amounts of sales, expenses, earnings, dividends, and the like. The columns may be subdivided to show their components or multiple columns may be clustered to permit

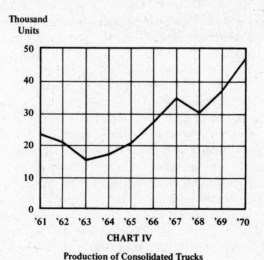

CHART IV

Production of Consolidated Trucks

Fig. 29. Curve

comparison of different types of data at one time or at different times.

Curve. When points along a horizontal axis are too close for a column chart to be feasible, the points are connected to form a curve. Thus the daily volume of trade on the New York Stock Exchange over a period of several weeks or more can best be shown by a curve. Two or three curves may also be overlaid on the same grid to show other quantitative variations over the same period. The curves can be separately identified by color or by the use of solid, dotted, and broken lines.

In using curves, two cautions should be observed: (1) The scale should start at zero; otherwise a rise or fall will seem steeper than it is; and (2) attention should be given to the scale that is used, for it is possible, by manipulating the scale, to make a curve seem steep or shallow.

GUIDES TO CHART-MAKING. Some principles governing the construction of charts are given below:

1. A chart is best drafted on graph paper, then copied on plain white paper where only a few necessary grid lines are retained.

2. All charts should be numbered and titled. Arabic numbers and capitals and small letters are customarily used for this purpose, for example, "Chart 1." Custom also places the number and title below the chart. However, practice occasionally varies and one may see the same typographic style and positioning used for both tables and charts.

3. Points on the scale, both horizontal and vertical, should be clearly marked, and the index or unit of measure (for example, "1960 = 100," "Thousands of Dollars") should be placed above the vertical axis or along the horizontal axis, as the chart requires.

OTHER GRAPHIC AIDS. In addition to the charts already described, the reporter may find use for maps, diagrams, or pictures. A map answers the question, "Where?" It may show the location of sites, the geographic distribution of a product, or a route. A diagram answers the question, "How?" Through the use of lines, circles, or other geometric figures, it may show the components of an organization, process, or operation and also indicate sequence or direction. A picture is the most realistic of the graphic aids and may consist of a drawing or photograph.

If the terms *Table* and *Chart* are used to label the tables and graphs respectively, the term *Figure* or *Exhibit* may be used to label any of the other graphic aids. If a number of the same kind of graphic aids are employed, however, they may be labeled *Map 1, Map 2, Diagram 1, Diagram 2*, etc. The term *Figure* may also be used to include *all* graphic aids.

All exhibits should be carefully and consistently numbered and titled and should be included with the text or at the end of the report according to the same criteria used in deciding where to put the tables and charts. Graphic aids placed at the end of the report should be arranged sequentially by classification and number. The exhibits themselves are improved in appearance and clarity if they are large enough to be examined easily, if unnecessary details are omitted, and if all the essential parts are legibly identified.

Review Problems

1. Assume that your company is anxious to relocate employees living near a plant about to be closed and consolidated with the plant at which you are now working. Your supervisor thinks you might be able to help by reporting on the housing situation in the general area in which you live. Write a letter report incorporating your findings.

2. Draw a pie chart to show the sources of Mythic University's income dollar as follows: tuition, 55.7 cents; income from endowment, 10.5 cents; gifts from alumni and others, 5.0 cents; and government sources, 28.8 cents.

3. Draw a bar chart to show the following percentages of change in international common stock prices for the ten year period June 1959–June 1969; United States, +36.0; Japan, +144.3; Germany, +60.8; United Kingdom, +63.4; Netherlands, +47.1; Italy, +14.8; France, +41.9.

4. Draw a column chart to show Acme Tool Company's sales in millions of dollars for the six years ending 1969 as 2.3, 2.8, 3.6, 5.5, 6.2, and 6.6.

5. Follow the price of some favorite stock on the New York Stock Exchange; then draw a curve showing its action over a two-week period.

6. Study the operations of a single department or section of a particular company in your locality; then write a report, assumedly at the request of the general manager, on the efficiency with which the work is carried on.

7. Write a documented report (including footnotes and bibliography) on one of the following subjects:

    a. Improving interpersonal communication through the application of listening techniques.

    b. The use of feedback in employee relations.

    c. Emotional appeals as instruments of persuasion.

8. Through study and first-hand research, write a documented report on one of the following topics:

a. Training employees to write.

b. The use of form letters or form paragraphs to systematize correspondence.

c. An analysis of employee house organs in a particular business or industry.

d. The use of graphics in annual reporting to shareholders.

e. An analysis of the language of stockbrokers' newsletters.

PART 4

HANDBOOK OF GRAMMAR AND USAGE

Section I
Review of Grammatical Terms

An understanding of grammar and sentence structure depends to a large extent on the student's knowledge of grammatical terms.[1] In this section the principal terms are defined and illustrated.

THE PARTS OF SPEECH

The parts of speech are the classification of words according to their function, meaning, and form. The eight parts of speech are noun, pronoun, adjective, verb, adverb, preposition, conjunction, and interjection.

1. NOUNS. A *noun* is the name of a person, place, or thing (*secretary, office, table*). (See also Sections II and III.)

Common Noun. A *common noun* is a name characteristic of all members of a class of persons, places, or things (*man, company, city, room*).

Proper Noun. A *proper noun* is the name of a particular person, place, or thing (*Mr. Jones,* the *Glidden Company, Philadelphia,* the *East Room*).

Special Classes of Nouns. A *concrete noun* is the name of an object; that is, something that can be seen or touched (*desk, bridge, house, plant*). An *abstract noun* is the name of a quality, condition, or idea (*intelligence, courtesy, abundance, darkness, democracy, Christianity*). A *collective noun* is the name of a group

---

[1] For a more thorough treatment of grammar and sentence structure in current usage, see Curme, George O.: *English Grammar,* College Outline Series (New York: Barnes & Noble, Inc., 1947).

(*committee, class, company, jury, herd*). A *compound noun* is a name consisting of two or more words (*Barnes & Noble, International Airport, vice-president, sergeant-at-arms, bookcase*).

2. PRONOUNS. A *pronoun* is a word used in place of a noun (*he, they, those*). (See also Sections II, III, and IV.)

Personal Pronoun. The *personal pronouns* are *I, we, you, he, she, it, they,* and their various grammatical forms such as *me, mine,* etc.

Relative Pronoun. The *relative pronouns* are *who, which,* and *that.* These pronouns not only substitute for nouns, but also link the nouns with the rest of the sentence. (Notice examples that follow.)

> Stenographers *who* work overtime will be paid time and a half.
> We are sending today the curtains *which* you recently ordered.

Demonstrative Pronoun. The *demonstrative pronouns* are *this, that, these,* and *those.* They are used to make pointed references to persons, places, or things.

> *This* is the desk I was talking about.
> *These* are not satisfactory.

Interrogative Pronoun. The *interrogative pronouns* are *who, which,* and *what.* They are used in asking questions.

> *Who* should write the letter?
> *Which* of the two models should we take?

Indefinite Pronoun. The *indefinite pronouns* include *one, some, few, all, any, anyone, somebody, none,* and so on. They are characterized by vagueness in their reference.

Reflexive Pronoun. The *reflexive pronouns* are those ending in *–self* or *–selves;* for example, *myself, oneself, themselves.*

3. ADJECTIVES. An *adjective* is a word by which we modify a noun or pronoun. (See also Section VI.) In addition to ordinary descriptive words, such as *large, warm, blue,* adjectives include (1) the articles *a, an,* and *the;* (2) participles; and (3) nouns and pronouns which modify other nouns and pronouns.

> The *brass* lamp has a *black* and *gray* shade. (Descriptive adjectives.)

The president's office is *an* ideal place for *a* conference. (Articles.)

Anyone *taking* a *reserved* seat will be required to show a ticket. (Participles.)

Which exhibitor is going to show *his* line of *nylon upholstery* fabrics at *Saturday's* convention? (Pronouns and nouns.)

4. VERBS. A *verb* is a word through which we assert something about a noun or pronoun. (See also Sections II and V.) The assertion denotes either an action

> he *walks,* we *deliver,* they *make*

or a state of being

> I *am* an accountant.
> The sediment *remains* in the tube.

Transitive Verb. A *transitive verb* is one that takes an object (see Rule 11).

> They *built* the factory in ten months.
> Please *send* a copy to Mr. Trent.
> Most employees *drink* coffee.

Intransitive Verb. An *intransitive verb* does not take an object.

> Mr. Peck *seemed* angry.
> A good worker *does* not *loaf* on the job.

Linking (Copulative) Verb. A *linking* or *copulative verb* connects the subject to a predicate noun or predicate adjective. (See Rule 10.) Examples of linking verbs are *be, appear, seem, look, taste.*

She *is* a new subscriber. (Linking verb followed by predicate noun.)

The new model *looks* good. (Linking verb followed by predicate adjective.)

Auxiliary Verb. An *auxiliary verb* is a verb that helps form another verb. The principal auxiliary verbs are *be, have, can, shall, will, do, may,* and *must,* and their various grammatical forms, such as *is, was, had, could,* and so on.

> He *might have* tried harder.
> We *shall be* pleased to serve you again.
> *May* we ask you to telephone us at our new number.

5. ADVERBS. An *adverb* is a word that modifies a verb, an adjective, or another adverb. (Also see Section VI.) Most adverbs (but not all) end in *–ly*. Certain adverbs have two forms (*slow, slowly; high, highly*). A few words, including *slow, late, well,* and *just,* are both adverbs and adjectives. Adverbs are easily identified by the fact that they answer the questions when? where? how? and to what degree? The adverbs in the following sentences are in italics:

> Please be *there* when I call. (Where?)
> I shall arrive *promptly.* (When?)
> He works *diligently.* (How?)
> It is not a *very* new idea. (To what degree?)

6. PREPOSITIONS. A *preposition* connects and shows the relationship between a noun or pronoun (the object of the preposition) and another word in the sentence. These are among the most common prepositions: *at, by, for, from, in, of, on, to,* and *with;* others include *around, beyond, before, against, through, in spite of,* and *because of.*

> We placed the papers *on* the desk.
> They promised delivery *by* Friday.
> In a few days you will hear *from* us again.

7. CONJUNCTIONS. A *conjunction* is a word that connects words, phrases, or clauses.

Co-ordinate Conjunction. A *co-ordinate conjunction* (*and, but, for, or, nor,* etc.) joins sentence elements that are grammatically equal, as noun with noun, adjective with adjective, verb with verb, phrase with phrase, clause with clause, and so on.

> This style shoe comes in brown *and* black. (Joins two nouns.)

> At home *or* on vacation, you will enjoy a portable radio. (Joins two prepositional phrases.)

> You may take your vacation now, *but* you will have to be back by the tenth of next month. (Joins two co-ordinate clauses.)

Co-ordinate conjunctions are sometimes paired with other words to form correlative conjunctions, for example, *not only . . . but also, both . . . and, either . . . or, neither . . . nor.*

> *Both* Mr. Tate *and* I have been invited.

> Please include in your estimate *not only* the cost of labor and materials, *but also* the shipping charges.

Subordinate Conjunction. A *subordinate conjunction* (*as, if, when, because, since, although,* etc.) joins a subordinate clause to another clause on which it is dependent.

> *If* you want to go, I shall not stop you.
> Please let me know *when* you want delivery.

Conjunctive Adverb. A *conjunctive adverb* (*however, therefore, furthermore, so, moreover, accordingly, nevertheless,* etc.) is an adverb used as a conjunction. It joins independent clauses only.

> We were going to start construction last week; *however*, the weather interfered.

> The goods were damaged when they arrived; *therefore* we sent them back.

8. INTERJECTIONS. An *interjection* is an exclamatory word (*oh, alas, bravo, hurrah,* etc.) which usually expresses an emotion. It has no grammatical function in the sentence.

> *Hurrah*, tomorrow's a holiday.
> *Oh*, what a mistake!

SUBJECTS AND PREDICATES

Two elements are necessary in order to make an assertion: a subject and a predicate. (Also see Section II.)

9. SUBJECTS. The *subject* is the name (noun or pronoun) of the person, place, or thing about which something is said. It may be simple, compound, or complete.

> The *customer* refused to pay the bill.
> *I* attended the conference.

Simple Subject. A *simple subject* consists of a single noun or its equivalent.

> *Mr. Penton* will see you soon.
> The *instructions* did not arrive on time.

Compound Subject. A *compound subject* consists of two or more simple subjects usually joined by *and, or,* or *nor*.

> The *plumbers* and *carpenters* will begin work on Monday.
> *Mary* or *Jane* will take the message.

Complete Subject. A *complete subject* consists of a simple or compound subject together with all its modifiers and other related words.

> A *cheerless reception room, like the one on the ninth floor,* is not likely to make a good impression on visitors.

> *Dealers and consumers all over the country* will welcome the improvement.

> *Anyone who objects to the plan* will be permitted to state his objections fully.

10. PREDICATE. The *predicate* is that which is said about the subject. It may be simple, compound, or complete.

> The machine *broke down.*
> Most customers *pay their bills promptly.*

Simple Predicate. A *simple predicate* consists of a single verb, including any of its auxiliaries.

> He *likes* bowling.
> I *shall leave* tomorrow.

Compound Predicate. A *compound predicate* consists of two or more simple predicates joined by conjunctions.

> We *have met* and *talked.*
> They *ordered* the goods, then *canceled* the order.

Complete Predicate. A *complete predicate* consists of a single or compound predicate together with all its modifiers and complements.

> The customer *made an error in copying the style number.*

> I *shall telephone Mr. Anthony today and ask if I may see him sometime next week.*

11. COMPLEMENTS. A *complement* is a word that completes the meaning of the verb. The most common types of complements are direct object, indirect object, predicate noun, and predicate adjective.

Direct Object. A *direct object* names the receiver of the action of the verb and represents a person or thing other than the subject.

> Mr. Battles endorsed the *check.*
> We liked the *design.*
> I mailed the *letter.*

Indirect Object. An *indirect object* tells to whom or for whom, or to what or for what the action is performed, but it does not employ a preposition.

> Please mail *him* the check.
> We thought we were doing *Joseph* a favor.
> You should give the *surface* two coats of varnish.

Predicate Noun. A *predicate noun* is a noun that completes a linking verb and represents the same person or thing as the subject.

> Mr. Bond is an excellent *speaker.*
> The street has become a *paradise* for shoppers.

Predicate Adjective. A *predicate adjective* is an adjective complement that follows a linking verb and modifies the subject.

> Our standards are *rigid.*
> The mixture smells *sweet.*

VERBALS

A *verbal* is a form of the verb used as a different part of speech. The three kinds of verbals are gerunds, participles, and infinitives.

12. GERUNDS. A *gerund* is a verbal noun; it ends in *–ing* (*working, riding,* etc.). The gerund is usually the subject or object of a verb or the object of a preposition.

> *Bowling* is a healthful sport. (Subject of verb.)
> Miss Robin likes *collecting* stamps. (Object of verb.)
> We are tired of *waiting.* (Object of preposition.)

13. PARTICIPLES. A *participle* is a form of the verb used as an adjective. The *present participle* ends in *–ing,* as does the gerund; the *past participle* usually ends in *–t, –d, –ed, –n,* or *–en.*

Thinking you were still at home, we telephoned you there. (Modifies *we.*)

He is the man most *wanted* for the job. (Modifies *man.*)

Torn between the two alternatives, the chairman found it impossible to come to a decision. (Modifies *chairman.*)

14. INFINITIVES. An *infinitive* is a part of the verb used as a noun, adjective, or adverb. It is usually preceded by the sign of the infinitive: *to.*

There are no letters for you *to sign*. (Adjective modifying *letters*.)

To resign now would be a futile gesture. (Noun, subject of *would be*.)

He is always quick *to act*. (Adverb modifying *quick*.)

PHRASES AND CLAUSES

Groups of related words within sentences are classified as phrases or clauses, depending on their grammatical structure.

15. PHRASES. In a strict grammatical sense, a *phrase* is a group of related words not having a subject or predicate. Phrases take their names from the kind of word with which they begin. Thus phrases begining with prepositions, gerunds, participles, and infinitives are called prepositional, gerund, participial, and infinitive phrases, respectively.

A *prepositional phrase* consists of a preposition and its object, plus modifiers. *Gerund, participial,* and *infinitive phrases* consist of a gerund, participle, or infinitive, respectively, plus their complements and modifiers.

Take the layout *to the advertising department*. (Prepositional phrase.)

We put off our decision *for another week*. (Prepositional phrase.)

Laying out the advertisement requires considerable artistic talent. (Gerund phrase.)

We regretted *putting off our decision*. (Gerund phrase.)

The man *laying out the advertisement* is well paid. (Participial phrase.)

Putting off our decision, we hoped that circumstances would be more favorable next week. (Participial phrase.)

Let me try *to lay out the advertisement*. (Infinitive phrase.)

We had good reason *to put off our decision*. (Infinitive phrase.)

16. CLAUSES. A *clause* is a group of words having a subject and predicate.

Main (Independent) Clause. A *main* or *independent clause* is a clause that can stand alone as a sentence.

> *I shall talk with you* after you finish the job.
> *You can have the check* whenever you wish.

A *co-ordinate clause* is one of two or more main clauses joined into a single sentence. The clauses may be connected by a co-ordinate conjunction, by a conjunctive adverb, or by a semicolon without a conjunction.

> It is a slow process, *but* we will finish the job. (Co-ordinate conjunction.)
>
> The salesman talked for a long time; *however,* we were not impressed. (Conjunctive adverb.)
>
> We expect the pattern to arrive any day; it should have been here last week. (Semicolon without conjunction.)

Subordinate (Dependent) Clause. A *subordinate* or *dependent clause* is a clause that is dependent on the main clause and can not stand alone as a sentence; it may begin with a subordinate conjunction or a relative or interrogative pronoun. According to their grammatical function, subordinate clauses are either noun, adjective, or adverbial clauses.

> I wanted to know *what we should do.* (Noun clause, object of the infinitive *to know.*)
>
> Please give the pass to Mr. Jones, *who will let you in.* (Adjective clause modifying the noun *Mr. Jones.*)
>
> *If you wish to discuss the matter further,* we suggest you visit us at your convenience. (Adverbial clause modifying the verb *suggest.*)

SENTENCES

A sentence is the expression of a complete thought by means of a group of words arranged according to grammatical principles.

17. STRUCTURE OF SENTENCES. *Sentences* are either simple, compound, or complex, according to the number and kinds of clauses that constitute them.

Simple Sentence. A *simple sentence* consists of a single independent clause.

> We appreciate your prompt reply to our letter.
> You are to be congratulated on your achievement.

Compound Sentence. A *compound sentence* consists of two or more independent clauses.

We like the design,/but we wish there were more colors to choose from.

You were right/and we were wrong.

We study our customers:/we give them what they want.

Each clause has its own subject and verb. Do not confuse a compound sentence with a simple sentence having one subject and a compound verb. The following is a simple sentence:

We know our customers *and give* them what they want.

Complex Sentence. A *complex sentence* consists of at least one independent clause and one or more subordinate clauses.

You may obtain the refund/if you apply within ten days.
We asked/what he wanted.

18. CLASSES OF SENTENCES. Depending on the manner of the expression, sentences are classified as declarative, interrogatory, imperative, or exclamatory.

Declarative Sentence. A *declarative sentence* makes a statement. All of the examples in Rule 17 on pages 289–290 are declarative sentences.

Interrogatory Sentence. An *interrogatory sentence* asks a question.

Who should get the memorandum?
Where will I find the secretary?

Imperative Sentence. An *imperative sentence* states a command. The subject *you* is usually not expressed.

Please follow our orders to the letter.
Be sure to mail the order card today.

Exclamatory Sentence. An *exclamatory sentence* expresses strong feeling.

You can not do that!
What must they think!

EXERCISE A

Identify the parts of speech of the italicized terms below.
1. We *appreciate your recent order for a* Winchester Electric *Razor.*

2. *The* order *will be filled immediately.*

3. The *product has been on* the *market* for *many years.*

4. *If* you *wish, we shall include* a gift *card and instruction* book.

5. We *are sure* you will be *well* satisfied *with* your *purchase.*

6. If, *however,* the *instrument* should *ever* need *servicing,* do *not* hesitate to call *on us.*

EXERCISE B

Identify the subjects and predicate verbs in the following sentences. Indicate also whether the sentences are simple, compound, or complex.

1. You will find enclosed with this letter our check for $14,000.00 in payment of our note of this amount maturing on January 28.

2. We have written to you many times, but we have not as yet had the courtesy of a reply.

3. When you have finished reading the booklet, may we ask you to pass it on to Mr. Grayson.

4. The client said he would return the documents which accompanied our letter.

5. After listening to the complaint, we seriously considered taking back the goods and refunding the money.

EXERCISE C

Name the verbals in Exercise B and identify them as infinitives, gerunds, or participles.

EXERCISE D

Identify each of the italicized words in the following sentences as subject, direct object, indirect object, object of a preposition, predicate noun, or predicate adjective:

1. Please send *me* a *copy* of your latest annual *report.*

2. *Mr. Henry* is *president* of the company, but *modest* nevertheless.

3. *We* like your *qualifications* and will keep *you* in *mind.*

4. *She* seemed *reluctant* to take the extra *pair* of drapes.

5. In *acknowledging the gift, Mr. Crown* paid *tribute* to the whole *staff.*

Section II
Agreement of Subject and Verb

Many errors in English occur because of failure to observe the rule that a verb must agree with its subject in person and number.

1. INTERVENING PLURALS. A singular verb should be used with a singular subject even though plural words come between them.

Incorrect

Our *order* for these goods *were* placed on March 9.

The *mislabeling* of sizes, especially in such articles as hats, blouses, and stockings, *are* most annoying to our customers.

Correct

Our *order* for these goods *was* placed on March 9.

The *mislabeling* of sizes, especially in such articles as hats, blouses, and stockings, *is* most annoying to our customers.

2. PLURAL COMPLEMENTS. A singular verb should be used with a singular subject even though the complement (a word that completes the predicate) is plural.

Incorrect

The most favorable *period are* the last three weeks of the year.

The main *advantage* of the new filing cabinet *are* the five full-size drawers.

Correct

The most favorable *period is* the last three weeks of the year.

The main *advantage* of the new filing cabinet *is* the five full-size drawers.

3. PLURAL SUBJECTS USED IN SINGULAR SENSE. A plural subject which expresses a unit of thought or measurement takes a singular verb.

Buy now and pay later is the philosophy of millions of Americans.

292

Twenty dollars is a lot of money to pay for a necktie.

Diamond Flakes gives sparkling new brightness to finest cottons and rayons.

4. **DELAYED SUBJECTS.** When the subject follows the verb, be sure that the number of the subject and the number of the verb are the same.

Incorrect	Correct
Still unsold from the original lot *is* three *generators*.	Still unsold from the original lot *are* three *generators*.
There *was* five packing *cases* in the shipment.	There *were* five packing *cases* in the shipment.

5. **COLLECTIVE NOUNS.** A *collective noun,* one that refers to a group of like persons or things, takes a singular verb when reference is made to the group as a unit; it takes a plural verb when reference is made to the individual members of the group.

Incorrect

The *committee was* unable to agree among themselves.

Correct

The *committee were* unable to agree among themselves.
The *staff were* called together.
The *staff has* no authority to act.

6. *With* **AND SIMILAR EXPRESSIONS.** A singular subject, even though followed by a phrase beginning with *together with, with, as well as,* or *in addition to,* takes a singular verb.

Incorrect	Correct
Mr. Farmer, with his lawyer, *are* going to court this morning.	*Mr. Farmer,* with his lawer, *is* going to court this morning.
Mr. St. Clair, together with his wife and two children, *were seen* boarding the train.	*Mr. St. Clair,* together with his wife and two children, *was seen* boarding the train.
Our secretary, as well as three clerks and a porter, *were dismissed.*	*Our secretary,* as well as three clerks and a porter, *was dismissed.* (But: *Our secretary and three clerks,* in addition to a porter, *were dismissed.*)

7. NEGATIVE EXPLANATORY PHRASES. When a negative explanatory phrase precedes or follows the subject of a verb and contains a noun differing from the subject in number, be sure that the verb agrees with the subject (not with the noun in the explanatory phrase).

Incorrect	*Correct*
The *players*, not the coach, *was* standing on the field.	The *players*, not the coach, *were* standing on the field.
Not Mr. Dryer but his *subordinates was* reprimanded.	Not Mr. Dryer but his *subordinates were* reprimanded.

8. WORDS SUCH AS *Each* AND *Every*. Such words as *each, every, everyone, everybody, no one, nobody, someone, somebody, anyone, anybody, either,* and *neither* (see Rule 9) should be followed by singular verbs. Other pronouns that relate to them should also be singular. In current practice, *none* is construed as singular or plural, depending on the sense in which it is employed in the sentence. The following examples are correct:

> Almost *everyone likes* to pay his bills promptly.
> *Every farmer, laborer, and consumer is involved.*
> *Somebody has* to come in on Saturdays.
> *Neither* of them *is qualified* to hold the job.
> No discount was offered and none *was* expected.
> *None* of the bank's officers *are* on the platform.

9. COMPOUND SUBJECTS. Two or more subjects joined by *and* are normally considered plural and take a plural verb. When, however, the subjects are joined by *or, either . . . or,* or *neither . . . nor,* the verb agrees in person and number with the nearer subject. These examples are correct.

You and I are going together.

You or I am to be held responsible for the error.

Either *the debtor or his co-signers are* required to be present at the meeting.

Neither *he nor they are* ready to take the responsibility.

10. RELATIVE PRONOUNS AS SUBJECTS. A verb following the

relative pronoun *who, which,* or *that* agrees in person and number with the antecedent of the pronoun, that is, the word for which the pronoun stands.

> It is *I who am* new at this job. (*Am* is first person singular to agree with *I.*)

> You may give the samples to *everyone who wants* them. (*Wants is* third person singular to agree with *everyone.*)

11. CONSTRUCTIONS SUCH AS *One of Those Who.* In a construction similar to *one of those who,* the verb following *who* (or *which* or *that*) is plural.

Incorrect

> He is *one of those persons who is* always shifting the blame.

Correct

> He is *one of those persons who are always* shifting the blame.
> (Of those persons who are always shifting the blame, he is one.)

> This is *one of the most daring solutions that have been* offered.

12. WORDS SUCH AS *Some* AND *Part.* Subjects such as *some, part, half, quarter,* etc., take either a singular or plural verb, depending on whether the portion referred to is considered as a unit or as representing the individual members of the unit. The following sentences are correct:

> *Some* of the paint *has been stolen.*
> *Some* of the papers *are missing.*
> *Part* of the apples *are* mine.
> *Part* of the shipment *is going* by express.
> *Three-fourths* of the legislators *are* against the bill.
> *Three-fourths* of the original estate *is* all that remains.

13. *Number* AS A SUBJECT. As a subject, *a number* takes a plural verb; *the number* takes a singular verb. The examples below are correct.

> *A number* of new designs *are expected* next week.

> *A number* of well-known businessmen *were involved* in the transaction.

> *The number* of people involved *was* not large.

EXERCISE

In each sentence where the verb does not agree with its subject, correct the verb. Two of these sentences are correct.

1. A test of the three different methods are the only way of arriving at a fair conclusion.

2. A thousand dollars for the machines are more than we can afford.

3. A number of scientists from the University of California was responsible for the new development.

4. I as well as my partners are interested in seeing the December figures.

5. What most people call the main office are really three wooden sheds joined together.

6. Of the barrel of sugar we started on Friday, only one-third is left.

7. Mr. Smith or his backers is sure to be present at the conference.

8. Every man, woman, and child who see the Corey Pen will want one.

9. The supervisor as well as the supervised need an occasional respite from the daily routine.

10. There is considerably more new orders on hand today than there was on the same date last year.

11. Neither of the models are selling well this season.

12. Mr. Jackson is one of the executives who has been chosen for the trip abroad.

13. I do not know whether you or Mr. Carson are supposed to be on duty.

14. Even better than the imported sample was the reproductions from our Bridgeport factory.

15. It is I who is thankful.

16. The original, not the carbon copies, are to be sent to the client.

17. The number of errors the trainees make are not important at this time.

18. Neither of you is going to sit by while Thompson does all the work.

19. Whichever of the two firms give the earliest delivery date will get the contract.

20. Mr. Carter, together with Mr. Sloan and Mr. Perry, are up for reelection.

Section III
Case of Nouns and Pronouns

The case of a noun or pronoun depends on its grammatical function in the sentence. The subject of a verb is in the nominative case. The object of a verb or the object of a preposition is in the objective case. A noun or pronoun that shows possession is in the possessive case.

1. NOMINATIVE AND OBJECTIVE CASES OF NOUNS. Nouns have the same form in both the nominative and objective cases. For this reason the nominative and objective cases of nouns are not a problem to the student in composition.

Nominative

These *papers* will have to be studied carefully.

Objective

We shall study these *papers* carefully.

2. POSSESSIVE CASE OF NOUNS. The possessive case of a noun is generally formed by adding an apostrophe and *s* in the singular.

> a girl's date, a boy's hair, a child's watch, a man's coat

In the plural, the possessive case of a noun is formed by adding an apostrophe to the plural form of the noun or by adding an apostrophe and *s* if the plural form of the noun does not end in *s*.

> girls' dates, boys' hair, children's watches, men's coats

In the instance of a singular noun already ending in *s*, or the sound of *s*, an apostrophe and *s* are usually added when the word has only one syllable; an apostrophe alone is added when the word has more than one syllable or when the addition of an *s* would make pronunciation difficult.[1]

> the lass's hair, Jones's report, Burns's absence
> the lasses' hair, Davis' report, ladies' suits
> for appearance' sake, two years' delay (not years's)

When joint ownership is indicated by two or more names connected by *and*, the possessive case is formed by adding an apostrophe and *s* to the last name only.

> Dave and Joe's repair shop; Smith, Kline & French's new product;
> Dunn and Capper's Department Store

3. POSSESSIVE OF INANIMATE OBJECTS. Except in certain idiomatic expressions (*a day's work, a week's wages*), it is not considered good practice to use the possessive case with the names of inanimate objects. Instead, use a phrase beginning with *of*.

Questionable	*Correct*
The garage's roof caved in.	The roof of the garage caved in.
The cabinet's finish was marred by the heat.	The finish of the cabinet was marred by the heat.

4. NOMINATIVE AND OBJECTIVE CASES OF PRONOUNS. Many pronouns, like nouns, have the same form in the nominative and objective cases (*somebody, anyone, another*, etc.). These are, however, some exceptions; these are listed in the following table:

Nominative	I	he	she	we	them	who
Objective	me	him	her	us	they	whom

5. PRONOUNS AS SUBJECTS. A pronoun that is the subject of a verb should be in the nominative case.

Incorrect	*Correct*
They and *us* are in full agreement.	They and *we* are in full agreement.
He, not *her*, should take the blame.	He, not *she*, should take the blame.
Us supervisors should stick together.	*We* supervisors should stick together.
Whom shall I say called?	*Who* shall I say called?

---

[1] Practice is sometimes at variance with this rule. The correspondent should, at all times, follow the wishes of his employer in this and other matters of usage.

Get the file from *whomever* has it.

Get the file from *whoever* has it. (Subject of the verb *has*. The whole clause, *whoever has it,* is the object of the preposition *from*.)

6. **PREDICATE PRONOUNS.** A pronoun complement following *is, was,* or other forms of the verb *to be* should be in the nominative case.

> It was *I*. That is *he*. *Who* will it be? (It will be *who*.)
> I thought it was *they*. It is not *she* who is at fault.

7. **POSSESSIVE CASE OF PRONOUNS.** With few exceptions (e.g., one's, everybody's), the possessive case of pronouns is not formed by the addition of an apostrophe. Notice the possessive forms listed below:

my, mine	our, ours
your, yours	your, yours
his, her, hers, its	their, theirs
whose	

Note. It's is the contraction of *it* and *is* and *it* and *has. Who's* is the contraction of *who* and *is* and *who* and *has.*

> *It's* going to be a rough year for competition.
> *It's* been a long time since I saw you.
> *Who's* going besides you?
> *Who's* been at my desk?

8. **PRONOUNS AS OBJECTS.** A pronoun used as the object of a verb or as the object of a preposition should be in the objective case.

Incorrect	*Correct*
between you and *I*	between you and *me*
instead of *they*	instead of *them*
to either him or *we*	to either him or *us*
Who do you mean?	*Whom* do you mean? (Object of *do mean*.)
I shall name *whoever* you wish.	I shall name *whomever* you wish. (Object of *wish*.)

We shall try to discover for *who* the gift was intended.

We shall try to discover for *whom* the gift was intended. (Object of the preposition *for*.)

9. PRONOUNS WITH INFINITIVES. A pronoun used as the subject or complement of an infinitive should be in the objective case.

> He asked *me* to leave. (Subject of *to leave*.)
> Miss Lipton took my partner to be *me*.

10. MODIFIERS OF GERUNDS. A noun or pronoun used to modify a gerund (see Section I) is generally in the possessive case. However, do not use the possessive form with the gerund when its use results in awkwardness; see the second example below:

Poor	Better
John's supervisor objected to *him* coming late so often.	John's supervisor objected to *his* coming late so often.

Poor	Better
Our supervisor objected to Miss Baker's and my taking more than fifteen minutes for a coffee break.	Our supervisor objected to Miss Baker and me taking more than fifteen minutes for a coffee break.
Mr. Glenn talking disturbed those who were trying to concentrate on the motion picture.	*Mr. Glenn's* talking disturbed those who were trying to concentrate on the motion picture.

Correct

> We found Mr. Glenn talking to a neighbor. (Here, *Mr. Glenn* is object of the verb *found*. *Talking* is not a gerund, but a participle modifying *Mr. Glenn*.)

11. PRONOUNS IN APPOSITION. A pronoun in apposition (that is, one that explains or characterizes a noun or another pronoun it closely follows) should be in the same case as its antecedent.

> The three of us—*Jack, Bill, and I*—will go together.

> The fifteen-year certificate went to only two employees, *Mr. Sax and me*.

> The car is ours—*Jane's and mine*.

12. ELLIPTICAL EXPRESSIONS. In an elliptical expression (one in which certain understood words are omitted), use the form of the pronoun you would use if all the missing words were present.

Incorrect	*Correct*
He can do as well as *me*.	He can do as well as *I* (can).
Miss Darby is more capable than *him*.	Miss Darby is more capable than *he* (is).
They sent the report to Mr. Humphrey rather than *I*.	They sent the report to Mr. Humphrey rather than (to) *me*.

EXERCISE

Wherever the incorrect case form of a noun or pronoun is given in the following sentences, substitute the correct form. Six of the sentences are correct.

1. I did not know whether it was she or him who wanted to see the report.
2. The Haines Company seems to be as prompt as us in making deliveries.
3. We should appreciate your calling on us when you are in the neighborhood.
4. It's going to be a busier season for them than for us.
5. Who's desk is it that is so littered with papers?
6. After you and me have had a look at the damage, we shall call in our engineers.
7. We should like to thank whomever is responsible for the work.
8. Whether or not you decide to subscribe, the book is your's to keep.
9. Will you please look up the Joneses reservation?
10. The man who we saw descend the stairs was Mr. Gray.
11. It will make no difference whether you give your check to we or them.
12. Who do you wish the gift sent to?
13. There was not much difference between their methods and ours.
14. His supervisor did not like Mr. Malloy having another job after hours.
15. If it was them who started these practices, I was not aware of it.
16. I purchased the draperies at Roger's and Hunt's Department Store.
17. Mr. Trotter will get better service if he gives the order to us rather than to the suppliers whom he has dealt with in the past.
18. Between you and I, the fall sales picture is rather bleak.
19. They left a sample for each of us—Mr. Courtney, Miss Graham, and me.
20. The customer for whom we have been saving the jacket failed to call for it.

Section IV
Reference of Pronouns

The correspondent should make the reference of every pronoun clear to the reader.

1. AGREEMENT OF PRONOUNS. A pronoun should agree with its antecedent in person, number, and gender—but not in case.

Incorrect	Correct
We, the employees of the Universal Corporation, desire to present this gift to *their* beloved ex-president, Mr. Mott.	*We,* the employees of the Universal Corporation, desire to present this gift to *our* beloved ex-president, Mr. Mott.
If you wire us your *instructions* for filling the order, we shall follow *it* to the letter.	If you wire us your *instructions* for filling the order, we shall follow *them* to the letter.

Faulty	Correct
France was unable to balance their national budget.	*France* was unable to balance *her* national budget.

2. AMBIGUOUS ANTECEDENTS. The noun for which the pronoun is a substitute should in every instance be unmistakable. Where possible, repeat the noun or use a synonym for it. In other instances, the sentence may be recast to avoid ambiguity.

Not clear	Better
When Frank introduced me to Mr. Johnson, I noticed that *he* appeared ill.	When Frank introduced me to Mr. Johnson, I noticed that *Frank* appeared to be ill. (*Or,* depending on the fact: . . . I noticed that *Mr. Johnson* appeared to be ill.)

Mr. Gates submitted the figures to his client, but *he* was not entirely satisfied with them.	Mr. Gates submitted the figures to his *client,* but his client was not entirely satisfied with them. (*Or,* depending on the fact: Mr. Gates was not entirely satisfied with the figures *he* submitted to his client.)

3. *Everybody, Each,* AND SIMILAR ANTECEDENTS. A singular pronoun should be used in referring to such antecedents as *everybody, nobody, each, someone, anyone, either, neither.* A singular pronoun should also be used in referring to any word or words preceded by the adjective *each* or *every.*

Incorrect	*Correct*
Everybody wants *their* own way.	*Everybody* wants *his* own way.
Nobody had *their* notes with *them.*	*Nobody* had *his* notes with *him.*
Each typist and stenographer will be held responsible for their own machine.	*Each* typist and stenographer will be held responsible for *her* own machine.

Correct

> *All* typists and stenographers will be held responsible for *their* own machines.

4. *Either . . . or,* AND SIMILAR CONNECTIVES. When two noun antecedents are connected by *or, either . . . or,* or *neither . . . nor,* the pronoun following should agree in person, number, and gender with the nearer antecedent.

Incorrect	*Correct*
Neither Daniel nor *William* had brought *their* tools.	Neither Daniel nor *William* had brought *his* tools.
He or his *assistants* will give *his* permission.	He or his *assistants* will give *their* permission.
I shall go to either Mr. Elwood or *Mr. Dodge* for *their* advice.	I shall go to either Mr. Elwood or *Mr. Dodge* for *his* advice.

When the application of this rule results in awkwardness, it is better to reconstruct the sentence.

Awkward	*Better*
Either Mr. Bryon or Miss Cash will lend you her key.	Get the key from either Mr. Bryon or Miss Cash.

5. *One* AS AN ANTECEDENT. After the indefinite pronoun *one,* it is correct to use *one* or *one's* in referring to it. It is also correct to use the pronouns *he, him,* or *his.* These examples are correct.

> *One* can not always be too sure of *one's* business associates.
> *One* can not always be too sure of *his* business associates.

6. VAGUE REFERENCES. Do not use a pronoun to refer vaguely to a preceding idea.

Vague	*Better*
Our beverages are sold only in cans, *which* eliminates loss from breakage.	Our beverages are sold only in cans. *As a result,* loss from breakage is eliminated.
We can not accept the article for credit because *it* would set a very bad precedent.	We can not accept the article for credit because *to do so* would set a very bad precedent.
You may order direct from your dealer or from the factory, but in *that* case you will have to pay the express charges.	You may order direct from your local dealer or from the factory, but *if you order from the factory,* you will have to pay the express charges.

A pronoun may refer to a clause or an entire sentence when no awkwardness results and when the reference is unmistakably clear.

Acceptable

> Mr. Strong consented without protest to the terms, *which* is exactly what we anticipated.

> They cut their prices and invaded our territory. *This* means war.

7. CONSISTENCY IN NUMBER. Once a collective noun is established as singular or plural, reference to it should be consistent.

Poor	*Better*
The company is agreeable to the plan, but *they* want some assurance that all the provisions will be carried out.	The company is agreeable to the plan, but *it* wants some assurance that all the provisions will be carried out. (The verb *is* establishes *company* as singular.)

Also good

> The trustees of the company are agreeable to the plan, but *they* want some assurance that all the provisions will be carried out.

8. PRONOUNS WITHOUT ANTECEDENTS. Do not use a pronoun for which there is no antecedent.

Poor	*Better*
In our building *they* have 12 elevators.	Our building has 12 elevators.

Poor	*Better*
In England *they* import many American farm products.	England imports many American farm products.

Also good

> English merchants import many farm products which are grown in the United States.

9. PRONOUNS WITH INDEFINITE ANTECEDENTS. In a statement which does not refer to particular persons or things, a pronoun—*we, you, one,* or *they*—may be used in a general sense (see Rule 5).

> *We* know what happens to *our* economy when *we* curtail credit.
> *You* can not be too sure of people's motives.

10. ANTECEDENTS IN SUBORDINATE SYNTAX. Do not use a pronoun to refer to a noun which occupies a subordinate grammatical position in the sentence.

Poor	*Better*
We were losing money through inefficient bookkeeping; so we did *it* with a Tycoon Electric Bookkeeper. (*It* refers to *bookkeeping,* but the reference is not immediately apparent.)	We were losing money through inefficient bookkeeping; so we invested in a Tycoon Electric Bookkeeper.
In the company's catalogue, *it* gives the price as $39.50.	In the company's catalogue, the *price* is given as $39.50.

Also good

> The company's catalogue gives the price as $39.50.

EXERCISE A

In each of the following sentences the reference of a pronoun is faulty. In each sentence, substitute a noun or pronoun that would make the reference clear.

1. When I called on Mr. Dain and his partner, I discovered I had already met him.

2. Each of the girls was given a letter to copy and told to do the best they could.

3. Miss Gair asked Alice for the file on the Ajax Company, but she was not sure where it was.

4. The printing bill for the posters was excessively high; so the next time we had it done by another company.

5. Mr. Park met Mr. Graham for the first time yesterday. Today he told me he felt as if they had been business associates for years.

6. We keep our office supplies at the rear of the cupboard and find it very hard to get at.

7. When you put a new ribbon in the typewriter, you should clean it at the same time.

8. The credit department is more efficient than the bookkeeping department largely because it has inexperienced employees.

9. Advertising on television has grown very expensive because it reaches so many people.

10. Everyone present had an opportunity to express their opinion.

EXERCISE B

Rewrite the following examples in order to clarify the reference of the pronouns.

1. Executives who bully their employees should not expect people to sympathize with them.

2. They asked us to include a supply of advertising material with their order, which of course we were glad to do.

3. Bills are payable on the tenth of each month and most of our customers do it.

4. Mr. Terry is always five or six days behind with his daily sales reports, which is very annoying.

5. Even on farms they often prefer electricity for cooking.

6. He advised us to sell to the Drew Company on open account and fortunately it turned out all right.

7. The building is centrally located, which makes floor space very much in demand.

8. At his office they said Mr. Johnson would not be back until Thursday.

9. He refused to accept the shipment. This was due to damage in transit.

10. The 9 o'clock flight to Chicago was canceled, which gave us a wait of two hours for the next plane.

Section V
Verbs

A verb states what the subject does or is (see Section I). For example,

> The pipe *leaks*. We *arrived* on time. Mr. Addis *is* young.

VERB TENSES

Tense is that property of a verb which establishes the time of the action. The principal tenses are present, past, future, present perfect, past perfect, and future perfect. (See table accompanying Rule 13.)

1. PRESENT TENSE. Use the *present tense* to denote present time or to state a timeless truth.

> I *attend* the meetings every Thursday.
> He *is working* as fast as he *can*.
> Warm air *rises*.

The present tense may also be used, in certain instances, to denote future time.

> I *leave* on Monday.
> He *is going* to be disappointed.

2. PAST TIME. Use the *past tense* to denote action definitely completed.

Incorrect	Correct
We *have shipped* your order on May 24.	We *shipped* your order on May 24.

3. FUTURE TENSE: *Shall* AND *Will*. Use the *future tense* to indicate ordinary future time. *Shall* is correct in the first person, singular and plural (I *shall* go, we *shall* go), and *will* is correct in the second and third persons, singular and plural (you *will* go, he *will go*, they *will go*).

> I *shall* arrive on Friday.
>
> We *shall* be glad to hear from you.
>
> They *will* not place their order until we give assurance of delivery by July 1.

To express determination, *will* is correct in the first person, and *shall* is correct in the second and third persons.

> We *will* have the contract fulfilled even if we have to sue.
> You *shall* go; I insist.

In questions, *shall* is correct in the first person, and *shall* or *will* in the second and third persons, depending on the form you expect in the answer.

> *Shall* we have the pleasure of seeing you again soon?
>
> *Shall* you be there? (The answer expected is "I *shall*.")
>
> *Will* he consent to be one of the judges? (The answer expected is "He *will*.")

4. FUTURE TENSE: *Should* AND *Would*. *Should* and *would* follow the same grammatical pattern as *shall* and *will*; that is, *should* is correct in the first person, and *would* is correct in the second and third persons.[1]

> I *should* be glad to have you call on me.
> We *should* appreciate your comments.
> I am sure they *would* welcome any suggestions.

Should is used in all three persons to denote moral obligation. *Would* is used in all three persons to denote habitual or frequentative action.

> You *should* report on time every morning.
> I *would* go there day after day, hoping to pick up a bargain.

---

[1] Many educated persons do not rigidly observe the distinctions between *shall* and *will* and between *should* and *would*. Hence usages such as these are acceptable: I *will* arrive on Friday. *Will* you be there? *Would* you care to see the report? We *would* appreciate your comments.

5. **PRESENT PERFECT TENSE.** Use the *present perfect tense* to indicate action begun in the past and continuing into the present, or action completed in the immediate past.

> I *have been attending* evening school for the past two years. (Action was begun in the past and is continuing into the present.)
>
> I *have written* the report and am waiting for it to be typed. (Action was recently completed.)

6. **PAST PERFECT TENSE.** Use the *past perfect tense* to denote action completed prior to a certain time in the past.

> Mr. Tindall *had come* to certain conclusions even before he attended the meeting.
>
> I *had done* everything in my power to avert yesterday's accident.

7. **FUTURE PERFECT TENSE.** Use the *future perfect tense* to denote action completed before a time in the future.

> By the end of the day, he *will have learned* his lesson.
> On Saturday I *shall have been gone* two weeks.

8. **TENSE OF INFINITIVES AND PARTICIPLES.** Be sure that the tense of the *infinitive* or *participle* is in proper relation to the time expressed by the main verb. Use the *present infinitive* or *present participle* to indicate action occurring at the same time as the verb; use the *perfect infinitive*, the *perfect particple*, or the *past participle* to indicate action prior to the time of the verb.

Incorrect	Correct
I wanted *to have mailed* the check, but I forgot.	I wanted *to mail* the check, but I forgot. (The present infinitive *to mail* denotes action concurrent with that of the verb *wanted*.)
They later believed it to be *stolen*.	They later believed it *to have been stolen*. (The perfect infinitive *to have been stolen* indicates action prior to that of the verb *believed*.)
Paying all his bills on time, Mr. Hill was sure he was entitled to special consideration by the credit man.	*Having paid* all his bills on time, Mr. Hill was sure he was entitled to special consideration by the credit man. (The perfect participle *having paid* denotes action prior to that of the verb *was*.)

FORMATION OF TENSES

In order to form the tense of a verb correctly, the writer needs to know its principal parts: present tense, past tense, past participle, present participle. The formation of the principal parts varies according to whether a verb is regular or irregular.

9. REGULAR VERBS. The *past tense* and the *past participle* of a regular verb are formed by adding *–d*, *–t*, or *–ed* to the *present tense* form. The *present participle* is formed by adding *–ing* to the *present tense* form. Note the examples of regular verbs below.

Present Tense	Past Tense	Past Participle	Present Participle
walk	walked	walked	walking
ask	asked	asked	asking
tempt	tempted	tempted	tempting
live	lived	lived	living
deal	dealt	dealt	dealing

10. IRREGULAR VERBS. The principal parts of irregular verbs are given in the dictionary. For example, *give* (present), *gave* (past), *given* (past participle), *giving* (present participle). If the dictionary omits the *past participle*, the form is the same as that of the *past tense*. For example, *bring* (present), *brought* (past tense and past participle), *bringing* (present participle).

11. PRINCIPAL PARTS OF COMMON IRREGULAR VERBS. Notice the principal parts of the following irregular verbs:

Present Tense	Past Tense	Past Participle	Present Participle
arise	arose	arisen	arising
begin	began	begun	beginning
blow	blew	blown	blowing
burst	burst	burst	bursting
cast	cast	cast	casting
do	did	done	doing
draw	drew	drawn	drawing
drink	drank	drunk	drinking
drive	drove	driven	driving
dwell	dwelt	dwelt	dwelling
eat	ate	eaten	eating
fall	fell	fallen	falling
fly	flew	flown	flying
forget	forgot	forgotten	forgetting

Present Tense	*Past Tense*	*Past Participle*	*Present Participle*
go	went	gone	going
grow	grew	grown	growing
know	knew	known	knowing
lay [2] (to put down)	laid	laid	laying
lead	led	led	leading
lie [2] (to recline)	lay	lain	lying
light	lit, lighted	lit, lighted	lighting
lose	lost	lost	losing
pay	paid	paid	paying
rise	rose	risen	rising
run	ran	run	running
see	saw	seen	seeing
set (to put in place)	set	set	setting
shine (to give light)	shone	shone	shining
sink	sank	sunk	sinking
sit (to be seated)	sat	sat	sitting
slide	slid	slid	sliding
speak	spoke	spoken	speaking
swell	swelled	swollen	swelling
take	took	taken	taking
tear	tore	torn	tearing
throw	threw	thrown	throwing
write	wrote	written	writing

VOICE

The voice of a verb indicates whether the subject is acting or is receiving the action of the verb.

12. ACTIVE VOICE. A verb is said to be in the *active voice* when the subject performs the action of the verb.

> John *mailed* the letter yesterday.
> Snow *covered* the crates.
> Edward *read* the books.

13. PASSIVE VOICE. A verb is said to be in the *passive voice* when the subject receives the action of the verb.

---

[2] One reason for the confusion between the parts of certain pairs of verbs like *lay* and *lie* is that one is transitive (takes an object) and the other is intransitive (does not take an object). (See Section I, 4, p. 283, for more information about transitive and intransitive verbs.)

The letter *was mailed* by John yesterday.
The crates *were covered* with snow.
The snowballs *were thrown* at him.

The following table compares the active and passive forms of the verb *ask*. (The practical uses of the active and passive voices are discussed in Chapter 5.)

	Active	*Passive*
Present	he asks	he is asked
	he is asking	he is being asked
	he does ask	
Past	he asked	he was asked
	he did ask	he was being asked
Future	he will ask	he will be asked
	he will be asking	
Present perfect	he has asked	he has been asked
	he has been asking	
Past perfect	he had asked	he had been asked
	he had been asking	
Future perfect	he will have asked	he will have been asked
	he will have been asking	
Infinitives	to ask, to have asked	to be asked, to have been asked
Gerunds	asking, having asked	being asked, having been asked
Participles	asked, having asked	being asked, asked, having been asked

MOOD

The mood of a verb indicates the way in which an idea is expressed. A verb has three moods, which are called indicative, imperative, and subjunctive.

14. INDICATIVE MOOD. The *indicative mood* is used to make statements of fact and to ask direct questions. This mood is the most frequently used of the three forms.

The passengers *complained* of the delay.
Mr. Tebbel *is going* to the convention.
Will you *pick* up the contract tomorrow?

15. IMPERATIVE MOOD. The *imperative mood* is used to express a command or a request. It usually takes the simplest form of the verb.

> *Please* sign both cards.
> *Enjoy* yourself.
> *Let's* dine late this evening

In order to express an emphatic command or a negative command, combine *do* with the imperative form.

> *Do drop* in at your convenience.
> *Do* not *write* to him yet.

16. SUBJUNCTIVE MOOD. The *subjunctive mood* expresses a condition, a wish, or a doubt.

17. FORMS OF THE SUBJUNCTIVE MOOD. In current usage, the subjunctive mood differs from the indicative mood mainly in the third person of the present tense, singular, as indicated here.

Indicative		*Subjunctive*	
I ask	we ask	I ask	we ask
you ask	you ask	you ask	you ask
he *asks*	they ask	he *ask*	they ask

The subjunctive of the verb *to be* is *be* in all forms of the present tense and *were* in all forms of the past tense.

> We suggest that he *ask* (not *asks*) the guard.
> I requested that he *be* (not *is*) seated next to the speaker.
> I wish I *were* (not *was*) going with you.

18. USES OF THE SUBJUNCTIVE MOOD. Use the subjunctive mood (1) in an "if" clause indicating doubt or impossibility of accomplishment, (2) in a formal wish or prayer, and (3) in a "that" clause expressing a request, command, decision, motion, or resolution.

If he *were* coming, he would have wired ahead.

I wish he *were* here.

I request that you *be* present at the meeting tomorrow.

The president demanded that Mr. Quinn *admit* his part in the scheme.

I move that the amendment *be* approved.

The Lord *be* with you.

EXERCISE

Indicate the correct form in each of the following sentences:

1. On May 24 Mr. Wilson (will be, will have been) with the company for twenty-five years.

2. I should like to (be, have been) present when the merger was negotiated.

3. After (receiving, having received) the quotation, we wired our brokers to place our order.

4. I (brang, brought) the minutes of the last meeting with me.

5. Apparently they (shall, will) not be satisfied until they have secured national distribution of their products.

6. One of the directors asked that he (is, be) excused before the meeting was over.

7. By the time I arrived, the meeting (was, had been) concluded.

8. If Mr. Clayton (was, were) as interested in sales as he is in costs, he might still be in business.

9. I (shall, will) see you tomorrow after lunch.

10. Now I have (began, begun) to think that we made a mistake in setting the time of the meeting so early.

11. Mr. Ward (led, lead) his company very ably during the war years.

12. When I was in charge of the plant, I (should, would) visit the finishing department every day.

13. We wanted to (test, have tested) the merchandise before placing a large order.

14. We (should, would) be pleased to know that you are coming.

15. The workmen (lay, laid) the cartons in neat rows and piled them up to the ceiling.

16. The entire shipment (had sat, had set) out in the rain for two hours before the expressmen came to cart it away.

17. Mr. Gann (filed, has filed) his income tax return only yesterday.

18. We wish Mr. Gates (was, were) prompter in meeting his financial obligations.

19. I asked Miss Sayre whether she (placed, had placed) the Martinson folder back in the file.

20. We believe you will want to (take, have taken) advantage of this offer before it expires.

Section VI
Adjectives and Adverbs

Adjectives and adverbs sometimes confuse the writer because they are similar (but not the same) in function and because they are sometimes spelled alike or nearly alike. (See Section I, 3, 5.)

COMPARISON OF ADJECTIVES

Almost all adjectives change their forms to indicate degrees of comparison. These degrees are three: positive, comparative, and superlative.

1. POSITIVE DEGREE. The *positive degree* of an adjective denotes the quality of an adjective in its simplest form, without comparison. Examples are *warm, sturdy, tempting*.

2. COMPARATIVE DEGREE. The *comparative degree* calls attention to more or less of the same quality of an adjective. It is regularly formed by adding *–er* to the positive form or by adding *–r* if the positive form ends in *e* or by prefacing the positive form with the word *more* or *less*. Examples are *warmer, sturdier, freer, stranger, ruder, more tempting, less tempting*.

The comparative degree is used in comparing two things.

> The company doctor reported that Mr. Garr's right eye was the *weaker*. (Not *weakest*.)

> We received a report from both Mr. Temple and Mr. Albert. Mr. Albert's was by far the *more* comprehensive. (Not *most*.)

3. SUPERLATIVE DEGREE. The *superlative degree* denotes the greatest or least degree of the same quality of an adjective. It is

regularly formed by adding *—est* to the positive form or by adding
—st if the positive form ends in *e* or by prefacing the positive form
with the word *most* or *least*. Examples are *warmest, sturdiest,
freest, strangest, rudest, most tempting, least tempting.*

The superlative degree is used in comparing three or more
things.

> I have the *biggest* desk in the office. (There are more than two.)

> These are the *most striking* designs we have ever shown.

The writer may occasionally use the superlative without intend-
ing any specific comparison.

> You were *most thoughtful* to write.

> He is a *most competent* draftsman.

4. REGULAR ADJECTIVES. Here are examples of adjectives which
form degrees of comparison regularly.

Positive	Comparative	Superlative
bright	brighter	brightest
	more bright	most bright
	less bright	least bright
kind	kinder	kindest
	more kind	most kind
	less kind	least kind
prompt	prompter	promptest
	more prompt	most prompt
	less prompt	least prompt
ordinary	more ordinary	most ordinary
	less ordinary	least ordinary
cautious	more cautious	most cautious
	less cautious	least cautious
qualified	more qualified	most qualified
	less qualified	least qualified

5. IRREGULAR ADJECTIVES. Adjectives that can not be compared
in the manner indicated above are called irregular adjectives. Notice these irregular adjectives and their comparative and superlative
forms.

Positive	Comparative	Superlative
good	better	best
bad	worse	worst

Positive	Comparative	Superlative
ill	worse	worst
much	more	most
many	more	most
little	less	least
far	farther	farthest
old	older, elder	oldest, eldest
late	later, latter	latest, last

SPECIAL USES OF ADJECTIVES

The writer should use adjectives logically and consistently.

6. ABSOLUTE ADJECTIVES. Certain adjectives like *unique, perfect, impossible,* and *final,* are absolute in their meaning and do not lend themselves to comparison.

Poor	*Better*
The treasurer's plan is *most unique.*	The treasurer's plan is *unique.* (*Unique* means "the only one of its kind.")
Our sales quota is becoming *more impossible* to reach all the time.	Our sales quota is becoming *less possible* to reach all the time.

7. COMPARISONS WITH *Other*. Comparison of two persons or things in the same class should logically employ the adjective *other.* (See also Section VII, 8.)

Incorrect	*Correct*
No applicant is so well-qualified as Mr. Gaynor.	No *other* applicant is so well-qualified as Mr. Gaynor. (Since Mr. Gaynor is an applicant, he must be compared with other applicants.)
Our line of shirts is better than any line on the market.	Our line of shirts is better than any *other* line on the market. (*Our line* is one of the lines being compared.)

8. ADJECTIVES WITH SPECIFIC VERBS. After certain verbs—*be, become, appear, seem, look, smell, taste, feel,* and *sound*—use an adjective, not an adverb, to describe the subject.

> The peaches you sent taste very *good* indeed (not very *well*).
> The inkwell looks *dry* (not *drily*).
> The machine appears *new* (not *newly*).
> He sounds *pleasant* over the telephone (not *pleasantly*).

"I do not feel *well*" is correct because *well* is an adjective when it is used to describe a state of health.

To describe the action of the verb, an adverb must be used.

> Mr. Edwards looked *carefully* at the sample.

9. EXPRESSIONS SUCH AS *This Sort of*. Before the singular words such as *sort, kind,* and *type,* use a singular demonstrative adjective. For example, use *this,* not *these* or *those.*

Incorrect	Correct
I do not like *these kind* of paper clips.	I do not like *this kind* of paper clips.

10. COMPOUND ADJECTIVES. An adjective modifier consisting of more than one word is usually hyphenated. (See Section IX, 46, 47.)

> He has a *one-half* interest in the business.
> I like his *matter-of-fact* manner.
> Please let us have an *up-to-the-minute* report.
> Did you order the *eight-by-ten* envelopes?
> *Sixty-five* dollars a week is the average rate.

COMPARISON OF ADVERBS

Adverbs, like adjectives, have three degrees of comparison: positive, comparative, and superlative.

11. REGULAR ADVERBS. The *comparative degree* of regular adverbs is formed by adding *—er* to the *positive* or by prefacing the positive form with the word *more* or *less.* The *superlative* is formed by adding *—est* to the positive or by prefacing the positive form with the word *most* or *least.* Here are examples.

Positive	Comparative	Superlative
quick or quickly	quicker more quickly less quickly	quickest most quickly least quickly
slow or slowly	slower more slowly less slowly	slowest most slowly least slowly
often	oftener more often less often	oftenest most often least often
happily	more happily less happily	most happily least happily

12. IRREGULAR ADVERBS. Notice the comparison of the following irregular adverbs:

Positive	Comparative	Superlative
little	less	least
much	more	most
well	better	best
ill	worse	worst
badly	worse	worst
late	later	latest, last
near	nearer	nearest, next
far	farther, further	farthest, furthest

Adverbs such as *now, then, there,* and *hitherto* can not be compared.

CORRECT USE OF ADVERBS

The writer should be careful to use adverbs correctly.

13. DOUBLE NEGATIVE. Avoid the use of two negative adverbs to express a single negative idea.

Incorrect

We will *not* accept *no* more hair brushes for exchange or refund.

We *don't hardly* know him.

Correct

We will *not* accept *any* more hair brushes for exchange or refund.

We *hardly* know him. (*Or:* We *don't* know him well.)

14. NEGATIVE COMPARISON. In formal writing, a comparison beginning with the adverb *not* should be completed by *so . . . as.*

Questionable

He is *not as* experienced *as* he pretends to be.

Correct

He is *not so* experienced *as* he pretends to be.

15. POSITION OF ADVERBS SUCH AS *Only, Nearly.* A limiting adverb—*only, nearly, just,* or *even*—should be placed immediately before the sentence element it modifies.

Poor

We *only* shipped the order two days ago.

He broke his ankle *nearly.*

Better

We shipped the order *only* two days ago.

He *nearly* broke his ankle.

Poor	Better
He *just* received the shipment yesterday.	He received the shipment *just* yesterday.
I *even* want you to do it at the risk of failure.	I want you to do it *even* at the risk of failure.

16. *Very Much* BEFORE PAST PARTICLES. *Very much* is preferred to *very* alone before a past participle that is not also regarded as a pure adjective.

Poor	Better
If you are going to be *very* delayed, please wire us.	If you are going to be *very much* delayed, please wire us.

CONFOUNDING OF ADJECTIVES AND ADVERBS

Because their forms are often the same or similar, the writer may confound adjectives and adverbs. However, study and practice should insure proper use.

Incorrect	Correct
This store will be closed *temporary*.	This store will be closed *temporarily*. (Adverb modifies verb *will be closed*.)
The record of results is *real* impressive.	The record of results is *really* impressive. (Adverb modifies adjective *impressive*.)
The machine is not performing too *good*.	The machine is not performing too *well*. (Adverb modifies verb *is performing*.)

EXERCISE

Rewrite the following sentences, correcting any errors in the use of adjectives and adverbs. Three of these sentences are correct.

1. The singing commercial does not harmonize too good with the dramatic presentation.

2. My client would hardly know what to do if I weren't at his elbow to tell him.

3. The lamps look beautifully when they are lit.

4. These kind of chairs have the most comfortable backs.

5. Between John's copy for the advertisement and Henry's, I like John's best.

6. We have not seen nor heard from Miss Craven since she went on vacation.

7. We are very concerned over his failure to answer our letters requesting payment.

8. Mr. Merry is not on our regular payroll, but he worked some for us last year.

9. The buffet is a real useful piece of furniture.

10. The machine operates easier now that it has been oiled.

11. Mr. Ellis has not performed his duties any different since he came here twenty years ago.

12. Both our branch stores are well located, but the uptown branch does the most business.

13. The new summer suits are far more lighter and cooler.

14. I scarcely never attend the Tuesday morning meetings any more.

15. Carson's American cheese blends especially good with milk and cream to make those rich casserole sauces.

16. Of all the solutions, Mr. Brent's was the most perfect.

17. We believe that our creditors are not taking our threats of action serious enough.

18. How big a variety of this style of flannel trousers do you have?

19. Mr. Baker has not nearly as many problems as he makes you think he has.

20. Let us see if we can blend the two fibers to obtain a tweed that does not feel too roughly.

Section VII
Coherence and Emphasis

The parts that make up the sentence should be selected, arranged, and connected so as to convey clearly and effectively the idea the writer intends.[1]

1. SENTENCE FRAGMENT. A sentence fragment is a group of words that do not express a complete thought. Thus, it is inaccurate to use or punctuate a sentence fragment as a complete sentence. Rather, incorporate the fragment into the sentence with which its thought belongs.

Poor	*Better*
At the height of our busy season he was spending three weeks on the beach at Bermuda. *While I worked evenings and weekends.*	At the height of our busy season he was spending three weeks on the beach at Bermuda while I worked evenings and weekends.
Mr. Smith asked to see the green Oriental rug. *The one we had sold the week before to the Stanton Department Store.*	Mr. Smith asked to see the green Oriental rug, the one we had sold the week before to the Stanton Department Store.

2. TELEGRAPHIC STYLE. Do not omit articles, nouns, or pronouns which are necessary for the grammatical completeness of the sentence. Such omissions give the impression of haste and discourtesy.

---

[1] For a more thorough treatment see Curme, George O.: *English Grammar,* College Outline Series (New York: Barnes & Noble, Inc., 1947) and Vivian, C. H., and Jackson, B. M.: *English Composition,* College Outline Series (New York: Barnes & Noble, Inc., 1961).

Poor	*Better*
Am enclosing order. Please ship goods by fastest route.	*I* am enclosing *my* order. Please ship *the* goods by *the* fastest route.

The *telegraphic* style may, of course, be used in telegrams, but even then words should not be omitted at the expense of clarity.

3. OMISSION OF ARTICLE. Do not omit an article which is necessary for clarity.

Not clear	*Better*
The vice president and director of sales agreed to attend the meeting in Atlantic City.	The vice president and *the* director of sales agreed to attend the meeting in Atlantic City.

If one person has both titles, the above sentence should be recast to read,

> Mr. Smith, the vice president and director of sales, agreed to attend the meeting in Atlantic City.

> *Or,*

> The vice president, who is also the director of sales, agreed to attend the meeting in Atlantic City.

4. OMISSION OF *That*. Do not omit the word *that* when it is needed to prevent misreading of the sentence.

Misleading	*Better*
Mr. Conklin believed Mr. Parrish should place the order immediately.	Mr. Conklin believed *that* Mr. Parrish should place the order immediately.
He said that over ten thousand entries were submitted in the contest and the prizes were distributed to fifty-seven winners.	He said that over ten thousand entries were submitted in the contest and *that* the prizes were distributed to fifty-seven winners.

5. OMISSION OF PREPOSITION. Do not omit the preposition in an expression of time.

Poor	*Better*
We shall write to Mr. Treadwell again August 12.	We shall write to Mr. Treadwell again *on* August 12.
We are open July and August until 6 p.m.	We are open *during* July and August until 6 p.m.

6. OMISSION OF VERB. Do not omit a verb or part of a verb which is necessary for grammatical completeness.

Poor	*Better*
The goods were ordered on May 9 and the confirmation received on May 15.	The goods were ordered on May 9 and the confirmation *was* received on May 15.
The table was mahogany and the chairs limed oak.	The table was mahogany and the chairs were limed oak. (*Or:* The tables were mahogany and the chairs limed oak.)

7. IDIOMATIC COMPLETENESS. Do not omit a preposition which is necessary to complete an idiomatic expression.

Poor	*Better*
Joe Hack's interest and devotion *to* the business are not to be questioned.	Joe Hack's interest *in* and devotion *to* the business are not to be questioned.

8. ILLOGICAL COMPARISON. Do not omit a word which is necessary to complete a comparison logically.

Poor	*Better*
Nylon is one of the strongest if not the strongest synthetic fiber yet developed.	Nylon is one of the strongest synthetic fibers, if not the strongest synthetic fiber, yet developed.
Business conditions to day are not similar to 1960.	Business conditions today are not similar to *those* (or *the conditions*) *of* 1960. (*Conditions* can not be compared with *1960*; they must be compared with *other conditions*.)
These tweeds are heavier than any I have seen.	These tweeds are heavier than any *others* I have seen. (*Or:* These are the heaviest tweeds I have seen.)
No one in our employ can type so rapidly as Mary Small of our stenographic pool.	No one *else* in our employ can type so rapidly as Mary Small of our stenographic pool. (Mary Small is one of the persons in our employ.)

9. OMISSION OF *As.* Do not omit the second as in a double comparison.

Poor	*Better*
The new binding is as beautiful, if not more beautiful *than* the old.	The new binding is as beautiful *as,* if not more beautiful *than,* the old. (*Or:* The new binding is as *beautiful as* the old, if not *more so.*)

10. POSITION OF MODIFIER. Put words, phrases, and clauses as close as possible to the words they modify.

Misplaced	*Better*
She *almost* worked five hours in typing the report.	She worked *almost* five hours in typing the report.
We found the order Mr. Smith referred to *in the waste basket.*	*In the waste basket* we found the order to which Mr. Smith referred.
The young man brought a number of samples of his work *applying for the position.*	The young man *applying for the position* brought a number of samples of his work.
The man who sells successfully *more often than not* is personally well adjusted.	*More often than not,* the man who sells successfully is personally well adjusted.

11. SPLIT INFINITIVE. An adverb should not be placed between the two parts of the infinitive unless placing the adverb elsewhere results in awkwardness.

Awkward	*Better*
We urge you *to promptly write* us if we can be of help. (Split infinitive.)	We urge you *to write* us *promptly* if we can be of help.
If you want *really to appreciate* these colors you should see them in the daylight. (Infinitive not split.)	If you want *to really appreciate* these colors, you should see them in the daylight.

12. DANGLING PHRASE. An introductory adjective phrase containing a participle, gerund, or infinitive should logically relate to the subject of the sequence. If it does not, either (1) change the subject so that the introductory phrase does relate to it or (2) change the introductory phrase to a dependent clause with its own subject and verb.

Dangling	*Better*
Traveling only 40 miles an hour, a blowout caused his car to swerve into the ditch.	*Traveling only 40 miles an hour,* his *car* swerved into the ditch when his tire blew out. (*Or: Although he was traveling only 40 miles an hour,* a blowout caused his car to swerve into the ditch.)

It was not "a blowout" that was traveling, as the first sentence seems to say, but the "car" or "he."

Dangling	*Better*
Upon comparing the check with the invoice, you appear to have taken the 2 per cent discount.	*Upon comparing the check with the invoice, we* noticed that you have taken the 2 per cent discount.

Dangling	*Better*
To gain advancement, we advise you to continue your education in the evening.	*If you want to gain advancement, we* advise you to continue your education in the evening.

13. DANGLING ELLIPTICAL CLAUSE. When the subject of a subordinate clause is omitted, the understood subject should be the same as the subject of the main clause. If it is not, either (1) supply the missing subject or (2) reconstruct the main clause so that the subject is that of the understood subject in the introductory clause.

Dangling	*Better*
While eating their lunch, Mr. Case came to say that they would have to work late that evening.	*While they were eating their lunch,* Mr. Case came to say that they would have to work late that evening. (*Or: While eating their lunch, they* were told by Mr. Case that they would have to work late that evening.)

14. SHIFTING POINT OF VIEW. Avoid beginning a sentence with one subject or point of view, then shifting to another with resulting awkwardness.

Poor	*Better*
When *you* examine the product closely, the *workmanship* is very good.	When *you* examine the product closely, *you* are sure to be impressed by the workmanship.

Poor

If *any of your workers* want the details of the offer, *you* will find them in the little booklet enclosed.

Better

If *any of your workers* want the details of the offer, *they* will find them in the little booklet enclosed.

15. PARALLEL STRUCTURE. Express co-ordinate ideas in similar grammatical form.

Poor

Please *sign* the enclosed copy of this letter and *we would be pleased* to receive it in the next day or so. (A command and a declarative statement.)

Better

Please *sign* the enclosed copy of this letter and *return* it to us in the next day or so. (Two commands.)

The office is *large, airy,* and *in a convenient location.* (Two adjectives and an adverbial phrase.)

The office is *large, airy,* and *convenient* to everything. (Three adjectives.)

To know what is wrong is better than *guessing.* (Infinitive and gerund.)

To know what is wrong is better than *to guess.* (Two infinitives.) (*Or: Knowing* what is wrong is better than *guessing.*) (Two gerunds.)

16. UNRELATED IDEAS. Do not use *and* to connect two seemingly unrelated ideas. Either provide a connective that will more clearly show the relationship, or write two sentences.

Poor

Mrs. Green maintains a large account with us, *and* she is now in Fort Lauderdale visiting her daughter.

Better

Mrs. Green, who maintains a large account with us, is now in Fort Lauderdale visiting her daughter. (*Or:* Mrs. Green, who is now in Fort Lauderdale visiting her daughter, maintains a large account with us.)

You were not at home when the package was delivered *and* the messenger left it with Mrs. Crandell next door.

As you were not at home, when the package was delivered, the messenger left it with Mrs. Crandell next door. (*Or:* You were not at home when the package was delivered, *and therefore* our messenger left it with Mrs. Crandell next door.)

Thank you for your interest *and* if we can be of further help, please let us know.

Thank you for your interest. If we can be of further help, please let us know.

17. **Ambiguous Conjunction.** Avoid using a connective that may be interpreted in more than one way.

Ambiguous	*Clearer*
While Miss Tice was sorting the cards correctly, she was not working fast enough.	*Although* Miss Tice was sorting the cards correctly, she was not working fast enough.
Since we have set a sales record for Ajax appliances, we have been given the franchise for the entire Milwaukee area.	*Because* we have set a sales record for Ajax appliances, we have been given the franchise for the entire Milwaukee area.

18. **Position of Correlative Conjunction.** Place correlative conjunctions (either . . . or, neither . . . nor, not only . . . but also) immediately before the sentence elements they are to connect.

Poor	*Better*
We were told *either* to see the administrator *or* his assistant.	We were told to see *either* the administrator *or* his assistant.
The idea will *not only* have to be approved by Mr. Cole, *but also* by Mr. Berry.	The idea will have to be approved *not only* by Mr. Cole, *but also* by Mr. Berry.

19. **Misplaced Emphasis.** The beginning and end of a sentence usually receive the most attention. The writer should therefore avoid putting weak words and expressions in those positions when emphasis is desired. Especially to be avoided is an anticlimactic phrase at the end of a sentence.

Weak	*Stronger*
The market in furs has been very poor this month because of the excessively warm weather. *However,* mink sales have been a notable exception.	The market for furs has been very poor this month because of the excessively warm weather. Mink sales, *however,* have been a notable exception.
There are three important points made in this report.	Three important points are made in this report.
Under this arrangement workers will average $5.00 more per week, *in effect.*	Under this arrangement workers will, *in effect,* average $5.00 more per week. (*Or: In effect,* workers will average $5.00 more per week under this arrangement.)

20. ENDING SENTENCES WITH PREPOSITIONS. It is often maintained that a sentence should not end with a preposition. However, a preposition may be placed at the end of a sentence if the sentence would sound awkward otherwise.

Awkward	*Better*
What kind of appeal do you think it is *to* which they are susceptible?	What kind of appeal do you think they are susceptible *to?*

When the preposition appears in the beginning or middle of the sentence, be sure not to repeat it at the end.

Incorrect	*Correct*
To whom did you send the table *to?*	*To* whom did you send the table?

21. WEAK PASSIVE VOICE. Use the active voice in preference to the passive voice when emphasis is desired. (See also Section V, 12, 13 and Chapter 5.)

Weak	*Stronger*
Your order *should be telephoned.*	*Please telephone* your order.

22. VARIETY IN SENTENCE STRUCTURE. Use periodic and balanced sentences occasionally, in addition to loose sentences, to achieve variety and emphasis.

Loose Sentence. A loose sentence is a sentence that can be ended at one or more places before the period and still make complete sense. Most sentences are loose sentences.

> We shall be glad to send you a supply of the pamphlets if you will tell us how many you want.

> These candies are made in our own kitchens, according to our own recipes, with the purest ingredients available.

> Our messenger left the package with the doorman, who said he would take it to you

Periodic Sentences. A periodic sentence is one that can not logically be ended at any place except after the last word. It gives emphasis to the main thought by holding it in suspense.

> For all your cooking and baking you will find the Parker stove an electrical wizard.

> Because delivery of the needed parts was held up, we had to suspend production.

Once you have tried the Regent portable typewriter, you will not want to write any other way.

Balanced Sentence. A balanced sentence is a sentence made up of co-ordinate or contrasting elements to achieve a rhythmic effect.

We have accomplished good results for others; we are sure we can do the same for you.

Take a lesson today, and you will be dancing tonight.

They sell better because they are worth more.

You can't be wrong if your shoes are Wright.

23. COHERENCE AND EMPHASIS WITHIN THE PARAGRAPH. Various literary techniques may be used to obtain coherence and emphasis in a series of sentences. (See also Chapter 6.)

Repetition. Repeat a word, phrase, or clause, or any sentence pattern. When sentence patterns are repeated, they are said to be in parallel construction. (See Rule 15.)

No receiver made will give you better picture quality. None will give you better reception far from the station, on a weak signal, or with bad interference. None will give you longer or more dependable service.

This beautiful publication, prepared for members, is unlike any other in the nation. It will bring you a privileged insight into the infinite diversity of nature. It will bring you special knowledge—more fascinating than fiction—gathered by outstanding naturalists from all corners of the world. It will bring you the inspiration of newly discovered interest and beauty in things both strange and familiar.

The pages that follow indicate what happened when these policies faced the test of a challenging market. How good were the concept and timing? How effective was the planning? How sound was the company's thinking? We believe you will be gratified as we are with the results.

Balance and Contrast. Equate one idea with another, or set one idea against another.

You asked for a furniture sale. We're bringing one to you. You asked for loveseats, sofas, lounge chairs, occasional tables, bedroom suites, and complete dining suites. You'll find them all included in this huge one-day event. You asked for lower prices. And now you're getting lower prices—as much as 50 per cent off the prices you would have paid for these very pieces only yesterday.

Just fifty years ago our operations were confined to one small building and three workers. Today we have 26 plants in as many cities and a working force of 125,000 men and women.

Climax. Arrange ideas in order of ascending importance.

We told you we had to have delivery by May 15, and you assured us that we would. Now, a week after the deadline, you write to say you will need another month. We can not wait another month. In fact, if you delay as much as another week, we shall be unable to carry out our contract, and we shall face a lawsuit in consequence.

Philadelphians like the *Bulletin;* they buy it, read it, trust it. The *Bulletin is* Philadelphia.

EXERCISE A

Which of the following sentences are grammatically complete?
1. Order today.
2. The men working overtime at the Wolverine plant.
3. Do you consider yourself the best person to judge?
4. Whenever it is convenient for you, you may drop by and pick up the sweater we have been holding for you.
5. The factory siren, affected by the heat and sounding no less than five times during the morning.
6. A fine quality cotton and Dacron raincoat, the best buy for your money.
7. Please call us if you wish to have the desk delivered before Thursday of this week.
8. Being sure to enclose the order blank and your check in full payment.
9. Imported from Italy, these lamps which you may see in our windows are the highest expression of native craftsmanship.
10. Knowing you have been looking for a home in our town for some time now.

EXERCISE B

Supply the necessary words or expressions that have been omitted from the following sentences. Four of the sentences are complete as they stand.
1. December we do our biggest business in toys and games.
2. His is one of the biggest, if not the biggest office in the building.
3. We do not know any man who will work as hard as George.
4. I doubt the customer will be satisfied with a substitute.
5. Do you think anyone else will give you as high an allowance as we will?
6. Bolts and screws needed for completion of order are expected Friday.
7. Marvin Jones makes as many calls, if not more, than any other salesman we have.
8. The invoices were sent and the check in payment received.

9. The secretary and treasurer were authorized to sign checks.

10. We manufacture a more complete line of webbing than any company in the world.

11. Have completed order and will ship by parcel post today.

12. If we are to believe these tests, the Intelligence Quotients of the clerical workers are as high as the executives.

13. I can tell you have been under a strain.

14. Mr. Tenney seemed very pleased to know that we were considering his application seriously.

15. The low-priced brand is as good if not better than the brand selling for ten cents more.

16. From the beginning he believed and worked for the project.

17. The welt on these slip-covers is an expensive touch that you will not find on any slip-covers in their price range.

18. The customer expressed a preference for percale pillow cases.

19. The clerks were amused and Mr. Griffith chagrined over the error in identity.

20. Mrs. Keith prefers typewritten copy to any handwritten copy.

EXERCISE C

Rewrite the following sentences for better arrangement, connection, or emphasis:

1. Basing our conclusion on the information we have received, Jones & Co. are believed to be capable of meeting their normal obligations.

2. Our inquiries are worth thousands of dollars properly handled.

3. He was one of the wealthiest cattle ranchers in the Southwest, it seems.

4. You may continue to use your present checks until exhausted.

5. Not only have they failed to match last year's sales, but the sales of two years ago as well.

6. This skillet is made of stainless steel and distributes the heat evenly.

7. Working around the clock, the dynamo was repaired and service restored.

8. Our salesmen only go where the market conditions are favorable.

9. Abelard & Company make ladies' sports clothes and they have been in business since 1935.

10. We think it will be to your advantage to again advertise electric clocks this month.

11. While you were gone for six months, you did not lose any of your seniority rights.

12. Mr. Kerr had an account with this bank which opened in July 1965 and closed in April 1970.

13. You will not only like the unusual styling, but the low prices as well.

14. When Mr. Stone examined the records of these employees, their poor performance ratings surprised him.

15. He asked us to submit our last profit and loss statement and that we should also give the name of our bank.

16. In order to be in a better position to meet competition, a complete selection of men's clothing was added to our line.

17. We received a letter from Miss Taylor dated August 19.

18. Please make the plates, set the type, and we should like to see the proofs by Thursday.

19. You may be sure that we shall treat such information in strict confidence, and if we can ever reciprocate, please feel free to call on us.

20. Mr. Tripp came in today to discuss renewing his note for $1,000.00 which matures tomorrow for an additional thirty days.

Section VIII
Correct Word Use

The correctness of a word is established by the common usage of literate people. Because there is no absolute yardstick, and especially because the uses and meanings of words change continually, opinions about correctness are not usually uniform. Fortunately for the student, an up-to-date dictionary is a reasonably authoritative guide to shades of meaning and degrees of acceptability. Two of the best desk dictionaries are *Webster's Seventh New Collegiate Dictionary* [1] and *The Random House Dictionary*.[2]

1. USING THE DICTIONARY. Like any other reference book, the dictionary is valuable only to the extent that the student knows how to use it—and does use it. If you follow these directions, you will avoid many mistakes in using words.

a. Study the table of contents and introductory notes in order to become familiar with the kinds of information in your dictionary and the manner in which the information is presented.

b. When you look up a word, note first its spelling and then its pronunciation. If there are alternative spellings or pronunciations, the preferred style is given first. If, because of variant spellings, a word is listed twice, the preferred spelling is that which introduces the full treatment of the word. Observe the division of the

---

[1] *Webster's Seventh New Collegiate Dictionary* (Springfield, Mass.: G. & C. Merriam Co., 1967).

[2] *The Random House Dictionary of the English Language* (College Edition) (New York: Random House, 1968).

word into syllables and especially the stress mark which tells you where to place the principal accent. Also refer to the pronunciation key which may be found, in simplified form, on the inside cover or across the bottom of each double page.

c. Before reading the definition of a word, notice carefully its part of speech and its irregularities in reflection, if any. In the case of a verb, learn whether it is transitive or intransitive.

d. Learn from the introductory notes whether the definitions are arranged with the most common meanings first or the oldest meanings first. In this way you will be able to find more readily the definition you want.

e. Find in the introductory notes the explanation of the various labels and signs so that you will be able to interpret correctly the information the dictionary gives you. It is important, for example, to know that a definition is *obsolete* (no longer in use) or that a word is *provincial* (characteristic of a certain part of the country), or that another word is *colloquial* (for informal use only).

f. The derivation (etymology) of the word either precedes or follows the definitions. Not only is the etymology interesting for its own sake, but it is often useful in helping you to fix the meaning of the word in your mind.

g. After some words, you will find a list of synonyms with careful distinctions among them. In other instances you will find cross-references to synonyms. Be sure to look up every reference.

h. If you do not see the word you are looking for among the main entries, you may find it as a "run-on" entry following the treatment of the word from which it is derived. For example, the words *massager, massageuse,* and *massagist* follow the definitions of the word *massage.*

2. FREQUENTLY CONFOUNDED WORDS. Do not confuse words that are similar in spelling or pronunciation, but not in meaning. Distinguish carefully between the words in each of the following sets:

accept (verb, to take)
except (verb, to leave out; preposition, leaving out)

affect (verb, to influence)
effect (verb, to bring about; noun, result)

all ready (completely ready)
already (by this time)

all together (in unison)
altogether (entirely)

allusion (reference)
illusion (deception)

appraise (to evaluate)
apprise (to inform)

assistance (help)
assistants (helpers)

baring (uncovering)
barring (excluding)
bearing (carrying)

beside (close to)
besides (in addition to)

biannual (twice a year)
biennial (every two years)

breath (noun, respiration)
breathe (verb, to respire)

calendar (tabulation of days)
calender (a smoothing machine)

capital (chief city, principal sum)
Capitol (state house)

cloth (fabric)
clothe (to dress)

clothes (apparel)
cloths (fabrics)

complement (that which completes)
compliment (commendation)

continually (recurrently)
continuously (without stopping)

correspondence (letters)
correspondents (letter writers)

costumer (costume maker)
customer (patron)

councilor (member of a council)
counselor (adviser)

credible (believable)
creditable (praiseworthy)

desert (dry area)
dessert (final course of a meal)

device (noun, contrivance)
devise (verb, to contrive)

discomfit (to foil)
discomfort (to make uneasy)

dual (pertaining to two)
duel (combat)

eminent (distinguished)
immanent (inherent)
imminent (impending)

flaunt (to display boastfully)
flout (to treat with contempt)

forth (forward)
fourth (next after the third)

formally (in a formal manner)
formerly (at some former time)

healthful (promoting health)
healthy (having health)

holy (sacred)
wholly (fully)

ingenious (clever)
ingenuous (frank)

its (possessive case of *it*)
it's (contraction of *it is* or *it has*)

later (tardier)
latter (the second of two)

lead (metal)
led (showed the way)

loose (not tight)
lose (to suffer loss)

material (the substance of which
    something is made)
matériel (supplies, especially mili-
    tary, as opposed to personnel)

moral (adjective, right and proper)
morale (noun, prevailing spirit con-
    ducive to dependable perform-
    ance)

passed (verb, went by)
past (adjective, adverb, preposition,
    beyond)

personal (private)
personnel (working force)

practice (noun, performance; verb, to perform)
practise (verb, to perform)

precedence (priority)
precedents (examples)

presence (being present)
presents (gifts)

principal (chief, head of a school, sum of money)
principle (fundamental truth)

prophecy (noun, prediction)
prophesy (verb, to predict)

receipt (written acknowledgment)
recipe (formula)

reign (to rule)
rein (part of a harness)

respectfully (with respect)
respectively (each in the order given)

stationary (standing still)
stationery (writing materials)

their (possessive case of *they*)
there (adverb, in that place)
they're (contraction of *they are*)

therefor (for that)
therefore (consequently)

to (in the direction of)
too (also)
two (next after one)

waive (to forgo)
wave (to flutter or cause to flutter)

who's (contraction of *who is* or *who has*)
whose (possessive case of *who*)

your (possessive case of *you*)
you're (contraction of *you are*)

3. FOREIGN WORDS. Note carefully the singular and plural forms of the following words, which are occasionally used in business correspondence:

Singular	*Plural* [3]
agendum	agenda
alumna	alumnae
alumnus	alumni
analysis	analyses
antenna	antennas, antennae
apparatus	apparatus, apparatuses
appendix	appendixes, appendices
automaton	automatons, automata
axis	axes
bacillus	bacilli
bacterium	bacteria
basis	bases

---

[3] Where two plurals are given, the first is preferred in *Webster's Seventh New Collegiate Dictionary*.

Singular	*Plural*
crisis	crises
curriculum	curriculums, curricula
datum	data
diagnosis	diagnoses
erratum	errata
index	indexes, indices
literatus	literati
locus	loci
matrix	matrices
maximum	maxima, maximums
medium	mediums, media
minutia	minutiae
parenthesis	parentheses
plateau	plateaus, plateaux
radius	radii
stratum	strata
syllabus	syllabuses, syllabi
synopsis	synopses
synthesis	syntheses
thesis	theses
virtuoso	virtuosos, virtuosi

4. COMMONLY MISUSED WORDS.[4] Here is explained the correct use of a number of the words and expressions that are commonly misused in business. Misuse may result from confused meaning, or incorrect spelling, or a substituted part of speech. (Also see the list of confounded words in Rule 2.)

Advise   *Advise* is stilted (and may also lead to error) when it is used in the sense of "to notify." It is used correctly in the sense of "to give advice."

    Questionable   Please advise us of your decision as soon as possible.

    Better   Please notify us of your decision as soon as possible.

    Correct   We advise you to sell the shares as soon as possible.

---

[4] For a more extensive treatment of misused words, see Shaw, Harry: *Errors in English and Ways to Correct Them,* an Everyday Handbook (New York: Barnes & Noble, Inc., 1962).

Affect, *effect*	A verb only, *affect* means "to influence." Do not confuse with *effect*. As a verb, *effect* means "to bring about"; as a noun, *effect* means "result."

	Incorrect	What will be the *affect* of the new policy on our current procedures?
	Correct	What will be the *effect* of the new policy on our current procedures?
	Correct	We shall be seriously *affected* by the new policy.
	Correct	We *effected* a change in our procedures as a result of the new policy.

Already, *all ready*	*Already,* an adverb, means "by this time"; *all ready* (two words) means "entirely ready" or that everyone is ready.

The workers have *already* arrived.
We are *all ready* for Saturday's rush.

Alright, *all right*	Alright is not in good usage; *all right* (two words) is correct in informal usage in the sense of "yes," "satisfactory," or "certainly."

It will be *all right* if you leave now.

Among, *between*	Use *among* in referring to three or more units; use *between* in referring to only two. Do not use *amongst*.

	Incorrect	The estate was divided *between* the three heirs.
	Correct	The estate was divided *among* the three heirs.
	Correct	It is hard to choose *between* Smith and Jones.

Amongst	Use *among*.
Amount, *number*	*Amount* refers to general quantity; *number* refers to countable units.

	Incorrect	A large *amount* of employees were absent last Friday.
	Correct	A large *number* of employees were absent last Friday.
	Correct	A large *amount* of work remains to be done.

And etc.	Omit *and*.

	Incorrect	All colors are available: blue, green, red, yellow, *and etc.*

Correct   All colors are available: blue, green, red, yellow, *etc.*

Anyplace   Colloquial. Better write *anywhere*. Similarly, write *somewhere* for *someplace*, *nowhere* for *noplace*.

Questionable   We deliver *anyplace*.

Better   We deliver *anywhere*.

Anywheres   Use *anywhere*.

Appraise, assess, evaluate   *Appraise* and *evaluate* mean "to ascertain the value or amount of." *Assess* means "to value for tax purposes."

The pawn broker *appraised* the ring at $2,000.00.

It is difficult to *evaluate* his work at this time.

The city *assessed* the property at $11,300.00.

Approve, endorse   *Approve* is a general term meaning "to sanction" or "to have a favorable opinion of." *Endorse* (sometimes spelled *indorse*) means specifically "to show approval by writing one's name on the face or back of" a document.

I *approve* his stand.

The check was not *endorsed*.

Apt, liable, likely   Use *apt* to denote natural tendency, *liable* to denote legal responsibility or exposure to possible disadvantage, and *likely* to denote mere probability.

An older woman is *apt* to be more content in a routine job.

If we do not live up to our contract, we are *liable* to be sued.

New sales quotas are *likely* to be set next week.

As, like   As a conjunction, *as* is followed by a clause; *like* is a preposition and is followed by a noun or pronoun which is its object. (See Section I, 6, 7.)

Incorrect   Please do *like* I tell you.

Correct   Please do *as* I tell you.

Correct   Please do it *like* me.

As per	Hackneyed. Use a more natural expression.
	Poor We packed your order *as per* your instructions.
	Better We packed your order *as* you instructed.
At about	Use *about*.
	Incorrect We shall meet you *at about* eight o'clock.
	Correct We shall meet you *about* eight o'clock.
Balance, remainder, rest	*Balance* in the sense of "remainder" or "rest" should be used only in referring to sums of money.
	Questionable Please send us the *balance* of the order next week.
	Correct Please send us the *remainder* (or *rest*) of our order next week.
	Correct The *balance* in our account is $5,500.00.
Bank on	Colloquial. Use "take stock in" or "rely on."
	Questionable I should advise you not to *bank on* their word.
	Correct I should advise you not to *take stock in* their word.
Beg	Hackneyed and too humble. Try to avoid it.
	Poor We *beg* to inform you that the goods will be shipped on May 12.
	Better We *are pleased* to inform you that the goods will be shipped on May 12.
	Better still The goods will be shipped on May 12.
Being that	Do not use for *because, since,* or *inasmuch as*.
	Incorrect *Being that* the rugs were inferior, we refused to accept them.
	Correct *Because* the rugs were inferior, we refused to accept them.
Best of any	The expression should be *best, best of those,* or *better than any other.*
	Incorrect The chromium model is the *best of any* we have tried.

	Correct	The chromium model is the *best of those* we have tried.
	Correct	The chromium model is the *best* we have tried.

But what   After *no doubt, no question,* etc., use *but that* or *that,* not *but what.*

	Incorrect	There is *no doubt but what* he will come.
	Correct	There is *no doubt but that* he will come.
	Correct	There is *no doubt that* he will come.
	Correct	I do not like the decision, *but what* can I do?

Can,
   may   Use *can* to denote ability, *may* to denote permission.

	Questionable	You *can* call for the films on Tuesday.
	Better	You *may* call for the films on Tuesday.
	Correct	If the date is agreeable, I *can* see you on the 19th.

Can not
   help but   The preferred expression is *can not help* or *can not but.*

	Questionable	We *can not help but* agree with you.
	Better	We *can not help* agreeing with you.
	Also correct	We *can not but* agree with you.

Can't hardly   Double negative. The correct expression is *can hardly.*

	Correct	He *can hardly* wait for the committee's decision.

Compose,
   comprise   *Compose* means "to make up" or "to constitute"; *comprise* means "to include."

	Incorrect	Twelve pages with accompanying tables *comprise* the report.
	Correct	Twelve pages with accompanying tables *compose* the report.
	Correct	The report *comprises* twelve pages with accompanying tables.

Contact   *Contact* as a verb is considered colloquial. In formal usage, write "get in touch with" or use a more precise term.

Contact as a noun is correct.

Questionable	Please *contact* Mr. White as soon as you can.
Better	Please *get in touch with* (or *write*, or *telephone*, or *call on*) Mr. White as soon as you can.
Correct	I shall be in *contact* with you frequently.

Copy, facsimile, replica

A *copy* is a general term meaning "a transcript, imitation, or reproduction of an original work." A *facsimile* is a more specific term and means "an exact reproduction," such as a photostat or other photographic print. A *replica* is also "an exact reproduction," but especially of a picture or statue by the original artist.

Miss Jones, will you please make two *copies* of this letter?

This letter in Mr. Day's handwriting is really a *facsimile*.

Ask Mr. Antonini if he will make a *replica* of his sculpture for our reception room.

Could of

See *might of, must of.*

Data

Data is the plural of *datum* and logically takes a plural verb. Pronouns that modify or refer to the word should also be plural.

Questionable	The *data* you asked for *is* ready.
Better	The *data* you asked for *are* ready.
Also good	The *information* you asked for *is* ready.
Correct	*These data have been* carefully *sifted.*

Different than

Although this expression is frequently used, the correct expression is *different from*.

Questionable	The Smith Company's plan is considerably *different than* yours.
Better	The Smith Company's plan is considerably *different from* yours.

Disinterested, uninterested

Careful writers distinguish between *disinterested* (impartial) and *uninterested* (not interested).

Questionable	He appeared to be *disinterested* in the price.

Correct	He appeared to be *uninterested* in the price.
Correct	Mr. Grant was chosen to arbitrate the case because he was the only *disinterested* person on the panel.

Doubt but what Better write *doubt but that.*

Questionable	I do not *doubt but what* you are right.
Correct	I do not *doubt but that* you are right.

Due to The use of *due to* as a preposition is not entirely sanctioned. Use *because of, on account of,* or *owing to. Due,* meaning "attributable to," is an adjective and as such should modify a noun. It is often used as a predicate adjective after the verb *to be. Owing* is also an adjective, but paradoxically custom approves the use of *owing to* as a preposition even when it frowns on *due to.*

Questionable	*Due to* the rain, the exercises could not be held outdoors.
Correct	*Because of* the rain, the exercises could not be held outdoors.
Questionable	He refused the goods *due to* the high price.
Correct	He refused the goods *on account of* the high price.
Correct	His refusal of the goods was *due* to the high price (predicate adjective).
Correct	*Owing to* the lack of raw materials, the plant had to be shut down.

Effect See *affect, effect.*

Endorse See *approve, endorse.*

Evaluate See *appraise, assess, evaluate.*

Facsimile See *copy, facsimile, replica.*

Farther, further *Farther* means "to a greater distance"; *further* means "to a greater degree" or "additional." In informal usage, however, *further* is often used in the sense of *farther.*

Correct	Our trucks carry goods *farther* than theirs.
Acceptable	Our trucks carry goods *further* than theirs.

	Correct	We did not pursue the matter *further*.
	Correct	If you do anything *further*, please let me know.

Favor   Archaic when used in the sense of "letter." Use the word *letter* instead.

	Incorrect	We have received your *favor* of October 7.
	Correct	We have received your *letter* of October 7.

Fewer   See *less, fewer.*

Figuratively   See *literally, figuratively.*

Former, latter   Use *former* and *latter* in referring to one of two persons or things. Otherwise use *first* and *last* respectively.

	Incorrect	In attendance were the president, the chairman of the board, and the treasurer. The *latter* was accompanied by his secretary.
	Correct	In attendance were the president, the chairman of the board, and the treasurer. The *last* (or, *The treasurer*) was accompanied by his secretary.

Help   Better not use for *employees* or *workers.*

	Questionable	The *help* agreed to work an extra hour on Friday evening.
	Better	The *employees* agreed to work an extra hour on Friday evening.

If, whether   In formal usage *whether* is preferred in an indirect question and is usually followed by *or*. *If* is used in informal speech and writing.

	Very formal	We do not know *whether* or not he is coming.
	Less formal	We do not know *whether* he is coming.
	Informal	We do not know *if* he is coming.

Imply, infer   *Imply* means "to express indirectly"; *infer* means "to deduce."

	Incorrect	I *imply* from what you say that you will not be present.
	Correct	I *infer* from what you say that you will not be present.

	Correct I *was implying* that he does not have the qualifications for the position.

Irregardless   Incorrect. Use *regardless.*

      Incorrect   I shall buy the stock *irregardless* of the business index.

      Correct   I shall buy the stock *regardless* of the business index.

Kind of a,
  sort of a   Write *kind of* or *sort of.*

      It is *a kind of* paint.

      What *sort of* coat do you prefer?

Kindly   There is some feeling against the use of *kindly* in the sense of "please." Literally, *kindly* means "with kindness."

      Questionable   *Kindly* send us all the spare parts you have.

      Better   *Please* send us all the spare parts you have.

      Correct   Our customers seem *kindly* disposed toward our new salesman.

Latter   See *former, latter.*

Lay, lie   See Section V, 11.

Leave,
  let   *Leave* means "to go away from"; *let* means "to allow."

      Incorrect   Please *leave* me do it for you.

      Correct   Please *let* me do it for you.

      Correct   *Leave* him alone.

Less,
  fewer   *Less* refers to bulk or mass; *fewer* refers to number of units.

      Questionable   There are *less* pieces of candy to the pound than we anticipated.

      Correct   There are *fewer* pieces of candy to the pound than we anticipated.

      Correct   You seem to get *less* for your money when you buy the big pieces.

Liable	See *apt, liable, likely.*
Literally, *figuratively*	*Literally* means "in the exact sense"; *figuratively* means "symbolically."

Incorrect	He is *literally* chained to his desk.
Correct	He is *figuratively* chained to his desk. (*Or,* He is chained to his desk.)
Correct	We have *literally* thousands of customers.

May	See *can.*
Might of, *must of*	Do not use *of* in the sense of *have.* The correct expressions are *might have* and *must have.*

Incorrect	He *must of* gone.
Correct	He *must have* gone.

Most all	The two words are contradictory. *Almost all* is the better expression.

Questionable	*Most all* the pressure cookers have been sold.
Better	*Almost all* the pressure cookers have been sold.
Also correct	*Most* of the pressure cookers have been sold.

No place	See *anyplace.*
Off of	Use *off,* alone.

Incorrect	The books fell *off of* the desk.
Correct	The books fell *off* the desk.

Oral, *verbal*	Although *verbal* is sometimes used in the sense of "oral," it really pertains to any use of words, written or oral.

Questionable	We have no signed contract; it was strictly a *verbal* agreement.
Correct	We have no signed contract; it was strictly an *oral* agreement.
Correct	Pictures have a more immediate impact than *verbal* communication.

Party	*Party* in the general sense of "a person" is colloquial. Use a more specific word.

Questionable	I told the *party* that telephoned that you would be back after two o'clock.
Better	I told the *man* (*woman, person,* etc.) who telephoned that you would be back after two o'clock.

Prefer

In a comparison, write *prefer to,* not the redundant *prefer rather than.*

Questionable	We *prefer* a plastic binding *rather than* a stapled binding.
Better	We *prefer* a plastic binding *to* a stapled binding.
Also correct	We would rather have a plastic binding *than* a stapled binding.

Principal, principle

As a noun, *principal* means "leader" or "chief"; it may mean, also, "a person who employs an agent to act for him," or "a sum of money on which interest is earned." As an adjective, *principal* means "highest in rank, authority, or importance." *Principle,* a noun, means "a fundamental truth or belief."

The *principals* in this transaction are Mr. Henry and Mr. Graves.

Interest is paid on the *principal* every three months.

Our *principal* source of tin is Bolivia.

We believe in the *principle* of equal wages for equal work, regardless of sex.

Raise, rise

Raise means "to lift up"; *rise* means "to move up." (See Section V, 11, footnote.) Note the following principal parts:

raise	raised	raised	raising
rise	rose	risen	rising

The company *raised* its prices last year.
Prices *have risen* sharply in the last year.
Mr. Henneman *rose* to go.

Rarely ever, seldom ever

The correct expressions are *rarely if ever, seldom if ever,* or *rarely* or *seldom,* alone.

Questionable	We *seldom ever* (or *rarely ever*) go there any more.

	Correct	We *seldom if ever* (or *rarely if ever*) go there any more.
	Correct	We *seldom* (or *rarely*) go there any more.

Reason is because
: *The reason is* should be completed by *that*, not by *because*. If you use *because*, leave out *the reason is*.

	Questionable	The *reason* we wired *is because* a letter would have arrived too late.
	Correct	The *reason* we wired *is that* a letter would have arrived too late.
	Correct	We wired *because* a letter would have arrived too late.

Remainder, rest
: See *balance, remainder, rest.*

Same
: Do not use *same* as a substitute for a noun or for *it* or *they.*

	Poor	We have your check for $35.00 and thank you for *same.*
	Better	We have your check for $35.00 and thank you for *it.*
	Better still	Thank you for your *check* for $35.00.

Shall, will
: See Section V, 3.

Should, would
: See Section V, 4.

Should of
: See *might of, must of.*

Sit, set
: *Sit* means "to be seated"; *set* means "to put in position." (See Section V, 11, and footnote.)

Mr. Seibert *has sat* at his desk all morning. Please *set* the file beside my desk.

Some place
: See *anyplace.*

These kind
: Incorrect. See p. 318.

This here, those there
: Incorrect. Omit *here* and *there.*

	Incorrect	We like *this here* table model.
	Correct	We like *this* table model.

Uninterested	See *disinterested, uninterested.*
Unique	See Section VI, 6.
Verbal	See *oral, verbal.*
Very	For the use of *very* with *much,* see Section VI, 16.
Whether	See *if, whether.*
Who, whom	See Section III, 5, 8.
Whose	Some prejudice exists against using *whose* as the possessive case of *which.* Write *of which.*

> *Questionable*   It was the showcase on *whose* top they had placed the marked-down items.
>
> *Correct*   It was the showcase on the top *of which* they had placed the marked-down items.
>
> *Also correct*   It was the showcase with the marked-down items on the top.

EXERCISE A

Correct the misspelling or misuse of the italicized words in the following sentences.

1. After the vacation period we shall again have our full *compliment* of cashiers.

2. We aim to provide *healthy* working conditions for all employees.

3. The clatter of typewriters was heard *continually* until we used sound-proofing to separate the executive offices from the central stenographic room.

4. *Lose* accounting methods are sure to cause business losses.

5. Our advertisements will point out the *principle* benefits of the new package.

6. They decided to free their patents and *wave* all rights to the royalties from them.

7. The inhalant works while you *breath.*

8. *Baring* unforeseen circumstances, you should receive the goods by mid-April.

9. If you *flout* your superior intellect, you will not make many friends.

10. A requisition is necessary for *stationary* or other supplies.

11. Our *Personal* Office is open from nine to five o'clock.

12. The *precedence* for executive stock-purchase plans were established a long time ago.

13. We intend to advertise in newspapers, magazines, television, and various outdoor *mediums.*

14. We shall keep you *appraised* of new developments.

15. His *illusion* was apparently to an advertisement we had run many years ago.

16. Mr. Adikes was *formally* a member of the Pomonok Country Club.

17. Our suggestion system has done much to improve employee *moral*.

EXERCISE B

Correct the misuses of words in the following sentences. Six sentences are correct.

1. Can we have your permission to proceed with the transactions outlined in this letter?

2. We shall appreciate your advising us of your decision.

3. Mr. Smith outlined for us the principles of collective bargaining.

4. The customer said he preferred model AC–5 rather than BC–8.

5. The will provided for a division of the estate between Mr. Dempsey's two daughters.

6. You might of been more tactful in your relations with the customer.

7. You will find the letter in the file beside the desk.

8. They can't seem to understand the seriousness of the situation.

9. Have you studied the affects of the new regulations?

10. We sent the statement back for correction, being that it was inaccurate.

11. The amount of buyers who come to New York varies with the season.

12. Can you have those data for me by four o'clock this afternoon?

13. At the time we did not know that a strike was imminent.

14. It will be all right if you send someone to represent you.

15. You should not imply from these circumstances that we can not complete the performance of our contract.

16. We need the sort of a man who is willing to work overtime one or two evenings a week.

17. We were able to meet the competition due to our superior workmanship and low prices.

18. You will find the new varnishes considerably different than the finishes you are now using.

19. We are literally snowed under with orders.

20. The reason you do not see the seams is because they are electronically welded.

Section IX
Punctuation

The purpose of punctuation is to make reading easier and clearer. The modern tendency is to use as few marks of punctuation as are consistent with that purpose.

Punctuation [1] is as necessary to good writing as pauses are to good speaking. On the other hand, punctuation can not compensate for shoddy writing. If an idea is not expressed clearly in the first place, a comma or semicolon will not make it clear.

PERIOD (.)

A period marks the end of a complete statement or unit.

1. ENDS OF SENTENCES. Place a period at the end of a sentence that is not a direct question or an exclamation.

2. ABBREVIATIONS. Place an abbreviation point (a period on the typewriter) at the end of every abbreviation. If the abbreviation comes at the end of the sentence, use only one period.

> Dr. Martin and Mrs. Gale were also present.
> The post office address is Trenton, N. J.

3. DECIMALS. Place a decimal point (period) between dollars and cents in figures expressing sums of money, also before a decimal fraction and between a whole number and the decimal.

	$14.55	$5,156.24	$.98
.275	.02	6.172	56.5 per cent

---

[1] See Shaw, Harry: *Punctuate It Right!*, an Everyday Handbook (New York: Barnes & Noble, Inc., 1963).

4. Numerical and Alphabetical Symbols. Place a period following the symbols denoting the parts of an outline or list.

> A. Types of Systems
>   1. Wear-out
>   2. Continuous
>   3. Campaign

5. After Indirect Questions. An indirect question is followed by a period—not by a question mark.

Incorrect	*Correct*
He asked whether we had reached a decision?	He asked whether we had reached a decision.

6. Following Requests. A request put in the form of a question usually is followed by a period—not a question mark.

> May we ask that you let us have your decision by Wednesday.
> Will you please send us a copy of your latest catalogue.

QUESTION MARK (?)

The question mark denotes a query or a doubt.

7. Direct Questions. Use a question mark after a direct question. The question mark is usually placed at the end of the sentence, where it takes the place of the period. The question mark may, however, be placed in the middle of the sentence as in the second example below.

> What would you advise us to do?

> But shall we do it? is a question that will require much thought.

8. Suggestions of Doubt. Use a question mark within parentheses to indicate that a date or other statement is questionable.

> The founder of the business was James Ryerson, 1823(?)–1888.

> I thought he said that the burst(?) test was unnecessary.

Do not use the question mark to indicate humor or sarcasm. The following is questionable:

> The speaker began with a humorous(?) story.

EXCLAMATION MARK (!)

The exclamation mark is used where special emphasis is desired.

9. INDICATING EMPHASIS. Use the exclamation mark at the end of a vigorously expressed statement.

> The sale ends tomorrow. Don't wait!

> He won three promotions in two years and increased his salary by 100 per cent in the same period. What a man!

10. EXPRESSING IRONY. The exclamation mark is occasionally used to express irony.

> They charged only $15.00 per person for the luncheon—a bargain!

11. AVOIDING MISUSE. The exclamation mark should be used with discretion (also see Rule 26). The first example below is poor; the second is much improved.

> We have written to you several times, but we have not yet heard from you!

> We have written to you several times, but we have not yet heard from you.

COMMA (,)

A comma is used to indicate a short pause within the sentence or to separate sentence elements which are not closely connected in the sentence.

12. PREVENTING CONFUSION. Use a comma to separate sentence elements that might be misread if the punctuation were omitted.

Incorrect	*Correct*
To begin with the boiler is badly in need of repairs.	To begin with, the boiler is badly in need of repairs.
Behind a cloud of dust shrouded the road.	Behind, a cloud of dust shrouded the road.

13. PLACEMENT IN SERIES. Place commas between members of a series of words or groups of words. The comma before the conjunction is advisable when the last two members of the series are joined by *and* or *or*.

The store was decorated with red, white, and blue banners.

We visited the plant, talked with the workers, made a careful study of the methods, and still failed to discover the seat of the trouble.

You can have your favorite style in large, medium, or small sizes.

The finishes are walnut, mahogany, oak, maple. (No conjunction.)

14. JOINING CO-ORDINATE CLAUSES. Put a comma before *and, but, for, or,* and *nor* (co-ordinating conjunctions) when they join two independent clauses. However, when the co-ordinate clauses are short, no comma is necessary.

Never in our history have we had so many applications for secretarial positions, but never have we had so few positions to fill.

We liked his work and we commended him for it. (Two short clauses; no punctuation.)

I made an exhaustive study of the leakage but could find no evidence of either dishonesty or carelessness. (No punctuation because *but* connects a compound verb—*made* and *could find*—not two clauses.)

15. SEPARATING CO-ORDINATE CONSECUTIVE ADJECTIVES. Use commas between adjectives in a series when each adjective separately qualifies the noun; do not use a comma when an adjective seems to qualify the next adjective or the whole phrase that follows. When adjectives are co-ordinate (and require a comma), you should be able to connect them by *and* without changing their sense.

Men seem to prefer the slim, unpleated, self-belted trousers. (Co-ordinate.)

Men seem to prefer the new slim, unpleated, self-belted trousers. (Partly co-ordinate.)

Have you seen our better lightweight cotton chenille robes? (Not co-ordinate.)

16. FOLLOWING INTRODUCTORY CLAUSES. When, in a complex sentence, the subordinate clause precedes the main clause, separate the two clauses by a comma. A comma is not ordinarily used when the subordinate clause follows the main clause.

Before you leave for the day, please cover your typewriter and close your desk. (Subordinate clause precedes main clause.)

Please cover your typewriter and close your desk before you leave for the day. (Subordinate clause follows main clause.)

17. SEPARATING INTRODUCTORY VERBAL PHRASES. Use a comma after a participial, gerund, or infinitive phrase preceding the main clause.

Knowing your past record, I am sure you will handle the job with distinction.

By making the parts out of plastic instead of metal, we save over ten thousand dollars a year.

In order to meet the deadline, we had to operate the plant in two shifts.

18. CONNECTING WORDS AND PHRASES. Use a comma after an introductory connecting word or phrase that is followed by a pause in reading.

Furthermore, we will guarantee the delivery date.
In consequence, he will not be allowed to work overtime.
Therefore you are not subject to these rules. (No pause.)

Introductory prepositional phrases not used primarily for connection should not be punctuated except to insure clarity.

During his visit he asked to see the new generator.

By noon, time was on our side. (The sentence could be misread if the comma were omitted.)

19. PARENTHETIC ELEMENTS. Use commas to set off interrupting words and phrases not essential to the sense of the sentence.

Let us assume, for example, that the subject of the discussion is time and motion study.

We believe, furthermore, that the annual dinner should be held at the Westleigh Inn, Litchfield, Conn.

The meeting will take place on the 23rd, that is, the day after tomorrow.

He succeeded, believe it or not, in making the sale without even showing a sample.

20. SETTING OFF NON-RESTRICTIVE MODIFIERS. Set off by commas a non-restrictive phrase or clause. A restrictive phrase or clause restricts or identifies the word it modifies and is, therefore, essen-

tial to the sense of the sentence. A non-restrictive phrase or clause is merely explanatory and not necessary for identity or sentence sense.

Non-restrictive

Miss Cleary's typewriter, which has been repaired three times in the past month, is out-of-order again. (If the words between the commas were omitted, the sense of the sentence would not be impaired.)

Mr. Samuels, who has had many years of experience in advertising, has been chosen as the assistant advertising manager.

The chairman, worn out by the bickering, finally called for a motion to adjourn.

Restrictive

A typewriter that has been repaired is as good as new. (The clause, "that has been repaired," is not set off by commas because it can not be omitted without damage to the sense of the sentence.)

A man with many years of experience in advertising has been chosen as the assistant advertising manager.

Any man imbued with a high sense of duty would be qualified to represent our cause.

21. SEPARATING NON-RESTRICTIVE APPOSITIVES. Use commas to set off non-restrictive words and phrases in apposition. When, however, the appositive is restrictive (essential to the identity of the noun to which it refers) no commas are used.

Mr. Samuels, a man of many years' experience in advertising, has been chosen assistant advertising manager. (Non-restrictive.)

Another applicant, a former salesman, was not very well qualified. (Non-restrictive.)

My friend John will be there to meet you. (Restrictive.)

Do you want to see Mr. Jones the bookkeeper or Mr. Jones the vice president? (Restrictive.)

22. EXPRESSIONS OF CONTRAST. Use commas to set off an expression of contrast.

It was Mr. Forbush, not Mr. Palmer, who asked for the refund.

The customer, far from being annoyed, was grateful for the sales talk.

23. INDICATING UNDERSTOOD WORDS. A comma may be used to show the omission of a word or words.

What you do is your responsibility; what I do, mine.

Some customers prefer the dictating machines with stands; others, without.

24. SETTING OFF SHORT DIRECT QUOTATIONS. Use commas to set off a short direct quotation. (See Rule 55.)

The advertisement said, "This offer is good for a limited time only."

He posted a warning, "Danger—No Smoking," near every installation in the chemical division.

25. INDICATING DIRECT ADDRESS. Use commas to set off substantives in direct address.

Boys, here is an opportunity to make money after school.

I want to assure you, Mr. Kane, that the matter will be adjusted to your complete satisfaction.

26. SEPARATING EXCLAMATIONS. Use a comma instead of an exclamation point after a mild interjection.

Well, what do you suggest we do about it?
Yes, you may send us the sample you offered.

27. WRITING DATES. In a date consisting of the month, day, and year, set off the year by commas. In a date consisting only of the month and year, omit the commas.

Frank Eraclito was appointed to the bench on March 26, 1970, for a term of ten years.

Frank Eraclito was appointed to the bench in March 1970 for a term of ten years.

28. NOTING ADDRESSES. Use commas to set off the components of an address.

He lived at 1765 Third Avenue, Albany, New York, until he was dispossessed.

Last year he rented a home in Orange County, New York, not far from his place of business.

29. FOLLOWING COMPLIMENTARY CLOSES. A comma is usually placed after the complimentary close. It is omitted when open punctuation is used in the date and inside address.

Very truly yours,

30. TITLES FOLLOWING NAMES. Both in the envelope address and inside address a title following a name on the same line is

Mr. David R. Brady, President

separated from it by a comma.

SEMICOLON (;)

The semicolon is used to indicate a long pause within a sentence or to separate independent sentence elements.

31. SEPARATING INDEPENDENT CLAUSES. In the absence of a conjunction, use a semicolon to separate the clauses of a compound sentence.

> This has been our policy for the past two years; it will continue to be our policy.

> You do not have to take our word for it; you can test the product yourself.

> You do not have to take our word for it. You can test the product yourself.

If two long main clauses joined by a conjunction are already broken up by commas, use a semicolon to separate the main clauses.

> If, after you see the client, you have any doubts about his credit standing, take the order conditionally, that is, subject to confirmation by the main office; but if the credit standing appears satisfactory, you may definitely accept the order for immediate delivery on 30-day terms.

32. PUNCTUATING CLAUSES WITH CONJUNCTIVE ADVERBS. Place a semicolon between the clauses of a compound sentence joined by a conjunctive adverb (*so, thus, therefore, nevertheless, however, furthermore, accordingly,* etc.).

> They placed their order early enough; however, a shortage of timers caused a three weeks' delay.

> I liked the samples very much; therefore I am going to order six dozen.

33. SEPARATING EXPLANATORY CLAUSES. Use a semicolon to separate two main clauses, the second of which begins with an expression similar to *namely* and *that is.*

He said that he had already obtained his next job; namely, he was slated to become Chief Chemist of the Tracer Chemical Corporation.

We suggest that you follow the original instructions; that is, you should sign each copy of the contract before a notary public and then return all four copies to us.

34. INTERNALLY PUNCTUATED SERIES. Place semicolons between elements in a series internally punctuated by commas.

Confusing

Installments are payable at our offices in New York City, Albany, New York, Trenton, New Jersey, and Dover, Delaware.

Clearer

Installments are payable at our offices in New York City; Albany, New York; Trenton, New Jersey; and Dover, Delaware.

35. FACILITATING READING. Place semicolons between co-ordinate sentence elements when these elements are already broken up by other punctuation.

Confusing

He said that he had borrowed money from his neighbor on March 15, that on the next day, wishing to repay the loan, he had visited his neighbor again, but that his neighbor, mistaking his intention, had refused to admit him to his house.

Clearer

He said that he had borrowed money from his neighbor on March 15; that on the next day, wishing to repay the loan, he had visited his neighbor again; but that his neighbor, mistaking his intention, had refused to admit him to his house.

COLON (:)

The colon is used to direct the reader's attention to a statement that follows. It also has certain conventional uses, as in expressions of time.

36. AFTER FORMAL INTRODUCTIONS. Use a colon after a formal introduction to a list, series, enumeration, explanatory statement, question, secondary title of a printed work, or long or formal quotation. The first word following the colon begins with a capital letter if it begins a sentence or if it is normally capitalized; otherwise it begins with a small letter.

Please enter our order for the following:

Five colors are available: peach, orchid, canary, pink, and white.

In substance this is what he said: "Do it if you want to, but don't come to me for help."

I can answer your request in a single word: Yes.

What we want to know is this: Are you prepared to give us a complete list of the wanted items with exact quantities and delivery dates?

The correct title is "United States Steel: Fifty Years of Progress."

37. FOLLOWING SALUTATIONS. Use a colon after a salutation in business correspondence.

Dear Mr. Prince:

38. EXPRESSING TIME. Use a colon in figures expressing time.

6:45 p.m.   11:20 a.m.

39. SEPARATING STENOGRAPHER'S INITIALS. A colon is usually used to separate the stenographer's initials from those of the dictator of the letter. (See Chapter 3.)

JHJ:HS

PARENTHESES ( )

Parentheses are curves employed to enclose incidental matter that is helpful but not essential in clarifying the text.

40. ENCLOSING EXPLANATORY REMARKS. Use parentheses to enclose explanatory remarks by the author. If the parenthetical statement comes within the sentence, use no punctuation before the first curve and do not capitalize the first word; if punctuation is necessary after the parenthetical remark, it should follow the closing curve. If the parenthetical remark comes after the end of a sentence, capitalize the first word and place a period inside the closing curve. The following examples are correct:

The rules for vacations (see page 39), which you should study carefully, apply to all employees, including high executives.

The rules for vacations apply to all employees, including high executives (see page 39).

The rules for vacations apply to all employees, including high executives. (See page 39.)

41. ENCLOSING SYMBOLS. Explanatory and illustrative symbols, as well as figures and letters used to enumerate points in the text, are usually enclosed in parentheses.

Use the cents sign (¢) in writing amounts under one dollar.

The goods delivered were (a) the wrong size, (b) the wrong color, and (c) the wrong style.

We seek these qualifications in the applicant: (1) under 25, (2) a college graduate, (3) a pleasant personality, and (4) an interest in making banking his career.

BRACKETS [ ]

Brackets are used to enclose incidental remarks, usually by someone other than the author of the main text. (Brackets can be made on the typewriter with the diagonal-line and underline keys [thus].)

42. ENCLOSING EDITOR'S REMARKS. Brackets are used in a text or a quotation to enclose material supplied by the editor.

The report concluded: "Arrangements should be made with the Frank G. Shattuck Co. [Schrafft's] for the exclusive right to serve refreshments on our premises during the 11 o'clock coffee break."

43. USING WITH PARENTHESES. If necessary, brackets may be used for parenthetical material within a statement already enclosed in parentheses.

Mr. Clary then stated his objections. (These have already been referred to as [a.] the shortage of capital and [b.] the pressure of competition.)

HYPHEN (-)

Hyphens are used to connect two or more words that make up a single expression and to separate the parts of words.

44. DIVIDING WORDS. Use the hyphen at the end of a line when division of a word is necessary. (See Section X, 4–8.)

45. CONNECTING COMPOUND WORDS. The hyphen is regularly used in expressing numbers and fractions, between prefix and proper noun or proper adjective, and between two or more words functioning as a single noun.

<table>
<tr><td>one hundred and thirty-eight</td><td>brother-in-law</td></tr>
<tr><td>sixty-seven</td><td>secretary-treasurer</td></tr>
<tr><td>one-third</td><td>sergeant-at-arms</td></tr>
<tr><td>three-fourths</td><td>anti-Communist</td></tr>
<tr><td>two and three-quarters</td><td>pro-American</td></tr>
</table>

46. JOINING COMPOUND ADJECTIVES. Hyphenate an adjective consisting of two or more words, provided a noun follows.

> He is a well-informed person.
> He is well informed.
> The car had a worn-out spark plug.
> One of the spark plugs was worn out.
> a matter-of-fact statement   a high-school graduate
> a third-grade clerk   a two-year-old baby

47. CONNECTING WITH SUSPENSION HYPHEN. When several modifiers of a noun are separated from it, but require connection by means of hyphens, the so-called *suspension hyphen* is used.

> The examination for third-, fourth-, and fifth-grade clerks will be held on October 3.

> We should like to reach both elementary- and high-school teachers.

48. OMITTING HYPHENS. The general tendency is to omit the hyphen between the parts of a single word when there is no danger of misreading or of confusion with other words.

> today   presuppose   recover (to regain)
> tomorrow   semicolon   re-cover (to cover again)
> anticlimax   postdate   re-elect (not *reelect*)

DASH (—)

A dash marks an abrupt interruption in the thought of a sentence. On the typewriter, form the dash with two hyphens; do not leave any space between it and the words it separates.

> It was the tenant—not the superintendent—who caused the damage.

49. FOLLOWING BROKEN THOUGHTS. Use the dash after a thought that is suddenly broken off or before an abrupt change in sentence structure.

> He worked six months for one employer, three months for another, and six weeks for a third; and only last April—but why go on? You have enough of his record to see the kind of worker he is.

50. PRECEDING SUMMARIZING TERMS. Place a dash before an expression that summarizes or explains the preceding statement.

> We finally agreed to his terms—3 per cent discount for cash.

> The advertisement has attention value, novelty, conviction—everything.

51. BEFORE CONCLUDING EXPRESSIONS. Use the dash before an expression that summarizes and concludes an involved thought in the same sentence.

> After you have served as a clerk for six years, and after you have held a junior administrative post for another four years, and after you take and pass your examination for senior administrator, and after you have been appointed to that position—after you have advanced in that fashion, I think you can say you have risen from the ranks.

52. EMPHASIZING INTERPOLATIONS. Dashes may be used instead of parentheses to give force to an interpolated remark.

> If he calls again—I think that will be the fourth time in a month— I shall not see him.

53. INTRODUCING EXPLANATIONS. A dash may be used instead of a colon to introduce and give force to a short explanation.

> The office was complete except for one thing—a desk.

QUOTATION MARKS (" ")

Double quotation marks are used to enclose verbatim quotations; single marks are used to enclose quotations within quotations. The quotation mark is usually a double mark ("); the single mark (') is the apostrophe on the typewriter.

54. ENCLOSING DIRECT QUOTATIONS. Use quotation marks to enclose word-for-word transcriptions of letters, speeches, and printed matter.

> A statement on all our sales slips reads, "Claims must be made within thirty days."

55. PUNCTUATING INDIRECT QUOTATIONS. Do not use quotation marks to enclose indirect quotations.

Incorrect	*Correct*
All our invoices state that "claims must be made within thirty days."	All our invoices state that claims must be made within thirty days.

56. ENCLOSING QUOTATION WITHIN QUOTATION. Use single quotation marks (' ') to set off a quotation within a quotation.

> The sentence read, "If you will just write 'Approved' and your signature at the bottom of this letter, we shall make the stock purchases as suggested above."

57. HANDLING BROKEN QUOTATIONS. Quotations broken by expressions such as *he said* should be punctuated as indicated in the following examples:

> "We are glad," the letter began, "that you wrote to us as you did." (A comma always precedes the interruption. A comma also follows when the part within the quotation marks would normally take a comma or no punctuation at all at that point.)

> "The person you mention was never in our employ," he testified; "therefore we are unable to give you any information about him." (A semicolon follows the interruption when the part within the quotation marks would normally take a semicolon at that point.)

> "The controller is out of town," his secretary said. "He is expected back on Monday." (A period follows the interruption when the part within the quotation marks would normally take a period at that point.)

58. OMITTING COMMAS. A quotation closely interlaced with the structure of the sentence is not ordinarily set off by commas. (See Rule 24.)

> Everyone answered "Yes" to the question.

> The directive said that the new office was to "co-ordinate the public relations activities" of the branch offices.

59. PLACING COMMA AND PERIOD. At the end of a quotation, the comma or the period is placed inside the quotation mark.

> "If you wish," he said, "we shall be glad to submit a revised estimate of the cost."

60. POSITION OF SEMICOLON AND COLON. A semicolon or a colon at the end of a quotation is placed outside the quotation mark.

We thought she said her name was "Wendy"; but her application reads "Mindy."

These colors are "warm": red, yellow, orange.

61. PLACING QUESTION MARK AND EXCLAMATION MARK. A question mark or an exclamation mark at the end of a quotation is placed either inside or outside the quotation mark, depending on the sense of the sentence.

Does he think he can win back Mr. Casey's friendship merely by saying, "I apologize"? (The question mark concludes the whole sentence.)

Mr. Price's answer was "Aboslutely not!" (The exclamation mark concludes only the quotation. A period is not necessary after the final quotation mark.)

62. HANDLING EXTENDED QUOTATIONS. When more than one paragraph is quoted, place a quotation mark at the beginning of each paragraph and at the end of only the last paragraph.

"There has never been an era in our nation's history without its social and economic problems. The present is certainly no exception.

"If we have failed in this country . . . it has been because we have failed to hold high the banner of our system before the peoples of the world."

63. DESIGNATING SHORT PRINTED WORKS. Use quotation marks to enclose the name of a chapter in a book, the name of a short story or magazine article, or the title of a pamphlet, folder, or other short printed work. (See Section X, 30.)

The title of the chapter is "The Last Half-Century of Advertising."

"Correspondence Efficiency," by Bradshaw Lee, is an article in the January issue of *Harvard Business Review*.

APOSTROPHE (')

The apostrophe is employed to denote possession, to indicate contractions, and to form certain plurals.

64. SHOWING POSSESSION. The apostrophe is used to show possession. (See Section III, 2.)

Mr. Gray's desk   men's hats
Philadelphia's parks   ladies' suits
Bliss's house   parents' problems

65. INDICATING CONTRACTIONS. The apostrophe is used in a contraction to show the omission of a letter or letters. (See Section X, 18.) Contractions are considered correct in informal writing.

it's (it is, it has)	we're (we are)
hasn't (has not)	Ass'n (Association)
can't (can not)	Sec'y (Secretary)

66. FORMING PLURALS. Use the apostrophe and *s* to form the plural of letters of the alphabet, numerals and symbols, and words used as things in themselves. The expression is usually underlined (or put in italics, if printed).

His *2's* were hard to distinguish from his *Q's*.
He used *&'s* instead of *and's* throughout the letter.

ELLIPSIS (. . .)

Ellipsis marks (plural: ellipses) are usually employed in groups of three (spaced periods on a typewriter) to show that words have been omitted. Ellipses are used in addition to other marks of punctuation, including the period denoting the end of a sentence; they are ordinarily treated as part of a quoted text and, therefore, are placed within the quotation marks.

67. INDICATING OMISSIONS. Use ellipses to indicate the omission of material from quoted texts.

I quote from the pamphlet: "Another help and an obviously simple one . . . is the use of form letters or form paragraphs. . . . What is more obvious than to prepare one really complete, courteous, and sincere reply which can be used by your secretary on a mere notation from you? . . ."

68. SUBSTITUTING FOR OTHER PUNCTUATION. In some narrative and sales messages, a series of periods is occasionally used instead of commas or other punctuation marks for effect. The business writer should use periods sparingly for this purpose.

Try Peppo . . . so light . . . so refreshing.

Now you can have all the travel comforts of tomorrow . . . at yesterday's fares.

BAR (/)

The bar is a diagonal line used between letters in some abbreviations, between alternative words, and in the writing of fractions and dates.

69. FORMING ABBREVIATIONS. The bar is used in certain standard abbreviations.

> B/P (bills payable)   c/o care of
> A/C (account)   1/3/71 (January 3, 1971)

70. SEPARATING ALTERNATIVE WORDS. The bar is placed between two words to indicate that either word may be used in interpretation. This device is confined largely to formal documents.

> Delivery will be made from the warehouse of the manufacturer and/or his duly authorized distributor.

71. WRITING FRACTIONS. The bar is also used in typewriting fractions. (See Section X, 45.)

> 3 3/4   16 5/8   2 2/3

EXERCISE

Punctuate the following sentences:

1. If we can be of further assistance to you we shall be glad to hear from you

2. The form properly filled out must be in our hands not later than March 19

3. If you should have an accident while away on a trip and need help in a hurry you can go to the nearest telephone call Western Union Canadian National Telegraphs in Canada and ask for the name address and telephone number of the nearest claim man

4. In the circumstances the receipt mailed to you on July 15 is void

5. Having noted during the past several months that the paper of your corporation was being offered in the open market by the commercial paper brokers I thought that if it would be an accommodation to you we could place a line of credit at your disposal

6. We have had requests from a number of agents for a sticker see enclosed that may be affixed to the outside of automobile policies that do not provide for trailer coverage

7. Accordingly we are enclosing a corrected confirmation of this transaction reading purchased 100 shares of Consolidated Copper Company common at 35 5/8

8. To save yourself a trip you should bring your birth certificate and two small photographs approximately 2″ × 2″ of yourself

9. Yes it will be necessary for you to sign the papers

10. The charge of $295.00 provides everything necessary in the way of plates driving license insurance etc

11. May we request that you send us your acknowledgment of the receipt of this check

12. Three copies are enclosed one white original and two green duplicates

13. With reference to your question is this the most advantageous time to start our advertising campaign I would say most emphatically yes

14. Mr. Stutz the principal creditor has threatened to institute bankruptcy proceedings

15. The company which has been in business since 1921 manufactures boys and girls hosiery underwear and blouses

16. If the decree is confirmed I doubt that there will be anything in the estate with which to pay the creditors if it should be reversed a remote possibility it is still problematic how much will be available for the same purpose

17. The shipment dates according to our records were September 24 1970 January 7 1971 and March 28 1971

18. The three copies that are marked respectively Original Duplicate and Collectors Copy are to be sent to the Collector of Internal Revenue State Office Building Albany New York the fourth copy that marked Taxpayers Copy is for your files

19. We have enclosed a plan of the S S Enterprise and have indicated two rooms C140 and C142 which we shall hold under option for you until August 12 at 3 p m at our offices 165 Broadway New York City

20. Henry the next time you go go by plane

Section X
Spelling and Related Matters

Closely associated with the correct use of words are spelling, word division, capitalization, the use of contractions and abbreviations, the underlining of words, and the representation of numbers. It goes without saying that correctness and consistency in these matters are important.

SPELLING

No business writer can afford to be deficient in spelling. Even when a stenographer is employed, the final responsibility for correct spelling rests with the person who signs the letter or report. Certainly he will be blamed for any errors in spelling or typing which he fails to catch.

1. LEARNING TO SPELL. With diligence and a systematic approach, spelling can be learned. Three important ways of learning to spell a word are (1) seeing the word correctly, (2) pronouncing the word correctly, and (3) writing the word correctly.

Seeing the Word Correctly. The writer who wants to improve his spelling should pay close attention to the structure of individual words. He should try to visualize each word and to remember its peculiarities. If he does, he will notice, for example, that *bookkeeper* consists of the two words *book* and *keeper* and therefore has a double *k;* that *argument* has no *e* after the *u* although the word *argue* does; and that *piece* has a *pie* in it. A great number of words lend themselves to similar observation and visualization.

PRONOUNCING THE WORD CORRECTLY. Often misspelling is due

370

to incorrect pronunciation. The person who mispronounces *attacked* as *attackted*, *mischievous* as *mischevious*, and *athletic* as *athaletic* is almost certain to misspell the same words.

The writer should practice pronouncing each word correctly until his concentration results in automatic accuracy. When in doubt about the correct pronunciation of a word, he should consult a dictionary. (See Section VIII.)

Writing the Word Correctly. Even though he knows how to spell a word, the correspondent may occasionally fail to write it correctly. As with visualizing a word correctly and pronouncing it accurately, writing a word correctly requires practice. The correspondent should write a word, with which he has difficulty, a number of times; he should repeat the procedure until he spells the word accurately and without difficulty.

It is very helpful to make up a list of troublesome words for periodic review.

2. BASIC SPELLING RULES. In addition to the ways already mentioned, the writer can improve his spelling by learning the fundamental spelling rules. Knowing only a half dozen of these rules will help him immediately in spelling hundreds of words.

Silent E. In adding a suffix to a word ending in a silent *e*, drop the *e* if the suffix begins with a vowel; retain the *e* if the suffix begins with a consonant.

advise + able = advisable	like + ness = likeness
come + ing = coming	achieve + ment = achievement
imagine + ary = imaginary	concise + ly = concisely

If a word ends in *ce* or *ge*, the silent *e* is retained before a suffix beginning with *a* or *o*. Examples are *changeable, noticeable, courageous*. Other exceptions to the rule are made whenever the silent *e* is needed to aid pronunciation or to prevent confusion with other terms. Examples are *mileage, eyeing, hoeing, dyeing* (compare *dying*), *lineage* (compare *linage*).

Final Y. When a word ends in *y* preceded by a consonant, change the *y* to *i* before adding any suffix except one beginning with *i*; when the final *y* is preceded by a vowel, retain the *y*.

deny	denied	denying	delay	delayed	delaying
pity	pitiful	pitying	attorney	attorneys	
petty	babies		alloy	alloys	
baby	pettiness		buy	buys	

Final Consonant. The rule of the "final consonant" applies to a single syllable word or a word in which the last syllable is accented. In either of these cases, when the final consonant follows a single vowel, double the consonant before adding a suffix beginning with a vowel. Do not double the consonant before a suffix beginning with a consonant.

begin	beginning	benefit	benefited	
occur	occurred	prefer	preference	(shifted accent)
commit	committed	commit	commitment	
allot	allotted	allot	allotment	

EI and IE. In words spelled with *ei* or *ie*, pronounced *ee*, use *i* before *e* except immediately after *c*.

achieve	believe	field	relieve	siege
ceiling	deceive	receipt	conceit	perceive

Exceptions to the rule are the words *either, neither, species, leisure,* and *seize.*

Plurals. The plural of nouns is usually made by adding *s* or *es* to the singular. (Again, consult a dictionary when in doubt.)

hats	bushels	pages	cupfuls	sashes	passes	hazes

The plural of nouns ending in *y* follows the rule for "final y"; for example, *lady, ladies.* The plural of words ending in *o* or *f* varies (*memos, tobaccos, heroes, briefs, leaves*). Other irregular plurals are evident in such words as *children, feet,* and *athletics* (same form in singular and plural). Compound nouns generally form their plurals by adding *s* to the last word of the group (*vice presidents, assistant managers, cross-examinations*); when, however, the first word in the compound noun is the important one, the plural ending is given to it (*passers-by, brothers-in-law, chairmen of the board*).

Suffixes. Students and correspondents often have difficulty in deciding whether or not the first consonant of a suffix is doubled when added to the end of a word. Here, the individual should remember that the consonant appears twice, only if the word ends in the same consonant. For example, formal*ly*, actual*ly*, wan*ness*; former*ly*, entire*ly*, obvious*ly*, useless*ness*.

Other word endings are troublesome because certain suffixes sound alike, but are not spelled alike. For instance, words ending in –*able* (*advisable, suitable, probable, returnable*) are much more numerous than words ending in –*ible* (*permissible, audible, eligible*), with which they are sometimes confused. Words ending in –*ent* and –*ant* (*persistent, resistant*) and –*ence* and –*ance* (*conference, attendance*) are also confounded and must be watched carefully.

3. WORDS FREQUENTLY MISSPELLED. Since the writer is likely to misspell the same words more than once, he is advised to keep a list of the words he has difficulty in spelling and to review it often. A comprehensive list of frequently misspelled words will be found in Harry Shaw's *Spell It Right!*, an Everyday Handbook (New York: Barnes & Noble, Inc., 1965). Also study the list of frequently confounded words in Section VIII, 2.

DIVISION OF WORDS

The hyphen is used to divide the syllables of a word at the end of a line; do not place the hyphen at the beginning of the following line. It is correct to divide a compound word between its main parts (*policy-holder, copy-writer, counselor-at-law, well-being, double-spaced* copy, *five-pound* sacks). It is also correct to divide a word after a prefix of two or more letters and before a suffix of three or more letters (*un-limited, sur-round, post-pone; surrounding, comfort-able, interpreta-tion*).

In best practice, divide as few words as possible. When in doubt about the division of specific words, consult your dictionary. It is important to avoid the pitfalls or hyphenation which are treated below.

4. PROPER NAMES. Do not hyphenate a proper name at the end of a line.

    Ander-son   John-ston   Westing-house   Chi-cago   New-ark

5. MONOSYLLABLES. Do not attempt to divide words of one syllable.

    ei-ghth   phra-se   cau-ght   help-ed   pass-ed

6. ONE-LETTER DIVISIONS. Do not split a word after or before a single letter.

    e-licit   e-nough   a-gainst   alread-y   residuar-y

7. HYPHENATED WORDS. Do not divide a word that is already hyphenated.

post-op-erative   re-or-der   well-be-ing   deep-root-ed

8. MISREADING. Avoid any division that would result in mis-reading of the word.

vehi-cle   intrave-nous   reor-ganize   ope-ra

CAPITALIZATION

Capital letters are used primarily for the beginnings of sentences and for proper names. There are also other uses, however, which careful writers observe. Where capitalization is optional, the writer should rely on the practice of his company or on his own judgment. In any case, he should maintain consistency. The rules discussed below are generally accepted in business.

9. SENTENCES AND QUOTATIONS. Capitalize the first word of every sentence and of every formal quotation. (For capitalization after the colon, se Section IX, 36.)

> In starting the meeting, the chairman said, "Please forgive me for taking you away from your desks."

This rule does not apply to a quotation that is not a complete sentence.

> The chairman said something about "taking you away from your desks."

10. TABULATIONS. Capitalize the first word in every part of a formal tabulation.

> You will find the following materials enclosed:
>
> Copy of our June 22 *Life* advertisement
> Publicity release for your local newspapers
> Salesman's Manual

11. SALUTATIONS. Capitalize the first word of the salutation and all proper names and titles. Do not capitalize the word *dear* following the pronoun *My*.

Dear Mr. Sellers: Dear Tom and Jim:
Dear Dr. and Mrs. Bragg: My dear Mrs. Crandell:

12. **Complimentary Closes.** Capitalize only the first word of the complimentary close.

Very truly yours,   Respectfully yours,   Yours sincerely,

13. **Proper Names.** Capitalize all proper names and names derived from proper names, including nicknames; the names of the months and days of the week; names of holidays; geographical names; names of buildings, organizations, and institutions; names of governmental agencies, departments, and high-ranking officials; names of historical documents and events; names of the Deity; words of kinship; and names of races and languages.

John Wyman, Ike Eisenhower, July, Friday, Thanksgiving Day, Tenth Street, English, Texas, Texan, Missouri River, American, Indian, Chrysler Building, General Motors, Smithsonian Institution, Federal Bureau of Investigation, the Chief Justice, Monroe Doctrine, World War I, Jehovah, Aunt Marie, Negro (*but* black), Caucasian (*but* white), French.

Many words derived from proper names are not capitalized when they have taken on a specialized meaning. Examples are *china* (dishes), *morocco* (leather), *pasteurize, platonic, macadam* (road).

The names of the seasons (*summer, fall, winter, spring*) are not capitalized. The points of the compass (*north, south, southeast,* etc.) are also not capitalized except when they are part of a street name or denote a specific region.

Last summer I spent my vacation in the *West*.
The farther *west* you go, the wider the hat brims.
2965 *North* Michigan Drive.

Words such as *street, avenue, river, bridge, hotel,* which are used as part of a proper name, are generally capitalized.

Park Avenue   Fiftieth Street   Golden Gate Bridge
Sheraton-Astor Hotel

Do not capitalize the article *the* preceding a proper name unless the article begins the sentence or is an integral part of the name.

the George Washington Bridge   *the* Chase Manhattan Bank
the General Electric Company

The Bank of New York   *The* Custom Shop   *The* Texas Company

14. LITERARY TITLES. Capitalize the first word of literary titles (including the names of books, reports, chapters, etc.) and all succeeding words except articles, prepositions, and conjunctions with fewer than four or five letters.

> *The Principles of Advertising*
>
> A Report on the Reorganization of the Sales Department
>
> *Twenty Thousand Leagues Under the Sea*
>
> A Day with General Electric (*or* A Day With General Electric)

TITLES OF RESPECT. Capitalize a title of respect or office when the title immediately precedes a proper name. Also capitalize a title of office following a name in the envelope address or inside address of the letter. In other instances of titles following proper names, practice leans toward capitalizing only the most important titles.

> Governor Graham   the Governor   Walter J. Graham, Governor of Idaho
>
> Professor Day   the professor   Julian Day, professor of economics
>
> Dr. Julian Day
> Professor of Economics (envelope address)

16. WORDS WITH NUMERALS. Capitalize words like *room, chapter, section, number,* and *part* (but not *page*) when they are followed by a numeral.

> Room 2045   Chapter III   Number 75   File 168B   page 8

17. ABBREVIATIONS. Capitalize abbreviations of titles preceding or following a name and the abbreviations of academic degrees. Other abbreviations are not ordinarily capitalized unless they are abbreviations of titles or words that would be capitalized in any case.

> Mr. David Farr, Ph.D.   Mr. William Trask, Jr.
> Henry Forsythe, Esq.   Dr. Paul G. Sage
> Col. Walter Elwood   Abraham Riggs, C.P.A.
>
> mfr.   asst.   yds.   encl.   F. (Fahrenheit)   A.D.   Geo.
> NBC.

Usage is divided with respect to the capitalization of certain common abbreviations, such as P.M., p.m.; R.S.V.P., r.s.v.p.; C.O.D., c.o.d.

CONTRACTIONS

A contraction is a shortened word form characterized by the substitution of an apostrophe for an omitted letter or letters. Examples are *can't, don't, we'll, they're*. Contractions are characteristic of informal correspondence, personal and business, but are considered out-of-place where dignity is desired.

Inappropriate	*Acceptable*
We're pleased to invite you to a special showing of gentlemen's cravats to be held at our Fifth Avenue shop beginning next Monday. There *you'll* see styles in neckwear exclusive with us.	*We are* pleased to invite you to a special showing of gentlemen's cravats to be held at our Fifth Avenue shop beginning next Monday. There *you will* see styles in neckwear exclusive with us.

Acceptable

I'm glad *you're* going to be here for our meeting on the 19th, because *I've* looked forward very much to the chance of seeing you again.

When in doubt, it is best to spell the words in full.

18. FIGURE CONTRACTIONS. The apostrophe to denote the omission of part of a figure is permissible in informal writing.

I was in the Class of '52.
If you think the last election was close, wait until '72.

ABBREVIATIONS

Although certain common abbreviations are accepted as standard, abbreviations should be kept to a minimum in ordinary business correspondence. Abbreviations are more widely used in catalogues, reports, technical manuals, legal documents, and the like.

19. PERIODS WITH ABBREVIATIONS. The period is the standard mark of punctuation after abbreviations. It has become common, however, to omit periods after abbreviations of government agencies, radio stations, and other organizations usually referred to by their abbreviated titles.

Cal. Calif. etc. Av. Ave. mph m.p.h. S.W. SW
s.w. NLRB HOLC WCBS

20. SPACING. Put a single space between the initials of a person's name or of the name of a state. In other abbreviations, the space is usually omitted.

Mr. S. M. Field   N. J.   S. D.   F.O.B.   B.A.

21. TITLES. The titles *Mr.* and *Mrs.* are always abbreviated. The title *Dr.* is usually abbreviated when used with a name. Titles such as *President, Senator,* and *Professor* are never abbreviated in very formal communications; they may be abbreviated in other correspondence only when they are used with initials or given names, but not with the last name alone.

Incorrect	*Correct*
Mister Jones	Mr. Jones
	Dr. Jones
Sen. Gray	Senator Gray
	Sen. George A. Gray
Prof. Black	Professor Black
	Prof. E. L. Black
	Professor E. L. Black

The abbreviated title *Rev.* and the title *Honorable,* whether abbreviated or not, are used only with the full name or with the last name and initials.

Incorrect	*Correct*
Hon. Plunkett	Hon. George E. Plunkett
Rev. Jones	Rev. Archer S. Jones

22. EXPRESSIONS OF TIME. Certain conventional expressions of time are commonly abbreviated.

a.m.   p.m.   B.C.   A.D.

23. NAMES OF PERSONS. Initials are usually used for middle names, but in any case do not use initials or other abbreviated forms that do not conform to the style customarily employed by the addressee himself. If a person signs his name *Charles H. Burke,* he should not be addressed as *Chas. H. Burke.* If he signs his name *T. Frank McNeary,* he should be so addressed and not as *Thomas F. McNeary* or *T. F. McNeary.*

24. COMPANY NAMES. In writing a company's name, use any

abbreviations or signs that appear in the spelling of the name on the company's letter head.

> Tripler & Co.   B. Altman & Co.   Barnes & Noble
> Bemis Bro. Bag Co.   Julius Wile Sons & Co., Inc.
> Monroe Calculating Machine Company, Inc.

25. NAMES OF MONTHS. It is better not to abbreviate the name of the month either in the heading or in the body of the letter.

Poor	*Better*
Dec. 14, 19—	*December* 14, 19—
your letter of *Feb.* 6	your letter of *February* 6

26. STATE NAMES. The following abbreviations are recommended for ZIP Code addresses.

AL	Alabama	MT	Montana
AK	Alaska	NE	Nebraska
AZ	Arizona	NV	Nevada
AR	Arkansas	NH	New Hampshire
CA	California	NJ	New Jersey
CO	Colorado	NM	New Mexico
CT	Connecticut	NY	New York
DE	Delaware	NC	North Carolina
DC	District of Columbia	ND	North Dakota
FL	Florida	OH	Ohio
GA	Georgia	OK	Oklahoma
GU	Guam	OR	Oregon
HI	Hawaii	PA	Pennsylvania
ID	Idaho	PR	Puerto Rico
IL	Illinois	RI	Rhode Island
IN	Indiana	SC	South Carolina
IA	Iowa	SD	South Dakota
KS	Kansas	TN	Tennessee
KY	Kentucky	TX	Texas
LA	Louisiana	UT	Utah
ME	Maine	VT	Vermont
MD	Maryland	VA	Virginia
MA	Massachusetts	VI	Virgin Islands
MI	Michigan	WA	Washington
MN	Minnesota	WV	West Virginia
MS	Mississippi	WI	Wisconsin
MO	Missouri	WY	Wyoming

27. SLANG ABBREVIATIONS. Except in the most informal letters, avoid slang abbreviatons and clipped words.

Poor	Better
Two of our workers were retired in the past year because of *t.b.*	Two of our workers were retired in the past year because of *tuberculosis*.
Since we built the new *lab* and hired a college *prof* to run it, new *biz* has been coming in at a rapid rate.	Since we built the new *laboratory* and hired a college *professor* to run it, new *business* has been coming in at a rapid rate.

28. **MISUSE OF ABBREVIATIONS.** Many abbreviations that are correct in combination with other terms are not correct when used alone.

Incorrect	Correct
The *sgt.* was given a two-weeks' leave.	*Sgt. William Graham* was given a two-weeks' leave.
We have a *no.* of similar cases pending.	We have a *number* of similar cases pending.

Also correct

Please consult our invoice *No. 1435*.

29. **COMMON ABBREVIATIONS.** All standard dictionaries list abbreviations either in the main vocabulary or in an appendix. Whenever in doubt about the spelling, punctuation, or use of capitals in abbreviations, consult your dictionary.

UNDERLINING

Words that would be set in *italics* in printed copy are underlined in typewritten or manuscript copy.

30. **PRINTED, THEATRICAL, VEHICULAR TITLES.** Underline the names of newspapers, magazines, books, plays, trains, planes, steamships, and so on.

The article in the *Daily Chronicle* was reprinted a month later in the *Reader's Digest*.

He will arrive on the *Metroliner* at 9 a.m. tomorrow.

We are sure that *Little Women* will make a good television play.

In the instance of the names of books, newspapers, magazines, etc., all capitals are sometimes used instead of underlining. The names of magazine articles and book chapters are uniformly put in quotation marks. (See Section IX, 63.)

We refer to your article, "Ways to Write Better Letters," in the September READER'S DIGEST.

31. FOREIGN WORDS AND PHRASES. Underline foreign words and phrases which have not been adopted into the English language.

Top hats used to be considered *de rigueur* for any formal occasion.

His *savoir faire* is a big asset to both him and us.

32. PARTICULARIZED REFERENCES. Underline words used as things-in-themselves and references to single letters.

The words *writing* and *convenience* were misspelled.
Be sure to dot your *i* and cross your *t*.

33. EMPHASIS. Underlining for the sake of emphasis should be used very sparingly. An exception to this rule is sometimes made in sales letters intended for mass circularization. (See examples in Chapter 12.)

NUMBERS

Since numbers are common to almost all business correspondence, many questions arise with regard to their correct representation. (See Chapter 2.)

34. EXACT NUMBERS. Exact numbers and amounts are generally expressed in figures unless they appear at the beginning of the sentence, in which case they should be spelled out.

Please send us 12 dozen oak chairs, your catalogue No. 2456B, at $156.00 per dozen.

Twenty-four years ago wholesale practices in this field were very much different from what they are now.

If spelling out the number at the beginning of a sentence proves cumbersome, recast the sentence so that the number is placed in some other position.

Poor	*Better*
Nineteen hundred and sixty-six was an especially trying year.	The year 1966 was especially trying.

Exact numbers that can be written as one word may be spelled out.

four dollars   seventy employees   twelve months
twenty-eight copies

35. ROUND NUMBERS. Round numbers are commonly expressed in words, or, in the case of numbers in the millions and higher, in both words and figures.

ten thousand people   the next twenty years   the first hundred dollars $170 million   a military budget of $70 billion

36. CONSISTENCY. In statistics containing several related numbers, do not mix words and figures.

At the year-end we held 570 corporate bond issues of 331 companies, the preferred stock issues of 143 companies, and common stock issues of 98 companies. (Not *ninety-eight* companies.)

37. CONTIGUOUS NUMBERS. Except in a series, two figures should not be placed together. Use figures for one number and spell out the other, or rewrite the sentence to avoid placing the two numbers together.

Poor	*Better*
In 1970, 19,000 workers at the Akron plant were given a new contract.	In 1970, nineteen thousand workers at the Akron plant were given a new contract. (*Or:* In 1970, a new contract was given to 19,000 workers at the Akron plant.)

When two numbers modify the same word, spell out one (preferably the smaller) and use figures for the other.

100 eight-cent stamps   36 two-story houses
ten 25¢ candy bars

38. REFERENCES TO TIME AND DATES. Use figures to express time with *a.m.* or *p.m.*, and to represent dates. Spell out expressions of time followed by *o'clock*.

10 p.m.   11:30 a.m.   5:15 p.m.   one o'clock
eleven-thirty o'clock

39. REFERENCES TO PLACES AND DIMENSIONS. Use figures to indicate room numbers, page numbers, street numbers, order numbers, serial numbers, etc., and dimensions and measures.

Room 332   page 46   670 Thames Street   invoice No. 1560
12 by 15 feet   a .38 caliber gun   32 degrees

40. EVEN-DOLLAR FIGURES. Do not use the decimal point without the ciphers. (See exception in Rule 44.)

$3.00 $7.00 $12 $89 $145 (*not* $145.)

41. MIXED AMOUNTS. Always use figures to express mixed amounts.

$41.85 $2.05 $104.60

When both mixed amounts and even-dollar amounts are used in a series, add the decimal point and two ciphers to even-dollar figures.

The checks were for $8.11, $15.60, and $17.00 respectively.

42. DOUBLE REPRESENTATION. Do not express amounts in both words and figures in ordinary business correspondence. (Double representation is prescribed, however, in the writing of checks and certain legal forms.)

Poor	*Better*
We are enclosing our check for $149.50 (one hundred and forty-nine dollars and fifty cents).	We are enclosing our check for $149.50.

43. AMOUNTS UNDER $1.00. Use the cents sign (¢) not the dollar sign and decimal point, to represent figure amounts less than one dollar. It is also correct to write out the word cents.

Poor	*Better*
$.56	56¢ *or* 56 cents
$.98	98¢ *or* 98 cents

44. COMMA WITH FIGURES. Place a comma between each group of three digits, counting from the right, except in dates, street numbers, policy numbers, serial numbers, and the like.

| 1,300 copies | 23,465 people | $1,405,087 | No. 4576895 |
| May 1971 | 5635 Broadway | Room 1712 | |

45. FRACTIONS. It is good practice to write out fractions that can be expressed in a single compound word; other fractions and those appended to the whole figure should be written as figures.

one-half   two-thirds   5/32   27 3/8

EXERCISE A

In the list below, find the misspelled words and respell them correctly. Twelve of the words are correct.

1. occurence	16. independant	31. togeather
2. dilemma	17. writter	32. superintendant
3. exhorbitant	18. ocassionally	33. seperate
4. mischievious	19. preform	34. undoubtably
5. labratory	20. sacreligious	35. treasurer
6. rhythm	21. hoping	36. embarass
7. untill	22. supercede	37. similiar
8. summarize	23. temperment	38. parallel
9. benefitted	24. facilatate	39. indispensible
10. hygiene	25. permitted	40. government
11. accidently	26. grammer	
12. interlectual	27. irrevelant	
13. convient	28. maintainance	
14. library	29. lose	
15. layed	30. receive	

EXERCISE B

Rewrite the following sentences, correcting all errors in capitalization, abbreviations, underlining, and the representation of numbers:

1. 19 years ago we opened our Wesley street branch three blocks North of our factory.

2. The author of the book, Motivation Research In Current Marketing Practice, is the same Prof. Aldridge who used to be Director of Research at the Ames institute.

3. The appointment of Wm. Somes as Account Executive was kept on the q.t. for a mo.

4. We sold about 2,000 sets of China from Jan. to Oct. of this y'r.

5. Mister Gustafson, Chairman of the Bd., will arrive by air france at 2 o'clock this afternoon.

6. The Chapter, Personal investments, was marred by the frequent misspelling of the word convenience.

7. Paragraph no. 16 in the Blackstone Company's What every Employee should Know relates to vacations and overtime pay.

8. The Daily Gazette is under the capable guidance of Editor Joseph Hanes, who used to be an Associate Editor of Life.

9. Thank you for your check for $75.10 (seventy-five dollars and ten cents) in payment of one doz. Morocco leather billfolds.

10. The pkge. was marked for Doctor Philip Baker in room 1427 of the Wellington hotel on east 54th street.

Answers to Exercises

SECTION I

A. 1. *appreciate,* verb; *your,* adjective; *recent,* adjective; *order,* noun; *for,* preposition; *a,* adjective; *Razor,* noun.

2. *The,* adjective; *will be filled,* verb; *immediately,* adverb.

3. *product,* noun; *has been,* verb; *on,* preposition; *market,* noun; *many,* adjective; *years,* noun.

4. *If,* conjunction; *wish,* verb; *we,* pronoun; *shall include,* verb; *card,* noun; *and,* conjunction; *instruction,* adjective.

5. *are,* verb; *sure,* adjective; *well,* adverb; *with,* preposition; *purchase,* noun.

6. *however,* conjunctive adverb; *instrument,* noun; *ever,* adverb; *servicing,* noun; *not,* adverb; *on,* preposition; *us,* pronoun.

B. 1. Subject, *you;* predicate verb, *will find.* Simple sentence.

2. Subjects, *we, we;* predicate verb, *have written, have had.* Compound sentence.

3. Subjects, *you, we;* predicate verbs, *have finished, may ask.* Complex sentence.

4. Subjects, *client, he, which;* predicate verbs, *said, would return, accompanied.* Complex sentence.

5. Subject, *we;* predicate verb, *considered.* Simple sentence.

C. 1. *enclosed,* participle; *maturing,* participle.

2. None.

3. *reading,* gerund; *to pass,* infinitive.

4. None.

5. *listening,* gerund; *taking,* gerund; *refunding,* gerund.

D. 1. *me,* indirect object; *copy,* direct object; *report,* object of preposition.

2. *Mr. Henry,* subject; *president,* predicate noun; *modest,* predicate adjective.

3. *We,* subject; *qualifications,* direct object; *you,* direct object; *mind,* object of preposition.

4. *She*, subject; *reluctant*, predicate adjective; *pair*, direct object (of infinitive).

5. *acknowledging*, object of preposition; *gift*, direct object (of gerund); *Mr. Clown*, subject; *tribute*, direct object; *staff*, object of preposition.

SECTION II

1. is
2. is
3. were
4. am
5. is
6. Correct.
7. are
8. sees
9. needs
10. are, were

11. is
12. have been chosen
13. is supposed
14. were
15. am
16. is
17. is
18. Correct.
19. gives
20. is

SECTION III

1. he
2. we
3. Correct.
4. Correct.
5. Whose
6. I
7. whoever
8. yours
9. Joneses'
10. whom

11. us
12. Whom
13. Correct.
14. Malloy's
15. they
16. Roger and Hunt's
17. Correct.
18. me
19. Correct.
20. Correct.

SECTION IV

A. 1. When I called on Mr. Dain and his partner, I discovered I had already met *Mr. Dain*.

2. Each of the girls was given a letter to copy and told to do the best *she* could.

3. Miss Gair asked Alice for the file on the Ajax Company, but *Alice* was not sure where it was.

4. The printing bill for the posters was excessively high; so the next time we had the *work* done by another company.

5. Mr. Park met Mr. Graham for the first time yesterday. Today *Mr. Park* told me he felt as if they had been business associates for years.

6. We keep our office supplies at the rear of the cupboard and find *them* very hard to get at.

7. When you put a new ribbon in the typewriter, you should clean the *machine* at the same time.

8. The credit department is more efficient than the bookkeeping department largely because the *bookkeeping department* has inexperienced employees.

9. Advertising on television has grown very expensive because *television* reaches so many people.

10. Everyone present had an opportunity to express *his* opinion.

B.   1. Executives who bully their employees should not expect sympathy.

2. They asked us to include a supply of advertising material with their order, and of course we were glad to comply.

3. Bills are payable on the tenth of each month, and most of our customers observe these terms.

4. It is very annoying to have Mr. Terry always five or six days behind with his daily sales reports.

5. Even on farms electricity is often preferred for cooking.

6. He advised us to sell to the Drew Company on open account, and fortunately his advice was good.

7. Because the building is centrally located, floor space is very much in demand.

8. At his office we were told that Mr. Johnson would not be back until Thursday.

9. He refused to accept the shipment because it had been damaged in transit.

10. The 9 o'clock flight to Chicago was canceled, and so we had to wait two hours for the next plane.

SECTION V

1. will have been
2. have been
3. receiving
4. brought
5. will
6. be
7. had been
8. were
9. shall
10. begun
11. led
12. would
13. test
14. should
15. laid
16. had sat
17. filed
18. were
19. had placed
20. take

SECTION VI

1. too *well*
2. Correct.
3. *beautiful*
4. *This kind of* chair has the most comfortable back. (*Or: These chairs* have the most comfortable backs.)
5. . . . I like John's *better*.
6. We have not seen *or* heard . . . .
7. very *much* concerned

8. . . . but he worked for us *for a short time* last year.
9. *really*
10. Correct.
11. *differently*
12. . . . does *more* business (than the other).
13. *far lighter* and *cooler*
14. scarcely *ever*
15. especially *well*
16. . . . Mr. Brent's came *closest to being perfect.*
17. *seriously*
18. Correct.
19. *so* many problems as
20. *rough*

SECTION VII

A. 1. Complete.
   2. Incomplete.
   3. Complete.
   4. Complete.
   5. Incomplete.
   6. Incomplete.
   7. Complete.
   8. Incomplete.
   9. Complete.
   10. Incomplete.

B. 1. *In* December we do our biggest business in toys and games.
2. His is one of the biggest *offices,* if not the biggest office, in the building. (*Or,* His is one of the biggest *offices* in the building, if not the biggest.)
3. We do not know any *other* man who will work as hard as George.
4. I doubt *that* the customer will be satisfied with a substitute.
5. Complete.
6. *The* bolts and screws needed for the completion of *the* order are expected *on* Friday.
7. Marvin Jones makes as many calls *as* any other salesman we have, if not more. (*Or,* Marvin Jones makes as many calls *as,* if not more than, any other salesman we have.)
8. The invoices were sent and the check in payment *was* received.
9. The secretary and *the* treasurer were authorized to sign checks.
10. We manufacture a more complete line of webbing than any *other* company in the world.
11. *We* have completed *your* order and will ship *it* by parcel post today.
12. If we are to believe these tests, the Intelligence Quotients of the clerical workers are as high as *those of* the executives.
13. I can tell *that* you have been under a strain.
14. Complete.
15. The low-priced brand is as good *as,* if not better than, the brand selling for ten cents more. (*Or,* The low-priced brand is as good *as* the brand selling for ten cents more, if not better.)
16. From the beginning he believed *in* and worked for the project.
17. The welt on these slip covers is an expensive touch that you will not find on any *other* slip covers in their price range.

18. Complete.

19. The clerks were amused and Mr. Griffith *was* chagrined over the error in identity.

20. Complete.

C. 1. Basing our conclusion on the information we have received, we believe Jones & Co. to be capable of meeting their normal obligations.

2. Properly handled, our inquiries are worth thousands of dollars.

3. It seems he was one of the wealthiest cattle ranchers in the Southwest.

4. You may continue to use your present checks until they are exhausted.

5. They have failed to match not only last year's sales, but the sales of two years ago as well.

6. This skillet is made of stainless steel, which distributes the heat evenly.

7. Working around the clock, the men repaired the dynamo and restored service.

8. Our salesmen go only where the market conditions are favorable.

9. Abelard & Company make ladies' sports clothes. They have been in business since 1935.

10. We think it will be to your advantage to advertise electric clocks again this month.

11. Although you were gone for six months, you did not lose any of your seniority rights.

12. This bank had Mr. Kerr's account from July 1965 to April 1970.

13. You will like not only the unusual styling, but the low prices as well.

14. When Mr. Stone examined the records of these employees, he was surprised by their poor performance ratings.

15. He asked us to submit our last profit and loss statement and to give him the name of our bank.

16. In order to be in a better position to meet competition, we added a complete line of men's clothing.

17. We received from Miss Taylor a letter dated August 19.

18. Please set the type, make the plates, and show us proofs by Thursday.

19. You may be sure that we shall treat such information in strict confidence. If we can ever reciprocate, please feel free to call on us.

20. Mr. Tripp came in today to discuss renewing for another thirty days his note for $1,000.00 which matures tomorrow.

SECTION VIII

A. 1. complement
2. healthful
3. continuously
4. loose
5. principal
6. waive
7. breathe
8. barring
9. flaunt
10. stationery
11. Personnel
12. precedents
13. media
14. apprise
15. allusion
16. formerly
17. morale

B.   1. *May* we have your permission to proceed with the transactions outlined in this letter?

2. We shall appreciate your *notifying* us of your decision.

3. Correct.

4. The customer said he preferred model AC–5 *to* BC–8.

5. Correct.

6. You *might have* been more tactful in your relations with the customer.

7. Correct.

8. They *seem unable* to understand the seriousness of the situation.

9. Have you studied the *effects* of the new regulations?

10. We sent the statement back for correction *because* it was inaccurate.

11. The *number* of buyers who come to New York varies with the season.

12. Correct.

13. Correct.

14. Correct.

15. You should not *infer* from these circumstances that we can not complete the performance of our contract.

16. We need the *sort of man* who is willing to work overtime one or two
evening a week.

17. We were able to meet the competition *because of* our superior workmanship and low prices.

18. You will find the new varnishes considerably *different from* the
finishes you are now using.

19. We are *figuratively* snowed under with orders.

20. The *reason* you do not see the seams *is that* they are electronically
welded.

SECTION IX

1. If we can be of further assistance to you, we shall be glad to hear from
you.

2. The form, properly filled out, must be in our hands not later than
March 19.

3. If you should have an accident while away on a trip and need help in
a hurry, you can go to the nearest telephone, call Western Union, and ask for
the name, address, and telephone number of the nearest claim man.

4. In the circumstances the receipt mailed to you on July 15 is void.

5. Having noted during the past several months that the paper of your
corporation was being offered in the open market by the commercial paper
brokers, I thought that if it would be an accommodation to you, we would
place a line of credit at your disposal.

6. We had requests from a number of agents for a sticker (see enclosed)
that may be affixed to the outside of automobile policies that do not provide
trailer coverage.

7. Accordingly, we are enclosing a corrected confirmation of this transaction reading, "Purchased 100 shares of Consolidated Copper Company common
at 35 5/8."

8. To save yourself a trip, you should bring your birth certificate and two small photographs (approximately 2″ × 2″) of yourself.

9. Yes, it will be necessary for you to sign the papers.

10. The charge of $295.00 provides everything in the way of plates, driving license, insurance, etc.

11. May we request that you send us your acknowledgment of the receipt of this check.

12. Three copies are enclosed: one white original and two green duplicates.

13. With reference to your question, "Is this the most advantageous time to start our advertising campaign?" I would say, "Most emphatically, yes!" (*Or, . . . would say most emphatically, "Yes!"*)

14. Mr. Stutz, the principal creditor, has threatened to institute bankruptcy proceedings.

15. The company, which has been in business since 1921, manufactures boys' and girls' hosiery, underwear, and blouses.

16. If the decree is confirmed, I doubt there will be anything in the estate with which to pay the creditors. If it should be reversed—a remote possibility —it is still problematic how much will be available for the same purpose.

17. The shipment dates according to our records, were September 24, 1970; January 7, 1971; and March 28, 1971.

18. The three copies that are marked respectively "Original," "Duplicate," and "Collector's Copy" are to be sent to the Collector of Internal Revenue, State Office Building, Albany, New York. The fourth copy, that marked "Taxpayer's Copy," is for your files.

19. We have enclosed a plan of the *S.S. Enterprise* and have indicated two rooms, C140 and C142, which we shall hold under option for you until August 12 at 3 p.m. at our offices, 165 Broadway, New York City.

20. Henry, the next time you go, go by plane.

SECTION X

A.

1. occurrence		17. writer	
2. correct		18. occasionally	
3. exorbitant		19. perform	
4. mischievous		20. sacrilegious	
5. laboratory		21. correct	
6. correct		22. supersede	
7. until		23. temperament	
8. correct		24. facilitate	
9. benefited		25. correct	
10. correct		26. grammar	
11. accidentally		27. irrelevant	
12. intellectual		28. maintenance	
13. convenient		29. correct	
14. correct		30. correct	
15. laid		31. together	
16. independent		32. superintendent	

33. separate	37. similar
34. undoubtedly	38. correct
35. correct	39. indispensable
36. embarrass	40. correct

B. 1. Nineteen years ago we opened our Wesley Street branch three blocks north of our factory.

2. The author of the book, *Motivation Research in Current Marketing Practice,* is the same Professor Aldridge who used to be director of research at the Ames Institute.

3. The appointment of William Somes as account executive was kept a secret for a month.

4. We sold about two thousand sets of china from January to October of this year.

5. Mr. Gustafson, chairman of the board, will arrive by Air France at two o'clock this afternoon.

6. The chapter, "Personal Investments," was marred by the frequent misspelling of the word *convenience.*

7. Paragraph No. 16 in the Blackstone Company's *What Every Employee Should Know* relates to vacations and overtime pay.

8. The *Daily Gazette* is under the capable guidance of Editor Joseph Hanes, who used to be an associate editor of *Life.*

9. Thank you for your check for $75.10 in payment of one dozen morocco leather billfolds.

10. The package was marked for Dr. Philip Baker in Room 1427 of the Wellington Hotel on East 54th Street.

Index